PS 379 SAL

THIS MAD
"INSTEAD"

THIS MAD

"INSTEAD"

Governing Metaphors in
Contemporary American Fiction

ARTHUR SALTZMAN

University of South Carolina Press

© 2000 University of South Carolina

Published in Columbia, South Carolina, by the
University of South Carolina Press

Manufactured in the United States of America

04 03 02 01 00   5 4 3 2 1

Library of Congress Cataloging-in-Publication Data

Saltzman, Arthur M. (Arthur Michael), 1953–
    This mad "instead" : governing metaphors in contemporary
    American fiction / Arthur Saltzman.
        p. cm.
    Includes bibliographical references and index.

    ISBN 1-57003-326-9 (cloth : perm. paper)
    1. American fiction—20th century—History and criticism.
    2. Metaphor.   I. Title.
PS379 .S25 2000
813'.5409—dc21

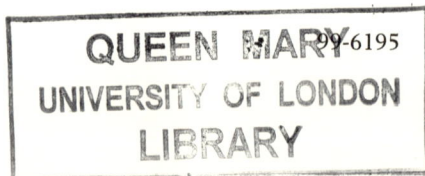

For Joy,
for pointing out the pivot above the canyon
and for ending a poem with "ask again"

"The end of the mechanical age," said Mrs. Davis, "is in my judgment an actuality straining to become a metaphor. One must wish it luck, I suppose. One must cheer it on. Intellectual rigor demands that we give these damned metaphors every chance, even if they are inimical to personal well-being and comfort. We have a duty to understand everything, whether we like it or not—a duty I would scant if I could." At that moment the water jumped into the boat and sank us.

Donald Barthelme,
"At the End of the Mechanical Age"

Contents

Acknowledgments		xi
Introduction	The Tongue's Ties	1
Chapter 1	Beholding Paul West and *The Women of Whitechapel*	19
Chapter 2	The Figure in the Static: Don DeLillo's *White Noise*	33
Chapter 3	In the Millhauser Archives	49
Chapter 4	Post Hoc Harmonies: Paul Auster's *Leviathan*	63
Chapter 5	The Nightmare of Relation: William Gass's *The Tunnel*	74
Chapter 6	The Trope in the Machine: Richard Powers's *Galatea 2.2*	94
Chapter 7	Kathy Acker's Guerrilla Mnemonics	110
Chapter 8	Down the Rabbit Whole: John Updike's Rabbit Novels	129
Conclusion	On the Ethical Behavior of Metaphor	181
Notes		189
Works Cited		209
Index		225

Acknowledgments

If I am fortunate in my achievements, it is because I am fortunate in my debts. I would like to thank the University of South Carolina Press (and Barry Blose in particular) for supporting this book and seeing it through its stages of development. I also wish to thank Irving Malin and Jerome Klinkowitz for treating my idiosyncrasies as insights and for offering thoughtful, sympathetic readings of the manuscript. Let me also mention those generous friends and colleagues at Missouri Southern and other institutions who have read and commented upon portions of the work in progress: Joel Brattin, Joy Dworkin, Bill Kumbier, Patrick O'Donnell, and Steve Spector. Dale Simpson, Larry Martin, Erik Bitterbaum, and Julio Leon battled for college funding on my behalf to defray permission costs, so I owe them in a most direct and practical sense. I am also indebted to the good ship MSSC and all who lunch in her, as well as to my daughter, Elizabeth, who has always shone for me, during and anyway.

Original versions of some of the chapters of *This Mad Instead* appeared in the following publications, which I gratefully acknowledge: *Twentieth Century Literature, Modern Fiction Studies, Critique: Studies in Contemporary Fiction, Beyond the Red Notebook: Essays on Paul Auster,* edited by Dennis Barone (University of Pennsylvania Press), and *Into the Tunnel: Readings of Gass's Novel,* edited by Steven G. Kellman and Irving Malin (University of Delaware Press). Other sources have granted me permission to borrow from copyrighted material:

Excerpts from *Don Quixote,* by Kathy Acker, copyright © 1986; *Empire of the Senseless,* by Kathy Acker, copyright ©1988; and *Great Expectations,* by Kathy Acker, copyright © 1982. Used by permission of Grove/Atlantic, Inc.

Excerpts from "Halley's Comet" and "Diffraction," from *Jaguar of Sweet Laughter: New and Selected Poems,* by Diane Ackerman. Copyright © 1991 by Diane Ackerman. Used by permission of Random House, Inc.

Excerpts from "Corson's Inlet," Copyright © 1963 by A. R. Ammons; "Poetics," copyright © 1969 by A. R. Ammons; "The Unifying Principle," copyright © 1972 by A. R. Ammons. From *Collected Poems 1951–1971,* by A. R. Ammons. Used by permission of W. W. Norton & Co., Inc.

Excerpts from *Ground Work: Selected Poems and Essays,* by Paul Auster. Copyright © 1990 by Faber and Faber, Ltd. Used by permission of Faber and Faber, Ltd.

Excerpts from "The Fish" and "Sandpiper," from *The Complete Poems 1927–1979,* by Elizabeth Bishop. Copyright © 1980 by Farrar, Straus & Giroux, Inc. Used by permission of Farrar, Straus & Giroux, Inc.

Excerpt from *Cleopatra's Nose: Essays on the Unexpected,* by Daniel J. Boorstein. Copyright © 1994 by Random House, Inc. Used by permission of Random House, Inc.

Excerpt from "Only the Polished Skeleton," from *On These I Stand: An Anthology of the Best Poems of Countee Cullen.* Copyright © 1947 by HarperCollins Publishers. Used by permission of Thompson and Thompson, New York.

Excerpts from *White Noise,* by Don DeLillo. Copyright © 1984, 1985 by Don DeLillo. Used by permission of Viking Penguin, a division of Penguin Putnam Inc.

Excerpt from *Holy the Firm,* by Annie Dillard. Copyright © 1977 by HarperCollins Publishers. Used by permission of HarperCollins Publishers.

Excerpt from *Living by Fiction,* by Annie Dillard. Copyright © 1982 by HarperCollins Publishers. Used by permission of HarperCollins Publishers.

Excerpt from *My Alexandria: Poems,* by Mark Doty. Copyright © 1995 by Mark Doty. Used by permission of University of Illinois Press.

Excerpt from "Loves," copyright © 1991 by Stephen Dunn, from *New and Selected Poems 1974–1994,* by Stephen Dunn. Used by permission of W. W. Norton & Co., Inc.

Excerpt from "The Colonel," from *The Country Between Us,* by Carolyn Forché. Copyright © 1981 by HarperCollins Publishers. Used by permission of HarperCollins Publishers.

Excerpt from *The Feminine Sublime: Gender and Excess in Women's Fiction,* by Barbara Claire Freeman. Copyright © 1995 by the Regents of the University of California. Used by permission of the University of California Press.

Excerpt from "The Fractal Lanes," from *Powers of Congress,* by Alice Fulton. Copyright© 1990 by Alice Fulton. Used by permission of David R. Godine, Publisher, Inc.

Excerpts from the Preface to *In the Heart of the Heart of the Country,* by William H. Gass. Copyright © 1968 by William H. Gass. Used by permission of David R. Godine, Publisher, Inc.

Excerpt from "Tribalism, Identity, and Ideology," by William H. Gass. Copyright ©1994 by the Modern Language Association of America. Used by permission of the Modern Language Association of America.

Excerpts from *The Tunnel,* by William H. Gass. Copyright © 1995 by William H. Gass. Used by permission of Alfred A. Knopf, Inc.

Excerpt from "Mock Orange," from *The Triumph of Achilles,* by Louise Glück. Copyright © 1985 by Louise Gluck. Used by permission of The Ecco Press.

Excerpt from "Donald Duck in Danish," from *Popular Culture,* by Albert Goldbarth. Copyright © 1990 by Ohio State University Press. Used by permission of Ohio State University Press and the author.

Excerpt from "Some Things," from *Heaven and Earth: A Cosmology,* by Albert Goldbarth. Copyright (1991) by The University of Georgia Press. Used by permission of The University of Georgia Press.

Excerpt from "Metaphor and Transcendence," by Karsten Harries, in *On Metaphor,* ed. Sheldon Sacks. Copyright © 1979 by the University of Chicago Press. Used by permission of the University of Chicago Press.

Excerpts from *The Collected Poems of Howard Nemerov,* by Howard Nemerov. Copyright © 1977 by Howard Nemerov. Used by permission of Margaret Nemerov.

Excerpts from *Galatea 2.2,* by Richard Powers. Copyright © 1995 by Farrar, Straus &Giroux, Inc. Used by permission of Farrar, Straus & Giroux, Inc.

Excerpts from *Collected Poems,* by Wallace Stevens. Copyright © 1954 by Wallace Stevens. Used by permission of Alfred A. Knopf, Inc.

Excerpts from *Collected Poems 1953–1993,* by John Updike. Copyright © 1993 by John Updike. Used by permission of Alfred A. Knopf, Inc.

Excerpts from *Pigeon Feathers and Other Stories,* by John Updike. Copyright © 1962 by John Updike. Used by permission of Alfred A. Knopf, Inc.

THIS MAD
"INSTEAD"

Introduction

THE TONGUE'S TIES

There is the world, the dream, and the one law.
The wish, the wisdom, and things as they are.
Howard Nemerov, "Unscientific Postscript"

If Shelley is right and the literary have their way with legislation, the burnished utopia that results will undoubtedly take one of two forms. One possibility is that everything will clearly be one thing and one thing only, altogether purged of adulterous correspondences. Imagine all existence chipped off the Platonic block. Words will no longer be the unrequited petitioners of things, and a new crop of linguists will arise to contemplate their reconciliation. Each utterance will enter a matrix of tightly stitched and inviolable complicities; nature's sundry clicks and fidgets will become so many tumblers in locks; verbal relations will take place with the efficiency of enzyme reactions. In a fastidiously rhymed environment, semantic hygiene will be guaranteed.

With all of our vines regularly trellised and our Tennessees jarred into compliance, poets will ease into complacency, their metrics always already etched in the senses and on display in a regimental sky. As John Barth puts it, "In a perfect funhouse you'd be able to go only one way" ("Lost in the Funhouse" 82), and so it would not be necessary to complete one's correlations after introducing them: "The brown hair on Ambrose's mother's forearms gleamed in the sun like" (70). "The smell of Uncle Karl's cigar smoke reminded one of" (71).

If this first version of paradise is earnest and regular as pavement, the second hums with inventory. In this scenario, every glance will generate manifold attachments, with familiarity breeding inexhaustible content. The "referential maniac," diagnosed in Vladimir Nabokov's "Signs and Symbols," will typify the citizens of an endlessly allusive universe:

> Phenomenal nature shadows him wherever he goes. Clouds in the staring sky transmit to one another, by means of slow signs, incredibly detailed information regarding him. His inmost thoughts are discussed at nightfall, in manual alphabet, by darkly gesticulating trees. Pebbles or stains or sun flecks form patterns representing in some awful way messages which he must intercept. Everything is a cipher and of everything he is the theme. . . . The silhouettes of his blood corpuscles, magnified a million times, flit over vast plains; and still farther, great mountains of unbearable solidity and height sum up in terms of granite and groaning firs the ultimate truth of his being. (284)

Not a noun will pass without its entourage, nor any atom escape epic attention. With every connection an embarkation, we will be radiant with perpetual insight. We will never be lonely again.

Whether being rid of the poet's associative itch or verifying its coinages as discoveries is the better destiny, books will no longer have to be refineries for the world's obdurate ore because accusations of ungainliness and arbitrariness alike will have been eliminated. Until then, the best guess is that writers will persist in their conventional enchantments: taking soundings, piling likenesses, adjectives, and images on nouns like fumbled balls, sweating over their labored shapes, offering up lathe-turned phrases as models of social improvement. The fact is that whatever a given author's politics, each employment of figuration endorses a partisan poetics, stumping for synthesis.

These two opposing attitudes toward figurative incursion come together in William Carlos Williams's brief poem "El Hombre" and Wallace Stevens's subsequent employment and embellishment of that poem, "Nuances of a Theme by Williams." Williams's poem can be viewed as part of the writer's campaign against "mere vegetable coincidence," which, says Williams, threatens to obscure "those inimitable particles of dissimilarity to all other things which are the peculiar perfection of the thing in question" (prologue to *Kora in Hell* 18). Williams would prefer to bring things into the visual and lexical fields unchaperoned by questionable devices:

> It's a strange courage
> you give me, ancient star:
>
> Shine alone in the sunrise
> Toward which you lend no part! (6)

The second stanza celebrates the liberation of the star not only from terrestrial mundanities but also from allegiances to imagery. In evoking the respective splendors of subject and sunrise, Williams appears to demonstrate his belief in ever-fractious atoms that elude unifying figures. "What I put down of value," he writes in *Spring and All*, "will have this value: an escape from crude symbolism, the annihilation of strained associations" (102); what inspires the poet is nature's "quality of independent existence," the dignity of "a world detached from the necessity of recording it, sufficient to itself" (121). We might have anticipated that the speaker in "El Hombre" would find the star's benign indifference discouraging, apathetic host that it is to the worshiper; however, because it reflects and authenticates his philosophy, its distance and silence shine like accomplishments. Unconstellated, undistractable, coldly *else,* the star imparts a "strange courage" to his convictions.

We think of Williams stalking the veritable until it emerges like a deer into the clearing. For him, every object, every perception, is unique and unprecedented. Meanwhile, with its inbred propensities for etymological association, syntactic arrangement, aural patterning—all the vast wardrobe of coherence—language is an especially suspicious artistic medium and must be frisked for the meanings it smuggles. "El Hombre" implies the dream of confinement to a bridled alphabet appropriate to that initial version of Eden, in which pure products emerge uninflected and entire into a bright, changeless noon.

In light of this ideal, larding with allusion is so much loose behavior; there is something illicit in the secret rendezvous of signs and multiple partners of signification. Many of Williams's best-known poems testify against the usual sense-making tactics of poetry on these grounds, staging their protests against the disfigurements of encroaching figures. "The Young Housewife" (136) is appreciated (somewhat voyeuristically) for her intriguing particularities: her shyness in spite of, or in ironic contrast to, her being uncorseted and outdoors in only a negligee; the relief, compositional if not psychological, in which she appears against "her husband's" wooden walls; even the inscrutable way she tucks a stray strand of hair behind her ear. All of that ordinary magnitude, "and I compare her / to a fallen leaf." The effect of that comparison is neither conclusive nor revelatory; on the contrary, it is anti-climactic, touched by the speaker's disdain for the feebleness of his own comparison. Can he manage no more than a cliché for lost promise? When the speaker next mentions the sound of his wheels crushing dried leaves as he drives off, the leaf conceit is exposed for the dry contrivance it is.

In "Spring and All," too, what had perhaps been intended as a descriptive overture leading to the more substantial argument of the poem—that is, the relationship urged between the contagious hospital and the difficult yet unstoppable regeneration of some humble bits of nature anonymously engaged in "the stark dignity / of entrance"—is unexpectedly prolonged:

> All along the road the reddish,
> purplish, forked, upstanding, twiggy
> stuff of bushes and small trees
> with dead, brown leaves under them
> leafless vines— (lines 9–13)

Five modifiers are summoned to rescue those bushes and small trees from neglect and to exploit them as consoling symbols of stubborn vitality. However, instead of rooting them securely by dictating the terms of possession, the words qualify and tussle with one another, start over, and then, with a blurt of exasperation, confess indefiniteness. ("Stuff," bitten off like an expletive, is the circuit breaker for this sorry run of descriptors.) Words are slippery, fickle attachments. When the speaker tries to collect himself and undertake the leafless vines, his vocabulary deserts him more quickly.[1] Peering over that ending dash like a bare cliff, we see "leafless" falter into "lifeless," while the preemptive "All" that opens this passage descends into the dubious summation "uncertain of all / save that they enter" a few lines later. Trust starkness, says Williams. Let no subterfuge interfere.

Wallace Stevens seconds Williams's assertion of a sanitized landscape when in his "Nuances of a Theme by Williams" he supports the pristine self-sufficiency of the ancient star of "El Hombre": "Lend no part to any humanity that suffuses / you in its light" (2.1–2). "If we could suddenly re-make the world on the basis of our own intelligence, see it clearly and represent it without faintness or obscurity, Williams' poems would have a place there," Stevens maintains in "Rubbings of Reality" (245); and we recognize in Stevens's idealization in *Notes Toward a Supreme Fiction* of "the sun when seen in its idea / Washed in the remotest cleanliness of a heaven / That has expelled us and our images" a parallel of Williams's solitary star (*It Must Be Abstract* 1.10–12). But such clarity comes at the expense of alteration. There is an "ambiguity produced by bareness" that even Williams's "passion for the anti-poetic" cannot expunge (Stevens, "Williams" 214, 213). Hence the very compulsion to provide glosses and extensions in "Nuances" implicitly contradicts the star's celebrated divorce from human projections. In Stevens's hands, "Shine alone" exfoliates into similes:

> Shine alone, shine nakedly, shine like bronze,
> that reflects neither my face nor any inner part
> of my being, shine like fire, that mirrors nothing. (1.1–3)

Associations accompany denials of association, so that the vaunted solitariness of the ancient star is refuted by the "taint" of context. Despite himself, the poet loads his every rift with "or." Things are insidiously fraught, and Stevens's objections to nuance are nuances too:

> Lend no part to any humanity that suffuses
> you in its own light.
> Be not chimera of morning,
> Half-man, half-star.
> Be not an intelligence,
> Like a widow's bird
> Or an old horse. (2.1–7)

"Widow's bird" or "old horse" may not represent the kind of intrusive flourish that Stevens disparages as a "crested image" in "How to Live. What to Do" (line 13), but those "nots" in the second stanza of "Nuances" tie his subject down to modifiers just as surely as any protracted conceit would have done.[2]

So too in "Add This to Rhetoric" Stevens begins by positing an untainted reality presumed to be standing somewhere apart from the constraints of the verbal: "It is posed and it is posed / But in nature it merely grows" (lines 1–2). The poem's progress is partly a criminal confession and self-denunciation, made somewhat less caustic by the belief that, like Crispin's pear, which "survives its poems" and their miserable entanglements (*Comedian as the Letter C* 5.28),

> Tomorrow when the sun,
> For all your images,
> Comes up as the sun, bull fire,
> Your images will have left
> No shadow of themselves. ("Add This to Rhetoric," lines 13–17)

Still, if we are to accept this reasoning, how do we account for the poem's protractions, its evident love of encumbrance? Why does the speaker so deliberately embroider his delivery of buildings, clouds, body, and sun with disqualified (and such exotic) adjectives and analogies (such as "Grisaille," "impearled," and "A fringed eye in a crypt")? Thus, despite—indeed, by virtue of—his extended insistence, a glowering artifice remains. "This is the figure and not / An evading metaphor" ("Add This to Rhetoric," lines 28–29) may mean to imply an essence apart, an unfigured figure, but all we have are words, cadence, craft, melodious guile. The separation of "figure" and "evading metaphor" is ingenuous at best.

As Nietzsche warned, truths consist of "a mobile army of metaphors, metonymics, anthropomorphisms"; they "are illusions of which one has forgotten that they *are* illusions" (quoted in Derrida 15). To again recall Stevens's intrepid comedian, the phrase "good, fat, guzzly fruit" is rescued along with the plum that provoked it (*Comedian as the Letter C* 5.33). It lingers just as lusciously in the mouth, a sweetly consoling interruption of a strict diet of untouched forms.

Disavowals of contact have the effect of applications: we are made to compare what has been introduced to us as incomparable.[3] In his *Adagia* (1934–40?), Stevens similarly displays the tension between rebellion against and allegiance to "poeticized" reality through a series of contradictory epigrams. For example, immediately after claiming that "the most beautiful . . . thing in the world is, of course, the world itself. This is so not only logically but categorically," he contends. "I believe in the image"

(193). "The ultimate value is reality," he declares, then goes on to state that "reality is not what it is. It consists of the many realities which it can be made into" (192, 202). On the one hand, Stevens sees the poet's talent as the "subtilization" of experience, which is principally a matter of apprehension of the world's complexity (201). On the other hand, when he argues that "metaphor creates a new reality from which the original appears to be unreal" (195), he appears to champion active manipulation of worldly materials. To say the least, Stevens is inconsistent when it comes to assessing his confidence in or his desire for the prospect of encountering or establishing a purely literal environment like a verbal pharmacy.

In sum, Stevens frequently refutes the appeal of the first version of Paradise considered above, not only because "in some sense, all things resemble each other," a belief that exalts the poet's occupation, but also because "perceptions of resemblance are effortless accelerations" of human intelligence, not distortions or distractions from legitimate intellectual business ("Three Academic Pieces" 71, 75). To perceive reality at all is to perceive it in costume. Thus, betrayals of Williams's restraining orders pervade Stevens's poetry. "An object the sum of its complications," as advertised in "Someone Put a Pineapple Together" (3.34), is an equation that, rather than subtracting the imagination's concoctions from perception, requires the imagination's participation if reality is to proceed toward its full definition. "Life consists / Of propositions about life," not by virtue of having renounced them ("Men Made Out of Words," lines 3–4). An Eden of unambiguous signification would be static, sterile. The real is too reckless for right angles to constrain; it "will from its *crude* compoundings come" (Stevens, *Notes toward a Supreme Fiction* 7.15; italics mine). The connoisseur of metaphor tacks into the truth. Following Dickinson, perhaps, we tell the truth "slant" not out of love of novelty but because the truth seems so inclined.

Close inspection of Williams's own poetry suggests that, for all of his vouching for the pure isolation of his materials, his method allows for a good deal of active interference as well. As he puts it in "A Sort of a Song," metaphor's role is "to reconcile / the people and the stones" (lines 7–8). "No ideas / but in things" may be the axiom we best remember from the poem, but metaphor inheres as a relational force nevertheless. Ideas are not dormant within things, they are deliberate assaults which, garbed as metaphors, take their cue from saxifrage, "my flower that splits / the rocks." We note that metaphor is delivered in "A Sort of a Song" by a brace of transitive verbs ("reconcile," "compose," "invent," "splits") of almost militant inspiration; the lurking snake, the model for his writing, operates through a series of motion-oriented adjectives. So Williams, too, betrays not just the inevitability but the catalytic responsibility of metaphor in his poetry as he struggles "to find some basis for avoiding the tyranny of the symbolic without sacrificing fullness of imagery" (quoted in Wagner 44).[4]

Whereas Williams typically busies himself with keeping figurative language inconspicuous as it goes about its organizational duties, Stevens, for all his considered interest in the subject, usually seems less stymied by this resistance to purgation. After all, as he tells the poet in "Prelude to Objects," a "diviner health" derives from the desultory business of "patting more nonsense foamed / From the sea." What is more, "We are conceived in your conceits" (2.1–3, 8). As Richard Poirier explains, "Because we assent to the fact that instability adheres to language, we become aware . . . that any exertions of authority over it . . . can be only temporary and sporadic" (*Poetry and Pragmatism* 137).[5]

A saving restlessness about language validates a faith in the transitional, whose lineage Poirier traces through Stevens, Frost, and Stein back to William James and Emerson. Borrowing from James, Poirier exalts "the reinstatement of the vague," and that vagueness, however dismaying to those who seek vivid resolutions and dependable arrivals in literary texts, is compatible with verbal extravagance. Fixity is an illusion that words perpetrate because they seem countersunk tight to the page; on the contrary, every text is "Fixed in the middle of the fall of things" (Nemerov, "Lion & Honeycomb," line 32).[6] Speaking of Frost's "For Once, Then, Something," Poirier notes that "there are enticements to significance here; there are, however, no entitlements" (*Poetry and Pragmatism* 146). To employ the title of his book on Frost, "the work of knowing" takes the place of conclusive knowledge, whose static quality implies dogmatism—hardly inspiring to the artistic quest. Instead, we are asked to produce, continually, more and other metaphors. In Frost's words, "Water came to rebuke the too clear water" in both the remembered well and the verbally rendered one ("For Once, Then, Something," line 15). As opposed to more rigid, more insistent textual strategies, "With simile-like arrangements things are seen as similar even as their nearness reveals difference. The turning is the main matter. Neither likeness nor unlikeness suffices. There is a gap between the extremes of uncovering and covering over in which similarities and differences oscillate" (Prunty 199). To find likeness is not to vanquish the environment; it is to respect the otherness that we recruit into formation. This results in local insights and stabilities suitable to the leaky ecosystem out of which they arise. So we discover that "the best metaphor goes to its compulsory equation with some unwillingness, something left out to contradict or to charm," which allows metaphor to suggest "both similarity and dissimilarity, the what-is-the-same floating uncannily, uneasily in the what-is-not" (Boruch 110).

Like Frost's fragile, quizzical "something"—the elusive presumption at the core of "For Once, Then, Something," as well as the ticklish "Something there is" that runs up against the tenacious wall in the opening line of "Mending Wall"—poetic refinements are not final.[7] To return to the opening lines of Nemerov's "Unscientific Postscript," which serve as my epigraph, "the dream" is clutched between "the world" and "the one law," much the way that Frost's blurry conceit is surrounded by the stony well. "The wisdom" referees between "the wish," through which the writer assembles his spells, and "things as they are," the hard rind of the real world that only fleetingly, grudgingly consents to his conjunctions. There is always a confession of doubt to upset equivalences. Adaptive, interrogative, often openly apologetic or deferential about their exaggerations, metaphors establish the most provisional of governments.

Metaphor can only reach out a gloved hand. But the essential coyness of resemblance does not minimize its effects. Tropes operate by beguiling what cannot be bullied. Likenings identify and preserve us. As Mary Kinzie explains, "The mutual attraction of the figurative for the literal has kept the tenor breathing through the vehicle or the physical world limber with power" (273). As in the case of Stevens's "amassing harmony" in *Notes toward a Supreme Fiction*, "It was not a choice / Between, but of" (*It Must Give Pleasure* 6.18–19). It is not a matter of metaphorical impositions contesting veritable obstructions so much as a matter of interactive and mutual expansions. Stevens's "Bouquet of Roses in Sunlight" are

> Too much as they are to be changed by metaphor,
> Too actual, things that in being real
> Make any imaginings of them lesser things.
> And yet this effect is a consequence of the way

> We feel and, therefore, is not real, except
> In our sense of it. . . . (lines 4–9)

Everything benefits from the transaction.

By way of evidence in recent prose, we find Annie Dillard's meditation on the impermeability of matter ironically sheathed in constant reference. Consciousness is not liberated by isolation but validated in concert: "The day is real; the sky clicks securely in place over the mountains, locks round the islands, snaps slap on the bay. Air fits flush on farm roofs; it rises inside the doors of barns and rubs at yellow barn windows. Air clicks up my hand cloven into fingers and wells in my ears' holes, whole and entire. I call it simplicity, the way matter is smooth and alone" (12–13). Sounds are too acutely suited and channeled here, rhythms too obviously reckoned for effect, for the writer to suggest that matter approaches innocent of fiddling. Dillard's lyrical language presses its attachments and becomes as much the object as the means of concern; her transports are *of* words and images as well as *through* them. This is sublimity pinned to the self's unique inflections. In place of Williams's ideal world of separate and legible signatures—his unique faith in nature's perfect diction—a textured, texted immanence presides. And if seeing is not conquering, it can still be investing things by and with the writer, an operation that is by turns anxious, embarrassed, and solemn, yet in any event undeterred. To return to terms suggested by Wallace Stevens, perhaps metaphor cannot after all "froth the whole heaven with its seeming-so," as the poet wonders in "Description without Place" (3.21); nevertheless, what Stevens refers to in *An Ordinary Evening in New Haven* as "the intricate evasions of as" (28.16) are by no means themselves evadable.

Witness in this regard the bold assertion of Ben Flesh in Stanley Elkin's *The Franchiser* that "I am going to link the world for you. I am going to have it make sense, but you must concentrate" (62). In truth, the title of the novel could serve most of Elkin's fiction, in that the effort to franchise—to possess, to situate, to ask that the world comport itself according to customary levels of commerce—transcends this individual businessman's savvy to represent the very indomitability of language that Elkin's heroes notoriously display. For despite the insidious ills Ben Flesh is heir to (specifically, multiple sclerosis and a temperamental prime rate), he is ever able to rally his faith in and through what words can conjure.

Whereas William Carlos Williams suggests that objects and entities are aloof and entire, bent to separate, inviolable activities like watches in pockets (activities that "like watches in pockets" fails to touch), the Elkin hero is an eager prospector of the analogous. Ben Flesh regularly drives his insights through a gauntlet of images. Although he tends to apologize for his "logorrhea" as being a symptom of his disease, he is no different from the rest of Elkin's characters who are traumatized by disconnectedness and distance, and whose symptoms feature verbal runs. The franchiser's rage for order, whereby the American landscape is colonized by the same fast-food restaurants, dry-cleaning establishments, and car washes—the nation's unsung limbic system—merely gives vocational certification to their common complaint.

It is the tension between their motivation to embrace the world and the novelty of the metaphors they employ to do so—between cliché and creativity—that is Elkin's trademark. To be sure, Flesh himself is treated to the same sort of associative swaddling when he is tricked out for formal presentation at his beleaguered dance studio:

> Mr. Flesh stands tux'd, his formal pants and jacket glowing like a black comb, his patent-leather shoes vaulted smooth and tensionless as perfect architecture. He might be standing in the skin of a ripe bright black apple. He feels, in the inky clothes, showered, springy, bouncy, knows in remissioned tactility around his shins, his clean twin sheathing of tall silk hose, can almost feel the condition of his soles, their shade like Negroes' palms. He is accessoried. In his old-fashioned dress white shirt his delicious burgundy studs are as latent with color as the warning lights on a dashboard. Onyx links, round and flat as elevator buttons, seal his cuffs, and dark suspenders lie on him with an increment of weight that suggests the thin holsters of G-men, and indeed there *is* something governmental in his dress, something maritime, chief-of-staff. The golden fasteners beneath his jacket could be captain's bars. A black bow tie lies across his throat like a propeller. (52–53)

Here is the franchiser enfranchised, attired in modifiers, dressed to *kvell*. Some of his accessories are modest enough, like the initial simile that unites the tuxedo to another enforcement of appearance (the black comb), or the string "showered, springy, bouncy," unexceptional as Williams's

bushwhacking in "Spring and All" . . . but Elkin's "and All" alerts us to the
exotics to come in the wake of "remissioned tactility." The "clean twin
sheathing of tall silk hose," the nouns and prepositional phrases whose
even cadence imitates the drawn-up stockings they express, has a sort of
decorousness about it, but it is immediately swaddled in references to
Negroes' palms, dashboard paraphernalia, and elevator buttons. There is
a certain caution in the "could be" of the paragraph's penultimate line, but
this is mock remorse, and the closing sentence suggests that the potential
military complex, were Elkin to persist, could be as extensive as any other.

The quirky ingenuity of Elkin's style—elastic, omnivorous, and dismissive of rhetorical protocols that would cordon off ordinarily segregated
registers—constitutes an elaborate objection to charges of incongruity.
Here is implied "the basic impartibility of human experience," according
to which hierarchies of high and low diction or high and low cultural allusion (not to mention the usual separations of noun and verb functions) are
refuted (Bailey 135–36). Ben Flesh's philosophy common denominates
America until, in the event that franchising proceeds to its logical extreme,
it is the same America everywhere, similed into seamless homogeneity.
The novel opens with an evidently disoriented Flesh traveling through
what could well be *anywhere*, thanks to the rank-and-file logos of Howard
Johnson's, Kentucky Fried Chicken, McDonald's, and so on, and realizing
that wherever he is, he is home (3). Flesh is quickly acclimated to the
democratic core; it is the same Eden everywhere.

The downside is that finding the landscape presaturated by geographic
and linguistic idioms threatens to consign the artist to utter predictability.
Driving about the undifferentiatable Elmiras, Springfields, and Omahas
he has helped to equate, Flesh occasionally feels stalemated, more laid up
than at home. His multiple sclerosis, whose flare-ups feature an inability
to distinguish textures, could symbolize a profound obstacle to the writer,
for whom precise, particular perception is critical. In much the same way
as the predictable frontier, the trite figure "is worn out not because it has
been used often before, but because it cannot bear the burden of new
attitudes" (Embler iv). In the case of Elkin's novel, the man whose career
relies on his aptitude for consumer urges has unwittingly contributed to
"civilization's demyelination" (*Franchiser* 140). As his and the country's
parallel diseases progress, Flesh becomes more and more the moody syn-
thesizer. As he mortgages his franchises to save his ill-conceived Travel
Inn, it is as though he were closing off lines of inference.

Likewise, the very innovations that enable Elkin to open his paragraphs to disparate cargoes could tend to restrict "the range of the strange" to which he is committed. Is the successful metaphor one that retains its peculiarity or one that, seeming to strike at the shared heart of things, is finally digested whole, leaving no trace of its erratic origin? We are faced with the contradiction of the brilliant disguise: our remarking upon the cleverness of the deception exposes it.

To some extent, the evolution of the reputation of metaphor anticipates this confusion. We need only contrast, say, Thomas Sprat's 1667 *History of the Royal Society,* which proclaimed all figures fat and rejected "all the amplifications, digressions, and swellings of style" as moral lapses (quoted in Hawkes 30), with post-Romantic contentions that metaphor is no mere ornament, no foreign liaison, but an essential aspect of language, in order to appreciate how, as Richard Wilbur puts it in "Praise in Summer," there is no evading "this mad *instead*" which "Perverts our praise to uncreation" (lines 7–8).[8] It should be noted that even as Wilbur's speaker laments (or pretends to lament) the inescapable interference of figured speech between self and nature, his closing plea does not rid itself of such "contaminants":

> Should it not be enough of fresh and strange
> That trees grow green, and moles can course in clay,
> And sparrows sweep the ceiling of our day? (lines 12–14)

Metaphor is not expendable. Put another way, preferring so-called literal language to figurative language falsely assumes their clear distinctiveness and easy divisibility. In *More than Cool Reason: A Field Guide to Poetic Metaphor,* George Lakoff and Mark Turner systematically refute notions of semantic autonomy and objective reference upon which purportedly ordinary or literal language is generally based (114–20). Similarly, Max Black contends that it is misleading to treat metaphor as some kind of violation of otherwise problem-free, "neutral" language. Words, like royalty, are born into their appointments.

Discouraging as this may be to students who indict writers for refusing to say plainly what they mean, there is no foundation to the notion that conscientious application of presumably unspoiled language could somehow tease the tangles out of texts. As Stevens concludes in the essay "Effects of Analogy," even the man "for whom reality is enough," who purportedly "sees without images" the true contours of the tangible, unwittingly launches figures of his own, and his imageless environment joins the other "pictorializations of men, for whom the world exists as a world and for whom life exists as life, the objects before which they come and speak, *with intense choosing*, words that we remember and make our own" (40; italics mine). The worldliest concerns resolve as words. Even square-hatted rationalists whose laundered thoughts evolve in unfurnished apartments find that their transcendence of figuration is itself a figure. Karsten Harries anticipates this condition when he defines metaphor in terms of impropriety and collision; his terminology identifies the paradox that the very wrenchings that metaphor employs in order to escape into an autotelic orbit also "destroy our experience of the work of art as a self-sufficient whole" (72–73). Harries conducts the problem still further: "What the poet has fallen into and what estranges him from that pure realm that beckons him with its promise of self-sufficiency is the necessary public and referential dimension of language. Poetry becomes a finally vain effort to rescue man from that dimension and to replace it with a purer environment, an environment that does not tolerate words but demands silence" (76). And a lucky thing that it is a vain effort, Harries implies, certainly insofar as literature is concerned. Attaining the goal would not be a successful amputation but a suicide.

"The plainness of plain things" examined in *An Ordinary Evening in New Haven* is not only a "savagery," then; it is also another sleight of poetry. "The poem of pure reality, untouched / By trope or deviation," the blank beneath "the trials of device," and every other wan concoction pretending toward the "vulgate of experience"—these are predefeated fabrications, and fabrications always (*An Ordinary Evening in New Haven* 4.1, 9.4–5). This puts the lie to the notion that improved access to Truth is somehow a matter of demanding higher fidelity diction.

For Max Black, too, no pristine standard exists; in fact, the simplest etymological excavation done on individual words proves that even the smallest of our linguistic building materials wear substantial figurative armor ("More about Metaphor" 22–27).[9] Try as you may, when you "say of what you see in the dark," there is no avoiding "the rotted names" (Stevens, *Man with the Blue Guitar* 32.4). Association is a rash that scratching expands.

Metaphor shields us from the onslaught of utterly discrete occasions. Significantly, contemporary readings of metaphor tend to prefer a "vehicular" emphasis over a static one when they consider its characteristics. Indeed, whereas the term *image* suggests something relatively resolved and nodally fixed, *metaphor* connotes motion, the ongoingness of the figurative operation within a text and in the reader's mind (Wheelwright 69, 71–72).[10] Seen in this manner, metaphor is not only a constituent of arguments and attitudes, it is a mode of development. It cruises for sequences that are by no means stationary—the "evanescent symmetries," as Stevens puts it ("Negation," line 9). We may think of a flight of geese, which, conjoined by some mysterious current of advertency, continue to alter and adapt to one another as they progress.

This orientation toward process, writes Richard Kuhns, is the fundamental difference between literary and philosophical employments of metaphorical strategies: "The effort in philosophy is to restrict metaphor; in poetry it is the opposite, to let metaphor work, pushing outwards the boundaries of inclusiveness as the poem is responded to. Poetic metaphor demands interpretive novelty and ingenuity, while the philosophic is usually responded to by an attempt to subdue through conceptual rigor" (237).[11] Instead of investing things with creative flexibility, "conceptual rigor" aspires to the same implacable status as the reality the imagination confronts. The motive for literary metaphor, by contrast, is to posit expressive intimations that contest the stolid "weight of primary noon / The A B C of being" (Stevens, "The Motive for Metaphor," lines 15–16). Truth blears in the upper latitudes of innovative relation. So it is that A. R. Ammons, in "Corson's Inlet," leaves himself open to "eddies of meaning" (line 19) in defiance of "sharp lines":

> no arranged terror: no forcing of image, plan
> or thought:
> no propaganda, no humbling of reality to precept. . . .
>   . . .
> still around the looser, wider forces work:
> I will try
> to fasten into order enlarging grasps of disorder, widening
> scope, but enjoying the freedom that
> Scope eludes my grasp, that there is no finality of vision. . . .
>   (lines 114–16, 122–26)

That vision is inconclusive does not disqualify its insights. Say rather that the tentativeness of vision—identified by its liberal admission policies, its eagerness to trope and associate, and all the broad vocabulary of specula-

tion—tries to coax the world out of its mute stringencies. In keeping with
Max Black's interaction theory, metaphor gives rise to an assimilative,
symbiotic link, the result being "a more inclusive, unifying context"
(Singer 23).[12] In the lively environment of articulation, the looser forces
are wider forces.

If metaphor were merely a self-confined dance of resemblance, its operations like those of a crystal compulsively repeating its essential structure,
insight would be solely a linguistic property, originating *and* terminating
at the level of words. When William Gass speaks of multidirectional
metaphors, he means to maximize their endowments. In the best metaphors, "both terms are resonant. If Hardy writes, 'She tamed the wildest
flowers,' then not only has 'she' become an animal trainer, the flowers have
become animals. Nor has 'taming' been left untouched, for such taming is
now seen in terms of gardening. Now if fictions are metaphors or models,
then perhaps they should occasionally 'fictionalize' the reader" (interview
with McCauley 35). Gass envisions a metaphor that provokes its own climate; reading, we are read—and revised—in return, in conjunctive empathy. The language is positively geared to astound.[13] At the same time, and
actually in keeping with this goal, ambiguity is not the artist's impasse but
part of his contribution. So as Marianne Moore reminds us, parrying objections (her own notorious one in "Poetry" included), "we must have the
courage of our peculiarities" (quoted in Morse 36).

Constitutive functions are often most evident when they misfire. Verbal elegance may lose its savor, turn reckless, or simply exhaust itself, and
the "madness" of or over the manufactured "instead" begin to dominate
our attentions. We may again recall Howard Nemerov, who in "Holding
the Mirror Up to Nature" ruefully regards those heartbreaking shapes that
resist imaginative implication:

> They will never become valentines
> or crucifixes, never. Night clouds
> go on insanely as themselves
>   though metaphors would be prettier. . . . (lines 3–6)

Earnestly laid as cornerstones, nouns flank an absence after all; verbs flirt
shamelessly, but their targets remain chaste. Regardless, "the clouds go on
clowning," the moon does not eclipse the masquerade that it is Artemis,
and in the "idiot dreams" of fabricated heroes "the buzzard circles like a

clock"—all testifying to the unquashability of tropes even at the moment we are alerted to their perjuries. From Dillard's dilated morning to Elkin's overdressed entrepreneur, imagination clambers past the parliamentarian in us. Implications prosper wherever the mind alights.

This, then, is the looming paradox: metaphor is inevitable (slipping Stevens's imperious "nots"), yet inevitably futile (frustrated even by Williams's meager bushes). The isolated star is an optical illusion, but what it illuminates is a profounder darkness. And yet, metaphor aspires beyond the role of ornamentation to become a means of knowledge. Hence Jacques Derrida's braiding of volatile terminology in his essay on "White Mythology": "What makes metaphor possible (what makes good and true metaphor possible) is what makes truth possible" (37).

My focus in *This Mad Instead* is on how the interplay of metaphorical breakthrough and breakdown is handled in a variety of fictions by an equally various selection of contemporary American writers: Paul West, Don DeLillo, Steven Millhauser, Paul Auster, William Gass, Richard Powers, Kathy Acker, and John Updike. Apart from the longer chapter on Updike's Rabbit novels (a longitudinal analysis of the development or deterioration of metaphor over the course of that thirty-year venture), I am mainly treating works written over the past fifteen years or so. In the matter of my selection and integration of texts, I find myself animated by something akin to Ammons's "looser, wider forces": guided by the elastic understandings and treatments of metaphor represented here, *This Mad Instead* is more of a broad invitational than a parochial school in terms of its program of eligibility.

Whatever their differences in terms of aesthetic philosophy or academic reputation, the works under discussion do share a deliberate attention to the sometimes enabling, sometimes distorting propensities of the verbal medium. Without exception, they deliver "insteads" whose madness and whose magic are closely allied. And while I hesitate to pronounce these to be the most salient, much less universally heralded, authors of the day, I believe that their individual courtings of, or bouts with, metaphor shed light not only on their own unique artistic projects but also on the so-called truth-value of fiction itself, and by extension, upon the self-conscious prominence of this issue on the contemporary literary scene.

Metaphor as the fortuitous error, the hopeful agnostic, the volunteer rose; metaphor as unruly ballistic, wayward agent, currency exchange. Conscientiously exploited, metaphors are wit's kindling; conscientiously extended, they may not only enhance but justify the verbal enterprise, wicking sense through the whole of the work. Hence the reward for the perspective that calls the fall into figuration a fortunate one: the figure in the carpet *is* the carpet after all.

Chapter 1

BEHOLDING PAUL WEST AND *THE WOMEN OF WHITECHAPEL*

To his painting *The Treason of Images* (1928–29), one of his most infamous weddings of cheek and dread, René Magritte assigns the warning *"Ceci n'est pas une pipe."* The joke, of course, is that this is indeed a *picture* of a pipe, but the consequences may be more profound for ekphrastic presumptions. As Murray Krieger defines it, *ekphrasis* is a miracle and a mirage together: a miracle in that the dream of "a tangible verbal space" seems to be attained and the temporal curse of narrative lifted; a mirage because the more effective the suggestion of an image, the more apparent the illusionary strategies and motives of the author (xvi–xvii). In other words, whereas art and writing share creative and parasitic penchants, those penchants finally run parallel. Joseph Conrad's announced goal of doing justice to the visible universe—"before all, to make you *see*" (147)— must be understood in light of the failure to equate two distinct mediations of vision, as well as two separate, however comparable, kinds of imaginative distillate.

The concept of *enargeia*, whereby one uses words to try to yield a description so vivid as to represent Ruskin's apprehension of "the very plain and leafy fact" (168) of the precedent world before the reader's eye, or inner eye, if you will, seems to imply that language is the somehow dis-

advantaged medium of expression, which approaches legitimacy principally in emulation (however futile) of the spatial arts.[1] Toward this end,
too, we may recollect Joyce Cary's Gully Jimson, for whom painting is substantial while "talk is lies. The only satisfactory form of communication is
a good picture. Neither true nor false. But created" (95).

Nevertheless, it might just as readily be argued that language is "privileged by its very intelligibility" (Krieger 12), and approximating the role of
reality's squire is a matter of insufficient or misdirected ambition. In her
book *The Search for Synthesis in Literature and Art,* Ann Colley deems it
a matter of the integrity of each mode of expression that convergences not
become victimizations (66). Irving Massey voices similar concerns in *Find
You the Virtue* when he variously suspects images of suppression, coer-
cion, and self-idolatry; accordingly, it becomes an ethical priority to introduce instabilities into one's inventions—to show their tumult intact—so
as to preserve "this errant quality of language, its redeeming elusiveness"
against pictorial impingements (3).

Paradoxically, commentators regularly assign such adjectives as "vital"
and "intense" to compliment a given painting's transcendence of fixity, as
if hue were coaxed to cry, while texts continue to labor under the stolid
terminology of arrest—structure, form, image—and the modernist myths
of condensed gestures and visionary instants. But the stubborn truth
remains that painting can imply but never reclaim the performance of
which it is but a trace; and no exercise of framing, no iconic clutch, can
truly control the dynamic properties of so restless an aesthetic as words
produce. (If Magritte's painting tells us it is not a pipe, verbal depiction
may be called upon to testify that it is not even a picture of a pipe, so that
the space it articulates is still further removed from any model.)[2] Its solid-
seeming deposits notwithstanding, narrative respects the predicate that
icons disguise. The writer's treadmill fate "is to keep on finishing a thing"
that can never reliably be called "a finished thing" (Stein 93–94).

Paul West is one writer who continually risks the vanity of setting up
shop in that divide between plastic being and verbal becoming, sustaining
both in an open-ended correlation. Not for him the stolid docks of convention. As West explains, the novel's novelty depends upon "the elastic-
ity of consciousness counterpointed by the as-is-ness of nature" (quoted
in Mooney 267). Stylistically, West follows Thoreau's counsel "to cut a
broad swath and shave close" (91) in that he combines unbridled imaginative premises and figurative ballistics with unmatched depth of verbal

focus. Therefore, while many of West's novels betray their indebtedness to historical personages (as do *The Very Rich Hours of Count von Stauffenberg* or *Lord Byron's Doctor*) or to virtual schemes (such as the Milky Way model for *Gala*) and ensure that the superimposition of fiction does not wholly obscure its origins, West's addiction to sonic textures and thickly imaged speculation—fiction as an exhibition game—is just as beguiling for its own sake.[3]

West's title for his collected essays and reviews, *Sheer Fiction*, encapsulates this doubleness. On the one hand, the brand of fiction West praises and practices is sheer in the sense of its permeability, its impressive commitment to erudition, research, and ulterior disciplines: "I've always hungered after, insisted on, *detail* in any writing, otherwise it's just a vacant trope unmoored," West said by way of concluding a discussion of the precise matrix in which each of his novels is situated (interview with Morrow 154). On the other hand, the fiction is sheer in the sense of being "solely" or "purely" fiction—purpled not by abusive hands but for regal display: imagination fully deployed, "the world written *up*, intensified and made pleasurably palpable, not only to suggest the impetuous abundance of Creation, but also to add to it by showing—showing off—the expansive power of the mind itself" ("In Defense" 47).[4] The self-evidence and self-justification Gertrude Stein relates to the visual arts—"An oil painting is something that looking at it it looks as it is, an oil painting" (89)—is hereby claimed for verbal art. This argument is also in keeping with Ronald Sukenick's several discussions about the opacity of words, in which case descriptive passages are their own destinations.[5] The novelist describes things "not to make us see those things but to test the language against them. . . . The pleasure of description is the pleasure of a linguistic skill, not that of a genre painting" (Sukenick 31). The writer need not worry about purging his prose of its figures in deference to depiction because surrogacy is too confining an ambition. It underestimates the creative propensity of the medium.

Nevertheless, while West's reputation for ostentation carries the day— William Gass and Stanley Elkin are two of a very small number of contemporaries who are capable of similar stratospherics and whose beleaguered characters are as operatic in their chains as West's—in the end there is no escaping the gravitational pull of derivation. Life and its particulars come before, as do words themselves laden with etymology and prior usage, so the test put to the author's talents is to treat belatedness not as a deterrence but as an occasion, a platform from which to launch the more difficult dives. "You can go very far away," West warns, "but the umbilical never snaps, and home base can always reel you in. Purple, however, makes the most of the ride" ("In Defense" 53). It is this interplay between stylistic prodigality and deterministic context, the ongoing isometrics between pioneering self-assertions and dutifully reproductive tracts, that creates the unique tensions of a Paul West novel.

West has demonstrated a long-standing concern with the problem of invoking or, more ambitiously, reconstituting images with words. Initially a painter himself, West continues to rely upon visual complements for his verbal constructions. Vision is authenticated when it is visible: "Once I get the right visual image, I know where I am; I know what I'm doing. But until I get it, I don't think I'm in the mood" (interview with Madden 157). It is not surprising to discover so many artists and artist-surrogates populating his fiction, especially in view of the fact that the nature of creative consciousness itself appears to be West's main thematic focus. *Portable People,* his collection of biographical "portraits," intentionally foregrounds the self-conscious duality of his art, in that it combines verbal sketches with visual illustrations (by Joe Servello); the reader/viewer engages these celebrities—the book is an eccentric human zoo of past and contemporary artists, actors, athletes, musicians, politicians, scientists, and other originals—not only as their depictions compare to their respective historical precedents but also through the mutual contextualization of the two media, which now ratify, now contradict, the respective impressions they make.

In conversation West is more cavalier than this about the compatibility of word and image, taking his cue from their shared attention to synthesis (interview with Madden 158). West seems to endow some of his own subjects in *Portable People* with extreme versions of this sort of confidence. Witness the declaration of West's John Clare that "line is infinitely mine, as unseeable apart from its earth as the outline of a strawberry from its fruit. . . . One of these all-alike days I will tread over it and, untripped, walk clean into the mind of God, all set out like a sensible vegetable garden" (13); or there is the bombast of his Auguste Rodin, whose God may be less decorous than Clare's but not less conducive to his inclinations: "God's dong, if such a thing can be, is a velvet hammer made of love that thumps the stars home, where they belong, in the moist pleat of the empyrean." Sexual, spiritual, and artistic exploits all rudely, confidently conspire: "None shall contain us, we shall be so massive in our roistering . . . with our humpbacked fists banged deep into the soft clay of eternity" (45, 46).

These excerpts suggest a giving over of reality to the artist's resolve. However, there is conflicting testimony to be found in West's other fictions, in which the appropriative assaults of the artist are more uncertain, their products more compromised. In "Short Life of Esteban Fletcher," for instance, West features the travails of a writer whose exclusive designs upon metafictional premises are swarmed under by pedestrian details. "Epiphanies and ecstasies he couldn't lift out of their homely circumstances," our narrator confides, and the contamination of his pure mental refuge by "the onrush of the knowable" plunges Fletcher into obesity and mental breakdown (87, 82). But our narrator considers this to be an object lesson of sorts and suggests that there exists nevertheless an avenue of profitable negotiation between the poetic artist and his prosaic environment: "A wiser commentator than I would point out that, having at last hit on the prose of life—its dry bread and drier protocol—he should have savored the mix, all those preposterous juxtapositions, and then advanced to re-see Infinity in a grain of, say, Dusseldorf mustard: its atoms, all alike, in their invariable, irreducible, divinely designed uniqueness" (87). The fact remains that the artist's materials may prove intractable, the glamour of his vision to the contrary. Yet there may be some consolation in the possibility that since subduing the world drains its energies or constrains it to doctrine, the obsolescence of West's Rodin in the postmodern hall of melting frames and authorial insecurities could be beneficial after all. George the Place in Flowers Where Pollen Rests, West's blind Hopi carver of kachina dolls, explains: "Of all carvers, I wasted least, hoping . . . to save in the doll, visible beneath even the most beautiful trimmings, the bulk of the original tree's heart, its basis in growth" (*Place in Flowers* 28).

George's hope implies that it is also possible to see the operations of metaphor themselves not as tending toward a rigid equivalence but as retaining, even underscoring, provisionality and fabrication. For if, as was noted in the introduction to this study, Richard Wilbur's sonnet "Praise in Summer" is correct that there is no dispensing with "this mad *instead*," which "Perverts our praise to uncreation," neither does metaphor effect a fusion that causes its original elements to vanish into the hybrid. "Uncreation," "wrenching things awry," and "it must needs derange" are the unerasable scars left by the poet's manipulations; and yet, even as our speaker laments (or pretends to lament, in any case) the inevitable interference of figuration between self and nature, his serenading the pristine depends on figures for its eloquence and impact. More than the harbingers of all that is "fresh and strange"—the trees, moles, and sparrows of the closing lines of the poem—metaphors are what are fresh and strange about them.

This is metaphor's essential predicament: its relational zeal, its pressing of kinship like a bankrupt cousin, potentially points toward a static synthesis. Militating against such an outcome, though, is another characteristic of metaphor that is just as entrenched as its synthetic urgency: "Metaphor, by redirecting consciousness to something beyond the immediate experience, opens up a space which protects an event, image, word, or individual from closing down over another. This space keeps desire alive and saves the entity from the stultifying consequences of a metamorphosis when one being or image merges completely with another" (Colley 3). In other words, metaphor may insinuate but never insist. Another pair of lines from Wilbur serves concisely to ground the dichotomy. In one poem he eagerly pursues the rewards of verbal contagion: "Odd that a thing is most itself when likened"; then he gives us pause on another occasion when he considers with pleasure "How we are enlarged by what estranges."[6] The idea is that aesthetic experience, like other human experiences, is dynamic. "The aesthetic 'attitude' is restless, searching, testing—is less an attitude than action: creation and recreation" with and among the terms set by the work and by the world (Nelson Goodman quoted in Steiner 29).

Especially when tended by so vigorously inventive a writer as Paul West, metaphor seeks to liberate words from habit; but we recognize the appeal against an equally demanding conscription regardless of its innovative or illuminating charms. William Carlos Williams stipulates as much in his prologue to *Kora in Hell* that no author must trust his own machinations too far: "The true value is that peculiarity which gives an object a character by itself. The associational or sentimental value is the false. Its imposition is due to a lack of imagination, to an easy lateral sliding" (14). Williams was introduced in the opening chapter of this study through his intention to guard against facile equations and reckless correlations based on sound, improvisation, or serendipity (what he decries as "mere vegetable coincidence"). He opposes the blurring of things that typically defines metaphor, preferring the precision of differentiation. Instead of this "easy lateral sliding" Williams proposes a brand of atomization which, as defended in a previously cited passage, respects "those inimitable particles of dissimilarity to all other things," and which, importantly, Williams does not speak of as the poet's frustration but as the "perfection" of the realities he encounters (prologue to *Kora in Hell* 18). "Only connect" is a naive creed because it underestimates both the subtlety of that enterprise and the contradictions inherent in disparate artistic commitments to originality and authenticity.

In keeping with these several exposures of verbal sleight of hand, Paul West's lavishly appointed style brings into focus the warring qualities of the language he so ingeniously employs. Particularly in *The Women of Whitechapel and Jack the Ripper,* a novel overtly dominated by the intersections between art, life, and writing, linguistic coherences are built only to be stripped to structure.

West's alternative title for *The Women of Whitechapel* was *The Eye of the Beholder,* which certainly suits a novel about Walter Sickert, the voyeur who draws too close to the sordid vortex he tries to capture on canvas. That discarded title also anticipates our discussion of metaphor in that speculation about the notion of a "beholder" yields differing degrees of appropriation. To behold is to seize, but it also reminds us of being beholden, or beholding to, which implies conditions of distance and obligation.[7]

West takes full advantage of the descriptive opportunities his subject and setting provide. He seems positively to revel in the gruesome eviscerations of fallen women perpetrated by his villain (a point regularly made by squeamish reviewers of the novel).[8] West steeps us in the crippled dictions and dark intestinal toil of London's brothel district; he relishes all of relation's plugs and sockets, the sticky hydraulics of political and sexual intercourse alike. But it is the elevation to protagonist of Walter Sickert that is West's most significant trump in *The Women of Whitechapel.* Set in relief against so squalid a background, Sickert's dreams of gentility seem strained and unformed; set against the author's ultracompetence, Sickert's artistic frustrations seem poignant, then frantic, as the seductions of Whitechapel contest, and grotesquely manifest, the plots founded at Windsor Palace.

The Women of Whitechapel is a startling mixture of history, rumor, conjecture, and authorial prerogative. The painter Walter Sickert has accepted the formidable job of seeing to the safety, welfare, and reputation of Queen Victoria's oafish grandson, Prince Eddy, as he slops his appetites about the seamier precincts of the empire. Sickert introduces

Eddy, who perpetually resides "in an infatuated blur" (25), to one Annie Crook, the disillusioned shopgirl who eventually bears him a daughter, Alice Margaret. The ambiguous signal is given, and Eddy, along with the child, is swept into protective custody; Annie, on the other hand, is shunted off to Guy's Hospital and Dr. William Gull, who plies the unwitting young woman with spiked grapes, then lobotomizes her, leaving her a moaning, anonymous hollow.

When Mary Kelly, a favorite consort and occasional model of Sickert's, composes a letter of complaint and, by implication, extortion to the Queen, complete with signatures from several fellow prostitutes, Gull's expert savagery is commissioned once again. With systematic grisliness, a lethal entourage moves out: Gull, with his locked box of a heart; his driver, Netley, a human bludgeon; and Sickert, the depraved familiar of these women, whose role is to coax the victims in and to witness without flinching the ghastly, sanctioned vengeance. What West proposes, then, is a corporate Ripper, the growth of whose myth only increases imperial deniability and further deflects the question of from what royal heights the crimes actually derive.

That the deaths of such women inspire little outrage from the society that consigns them to oblivion anyway, as well as the fact that they exemplify differences in the manner but not in the philosophy of political expediency, receives consistent attention throughout the novel. But it is Sickert who most directly embodies West's central questions. His initial yearning for "abstraction incarnate" implies the contradiction that will put the lie to the notion of "purity of phenomenon" and the dream of an uninflected, or uninfected, work of art (8).[9] Not only will the pre-Raphaelite dream of bringing an "ever-basting light" to the canvas be dissolved by the perversities of the painter, but so too will the very idea of the artist's bringing the world into captivity succumb.

Operating on the verge of official esteem, Sickert is nonetheless absorbed by the unwholesome, the debauched; he is professionally and personally dedicated to "the muse of the unsavory" (68), and in his "passion for what's beneath" he eagerly decants the erotic seepage of the world (281). A gross impressionist, he prefers Italy and France, "where art had heat and fat," to England, which he finds "draughty and proper and bland" (36). Life accurately understood and engaged is "a delicious wound" to be entered like a compliant whore (53). In other words, aesthetic transcendence strikes him as sterile. It denies his natural inclination "to be sen-

tiently in the thick of life . . . to feel it swilling and billowing about him as
it issued from the sluices of God. . . . An artist, he was convinced, needed
such a sense of the remorseless copiousness of things, and, lacking it,
would degenerate into a suburban pit-a-pat expert, an orthodox butterfly"
(51). "These were the gestures of the life he cleaved to, believing that he
painted frippery unless he delved and came up with moss and rot, bone
power and love manure" (209). His slovenly habitat feeds this insistence,
where his clutter of canvases are not stages in spiritual hygiene so much
as a sordid glut or "chromatic spoor" befitting Sickert's paradoxical quality of "dapper malignity" (21, 42).

The birth of Alice Margaret, fruit and proof of yoked opposites, is ren-

Thus Sickert is West's arch assimilator, who even as he aspires to court
favor remains a willing conduit for the corruptive spectacles of Cleveland
Street. Ellen, his intended, is not the cure but a chaste counterpoint to his
obsessions; in the narrows of her gentility the artist finds precise ground,
as it were, for his figures of putrefaction. And Sickert is forever conscious
of—both disturbed and aroused by—the dangers inherent in such collisions: "Only a deity, Sickert thought, could endure the massive contradictions of the double nature he envisioned, both enchanted and revulsed by
the clashes in his creation" (285). If a "slimy and unstoppable" experience
is basic to life, and if one only approaches "the disheveled shamefulness
the artist needs in order to be the true pariah of his genius" when he
perches "on the brink," there is also the threat of being overwhelmed that
jeopardizes what it informs (57, 44).

The birth of Alice Margaret, fruit and proof of yoked opposites, is rendered in the novel as a swamp of exposed innards and bloody membranes.
It mirrors the growing chaos of Sickert's paintings and, as it turns out,
raises the cost of Sickert's addiction to "worstness" (124). Initially Sickert
contented himself with being "a mature pachyderm of witness" (38),
whereby paint could translate, if not sanitize, the sordid; but as his art
is increasingly exposed to fiendish political urgencies, it loses its highly
touted capacity for conferring order: "It was no use painting people, urging them around on a palette and daubing them into places they had never
thought of going," he thinks bitterly. "Beyond color there was another
realm, of incalculable deeds, where lives fell apart and lovers saw each
other for the last time" (109). This is the same artist who had had sex with
Mary Kelly, then, in a profound example of the natural ease with which
life and art might coalesce, combined her effluvia with his paints (27); he
is the artist who had confidently believed that, from boudoir to studio,

"people were his metier, greasy and palpitant" (41). Now rot and confusion assault him:

> The work of oblivion goes ahead, grinding his conscience down into chalky atoms, soon to blow away while the dedicated painter reduces all hues to a drainage green, like an angry child who rubs all the colors together until nothing remains recognizable. He was thinking of Dark Annie disemboweled, of the sheer visual turmoil that came to birth before his eyes in the *Crusader*. If all the forms of life were melting down, surely what they melted into should be something just as holy as the forms: the molten wax of waxworks, crammed with possibility and hope and shape, magnificently latent; but he did not have that feeling at all, he was adrift in a world of destruction and decomposition, an artist in a shambles, and he could not understand how someone such as he, a connoisseur of life's mutterings and sulks, its puddles and distempers, should be feeling so little awe before the image of the human flayed. His indignation depended, he saw, on the holiness of the human effigy, as on that of the rabbit, elm, or thrush. Shape, he saw, was the thing God-given, and not flesh, not offal, not blood. He loved the dry. (289)

It is not that Sickert had been devoted to isolated sublimity or shunned the tint of viscera; rather, his longing for shape and "the dry" marks his desperation at being implicated in the revolting deeds of the Ripper.

But as the passage above also notes, Sickert cannot deny the possibility that the flayed corpses left in the wake of the *Crusader* are products of his own aesthetic. Sickert and the sinister Gull apply themselves to "the helpless pliability of human stuff" with identical zeal (100). (At times the slashing Gull seems wholly given over to aleatory techniques; at other times he broods over his use of the razor like a topiarist; occasionally caprice leads him to gouge hieroglyphics to set off the detectives.) In *The Women of Whitechapel*, whoring, portraiture, and vivisection are all performed within the same gluey medium.

Furthermore, the artist who blends his paints with his lover's discharges and the butcher who resews doped grapes with human hair betray the same fundamental passions and perspectives. Sickert and Gull both "loved tissue and muscle, flesh and skin, and felt like someone reading poetry while the rest of the world read prose" (101). Despite Sickert's pangs of guilt, both are intrigued by the same human sluices. They share a clinical distance critical to art, surgery, or murder; and if Gull rummaging in the bowels of a given victim is scrupulous and ruminative—he is like Joyce's removed artist-God paring his fingernails, or in his case meditatively scraping the blood from beneath them—Sickert is no less "a man turned abacus" in the coerced observance of the scene (295).

Both men proceed from "the argument from design" at its most diabolical. With geometric ruthlessness and considerable pleasure, Gull distributes the corpses about London's East End to duplicate the Masonic emblem he carved into one of the faces. The doctor who declared each of his lobotomies "an experiment in fusion" brings the same detached sense of justification to the broadening of his duties by court mandate. He envisions a horrifying coup on the part of these women, in which they seize his knives and needles and castrate and core him; but he consoles himself with the likelihood that they would leave him his eyes to behold them (131).[10] For his part, Sickert, "almost a past master of the done for," wonders if some day he will "drown in all his browns: all those sauces, soups, and glues his mind had lingered on, in a coprophile's tizzy" (285). Yet he too remains transfixed. Moral foundering aside, the craving for "what's beneath" remains. In truth, as Gull's go-between, Sickert proves to be more than complicit in the Ripper's crimes. He is fluent.

Clearly, no serenely symbiotic relationship between art and life can survive the plot of *The Women of Whitechapel*. West's message seems to be that if imagination cannot simply represent, neither can it transmogrify with impunity. "If only, instead of plopping into textbooks, such things settled into the still-soft pigments of art instead, not as events but as pomegranates, thrushes, frogs" (148). If only, that is, human history were as pliable as human flesh and its artistic mediations. But the novel's course of events, all panoramic grimness and psychic shatter, will not rest in any frame, much less conform: "No picture was static, he was convinced; the paint was always on the move, never mind how dry, or seemingly so. Atoms shifted and gases soared; the air was catalyst, and the humidity, and what looked like an autonomous work, to be hung or slashed, was much more of an extrusion from the atmosphere than it seemed; it was the soil rising up, the wind settling down, the puddle at the halt, air on parade" (214). Fidelity to reality is hereby redefined in terms of a dynamic model instead of a static one, which coincides with a shift from *enargia* to *energia* as a mimetic standard, the latter attuned to analogies with organic, autotelic processes rather than to nature's outer appearances (Schnitzer 5). Every picture is a motion picture, in other words. Images and the intentions of their makers are "crammed with flecks of the random" (278), and it is impossible for Sickert to justify an aesthetic philosophy that ignores the awful turbulence at the heart of things.[11] (We recall Netley's careful arrangement of one jettisoned corpse to give it the appearance of spontaneous disarray: a "stilled" life composed for effect yet retaining evidence of the turmoil that had occasioned it.) If the word-by-word chugging of prose cannot adequately reprise experience, how can a visual artifact pretend to do so? "*Splotches moved* if you looked at them long enough," "the ghost of Leonardo" whispers to Sickert (272). Things keep bleeding in the wake of dissection.

The demolition of Sickert's detached, resolute vantage point may be read as an implicit critique of the modernist aesthetic, which, like the self-legitimating authority and imperial concentration of the aristocracy, is predicated upon the subjugation of tensions and disharmonies (in art, in politics) and the recuperation of contradictions. Here the obstreperous Other—the women of Whitechapel—whom the state deems negligible, then disposable, continues to implicate the artist, who cannot manage the mandatory transformation from mimetic technician of that marginalized population to absolute instrument of their elimination. Nor does the "master narrative" of Jack the Ripper suppress competing fables.

Because the events of the novel resist conversion into art's kindlier element—given, in fact, the insurgencies of paint and perspective in *The Women of Whitechapel*—Sickert relies upon a method of deflection. The vanity of conferred form is bargained down to an art that filters without seceding from atrocity: Sickert discovers "that a man might engage in unspeakable things and still survive," if not be fully restored to his former affability; moreover, and just as crucial to Sickert, he might "retain his grasp of the cursive line" (304). Specifically, by devoting himself to a series of paintings about the so-called Camden Town Murder of 1907, he fashions a sort of historical palimpsest that simultaneously accommodates and disguises his obsession with the Ripper murders of 1888. The law does not come for him, and no lasting suspicion lights upon him, so Sickert chooses indirect repentance: confession by allusion. What sickness

Sickert cannot subdue he tries to defraud. But once again, art does not exorcise his demons; it authenticates them. Interpreting "histrionic dissipation" as "holy nausea" does not quiet his anxiety or excuse his participation (414, 387). Concealed but not purged in Sickert's parabolic paintings, these chilling intimations of mortality continue to define, and therefore disqualify, the artist's recoil.[12]

When it is compared to the fates suffered by the other principals of *The Women of Whitechapel,* not to mention the anonymous litter of corpses left by the Ripper, the haunting of Sickert seems lenient. The illegitimate daughter of Prince Eddy and Annie Crook, having lost even the vaguest claim to station, is taken in by Sickert himself. We learn that later, in what is perhaps another ironic comment on Sickert's protective impulses, which had saved none of the Whitechapel women, Alice Margaret bears him a child, "like some pure quotient from the disasters" (410). Rumors that surround Prince Eddy conflict, but whether he succumbs to syphilis, poison, or influenza, his end is as unsavory as one might have reasonably expected. Gull, whose moral descent never caused his faith in a "symmetrical and shapely" fate to falter, is eventually betrayed by his fellow Masons at a dinner ostensibly given in his honor; he will die in an insane asylum. But no outcome can match Netley's for spectacle. Sickert comes upon him at the moment of supreme gothic masochism as, with a rose clenched in his mouth and masked and bloodied for some impenetrable ritual, Netley hangs himself from a girder—a formidable performance that, as his body continues to twist and sway, is one of the novel's most nightmarish testimonies to art's inability to arrest motion or meaning. (He survives the "accident" only to be killed years later when his horse kicks him in the head and he is crushed by his own coach.)

In the end, Sickert is relegated to unanswered dreams of completeness and of reifying past company in just postures. A lifelong prisoner of "climactic vicariousness" (419), he is consigned to a perverse, relentless interest in stories of hackings out of *The Illustrated Police News.* In dark alleys he pantomimes the mythical Ripper, but it is unclear to him whether he is doing penance for past transgressions or invoking artistic license and the search for understanding in order to thrill to their memory over and over. Even the dead, "with a final date appended to their strivings" and apparently "peaceful as carbon," constitute a frieze ever in danger of becoming unfrozen in his mind, "dragging him into a past buried but active in the grave" (408, 419).

At the core of *The Women of Whitechapel* is the stubborn motility of images and intentions. Sickert considers redemption through "altruistic self-abasement" (397) that keeps sliding into useless compulsion. His decision to avenge himself upon Jack the Ripper by "strik[ing] him dead in pigment" (417) must likewise be measured against the unruliness of color and shadow, the duplicity of line, and the intransigence of that malevolent light, "unkillable and inopportune," that discloses the awful declensions of the flesh (418).

Sickert will try to paint while blindfolded to avoid the dictatorship of private thesis. It is instructive to recall the conviction that had once sustained him: "That was what made an artist of him, when, without even trying, he absorbed a hundred thousand disparate particulars and, in a flash or years later, returned a few of them to currency sea-changed, or paint-changed, into something that broke the heart and healed it all in one gaze" (143). It is now years later, and that proposed chemistry has been undermined by the limits of depiction.

Chapter 2

THE FIGURE IN THE STATIC
Don DeLillo's *White Noise*

In the course of naming contemporary novels he admires, Don DeLillo credits their importance to their common capacity to "absorb and incorporate the culture without catering to it" (interview with Begley 290). In DeLillo's own fiction, the challenge has always been to find a way of simultaneously engaging and resisting "the ambient noise," and that challenge has been answered by means of novels whose cunning does not compose its materials into some decorous conclusion. The DeLillo protagonist must locate some reliable avenue of free agency, some outpost of personal dimension, in face of ambiguous threats disclosed (although never completely elucidated) by the same sensitivities that recognize the need for aesthetic refuge.

For DeLillo himself, the paradox lies at the heart of the writer's profession: he must break the grip of idiom while continuing to exploit its pressures artistically. "Words on a page, that's all it takes to help him separate himself from the forces around him," he declares (interview with Begley 277). And yet, even as the writer hammers privileged habitats and crafts vantages above the vague extratextual roil—"How liberating to work in the margins outside the central perception," claims archaeologist Owen Brademas in *The Names* (77)—his task is to assimilate, not to exclude.[1]

Thus DeLillo goes on in this same interview to compromise the so-called ideal segregation of the novelist:

> You want to exercise your will, bend the language your way, bend the world your way. You want to control the flow of impulses, images, words, faces, ideas. But there's a higher place, a secret aspiration. You want to let go. You want to lose yourself in language, become a carrier or messenger. The best moments involve a loss of control. It's a kind of rapture, and it can happen with words and phrases fairly often—completely surprising combinations that make a higher kind of sense, that come to you out of nowhere. (Interview with Begley 282)

Notice the trammeled quality of DeLillo's "rapture": he is describing a release saturated with words which retain the effects of everyday use. Whatever transcendence he pretends to is derivative, obligated to the medium whose undertow he means to supervene.

As DeLillo redefines the terms of access and surrender to language, arbitrating his contradictory drives, he arrives at metaphor, which encapsulates the anxious status between planned exactitude and exhilaration, between decision and accident, out of which he prefers to constitute his projects. In *White Noise,* however, the task is further complicated by the way in which figures are disarmed by the flood of data, cultural debris, and otherwise indigestible stimuli that contribute to the condition that titles the novel. Whereas metaphor depends upon uniqueness and verbal defamiliarization to earn attention, white noise thwarts distinction, for the proliferation of language, typically through such vulgarized forms as advertisements, tabloid headlines, and bureaucratic euphemisms, submerges difference into the usual cultural murmur. There is always more, but always more of the same. The danger, as it is defined in *Great Jones Street,* is "sensory overload"(252): technological fallout in all its multifarious forms, including such linguistic manifestations as secret codes, arcana, and all the kabbala of conspiracy. "I realized the place was awash in noise," Jack Gladney notes as he moves through the burnished interiors of the supermarket. Here everything has an exclamatory glow about it, a euphemistic sheen to needs manufactured and met. But dread penetrates: "The toneless systems, the jangle and skid of carts, the loudspeaker and coffee-making machines, the cries of children. And over it all, or under it all, a dull and unlocatable roar, as of some form of swarming life just outside the range of human apprehension" (*White Noise* 36).[2] Anxiety is awareness that remains on the far side of enlightenment. During an interaction with an automatic bank teller, Jack thinks, "The system was invisible, which made it all the more impressive, all the more disquieting to deal with." Hence, there is not much consolation in the sense that "we were in accord, at least for now. The networks, the circuits, the streams, the harmonies," if such congruities reduce their consumers (46).

Faced with that prospect, the DeLillo protagonist tends to respond with atavistic recoil, seeking out communes, caverns, and other enclaves of pristine, primitive behavior. Reacting to chemical disaster, Jack realizes that he and a fellow victim of the dispersal are speaking to one another from an "aboriginal crouch" (137), a posture of withdrawal that seems to suggest a kind of Ur-conspiracy on the most instinctive level of human exchange.[3] Ironically, then, efforts to escape depersonalization end up verifying its influence. For Gary Harkness in *End Zone*, the disease is "team spirit"; for rock star Buddy Wunderlick in *Great Jones Street,* it is the tide of adoration of his fans; for Bill Gray in *Mao II,* it is the phenomenon of the crowd, the reinforced huddle and animate pack in whose context, argues Elias Canetti in *Crowds and Power,* "liberation can be found from all stings" (327). Its mutuality and density are pitted against surrounding tensions, as seen in the phenomenon of the arena: "There is no break in the crowd which sits like this, exhibiting itself to itself. It forms a closed ring from which nothing can escape. The tiered ring of fascinated faces has something strangely homogenous about it. It embraces and contains everything which happens below; no-one relaxes his grip on this; no-one tries to get away. Any gap in the ring might remind him of disintegration and subsequent dispersal. But there is no gap; this crowd is doubly closed, to the world outside and in itself" (Canetti 28). The crowd is an agreement whose main objective is to "form a shield against *their* own dying" at the cost of *one's* own dying (*White Noise* 73; italics mine).

"There's something about a crowd which suggests a sort of implicit panic," DeLillo contends. "There's something menacing and violent about a mass of people which makes us think of the end of individuality, whether they are gathered around a military leader or around a holy man" (interview with Nadotti 87). It is a theme to which he often returns in his fiction, perhaps most memorably in *Mao II,* which is a novel obsessed by the terrifying *and* the numbing impact of human surfeit: "The rush of things,

of shuffled sights, the mixed swagger of the avenue, noisy storefronts, jew-
elry spread across the sidewalk, the deep stream of reflections, heads floating in windows, towers liquefied on taxi doors, bodies shivery and
elongate, all of it interesting to Bill in the way it blocked comment, the
way it simply rushed at him, massively, like your first day in Jalalabad,
rushed and was. Nothing tells you what you're supposed to think of this"
(94). Crowds may confer magnitude, or at least the illusion of magnitude,
but its price is clarity—a hemorrhage in the field of vision. Images and
ideals are exaggerated, leaving the human equivalent of white noise.

   In his novella *Pafko at the Wall,* which would become the opening section of the novel *Underworld* (1997), DeLillo explains, "Longing on a large
scale is what makes history" (35), and crowds (here, the crowd gathered at
the Polo Grounds for the Giants' pennant-clinching victory) are the collaborative embodiment of that longing. Here as well, the crowd operates as
a self-conscious entity in search of historical dimension of its own, not just
the satisfaction of standing witness to history. Indeed, the baseball crowd
has historical reach: it is temporally extended through retellings of the
game down through the generations and spatially extended through radio
broadcasts into remote, anonymous precincts, later to be reborn as mythic
coherences ("I remember where I was when Bobby Thompson's shot was
heard 'round the world").[4] Once again, the media fortify this sensation of
significant assembly, of "the kindred unit at the radio, old lines and ties and
propinquities" on which the announcer bases his faith: "He pauses to let
the crowd reaction build. Do not talk against the crowd. Let the drama
come from them" (*Pafko* 55, 58). And once again, the expense of team
spirit is a waste of self, as our announcer realizes when, in the wake of cel-
ebration, he has to "get down to the field and find a way to pass intact
through all that mangle" (62). In DeLillo's fiction, one tries to defect from
the failure of differentiation, but his defection threatens disappearance.

   A denuded language deprived of texture and abiding context is both
another example and a means of disseminating the disease of attrition.
Whereas the language of *Ratner's Star* constituted a naked assault on the
sensibilities of the uninitiated—Billy Twillig is occasionally frightened by
the "intimation of compressed menace" contained in scientific jargon—
the language of *White Noise* is more threatening for being so commonplace. It lulls us into its death. Circumambient infection seems to have no
origin, when in fact, no meditation escapes linguistic mediation; and
because commercials, official press releases, academic pedantries, and the

like foster verbal regimentation, that mediation must be viewed as co-optation of private motives. Even transcendence is leveraged at this level; satori is scripted according the tawdriest common denominator, as Jack witnesses through his daughter Steffie's talking in her sleep: "I was convinced she was saying something, fitting together units of stable meaning. I watched her face, waited. Ten minutes passed. She uttered two clearly audible words, familiar and elusive at the same time, words that seemed to have a ritual meaning, part of a verbal spell or ecstatic chant. *Toyota Celica*" (155). The familiar is elusive on the one hand, inescapable on the other. Advertisers have preprogrammed the content and destination of our associations, so even when we imagine, we tend to imagine in the direction of media-induced debts, as evidenced by Jack's own relation of seeing his sleeping children to a "TV moment" or of cloud formations to brand-name mints and gums (Frow 183, 188). Although Steffie appears to be mumbling "a language not of this world," closer inspection reveals that it is utterly of this world, a carrier of the same grim stimulants, at once as synthetic and as deadly as Nyodene D.

Thus the novel is filled with disappointed verges—DeLillo builds to the point of revelation, only to resubmerge into the usual blather. Gladney's sentences exhibit "something like shock, a seeming inability to sort into contexts and hierarchies the information he receives and the thinking he does" (LeClair, *In the Loop* 211), which is to say that they repeat what they mean to address critically. For instance, here is Jack completing a frantic bout of dispossession of his personal ballast:

> I stalked the rooms, flinging things into cardboard boxes. Plastic electric fans, burnt-out toasters, *Star Trek* needlepoints. It took well over an hour to get everything down to the sidewalk. No one helped me. I didn't want help or company or human understanding. I just wanted to get the stuff out of the house. I sat on the front steps alone, waiting for a sense of ease and peace to settle in the air around me.
>
> A woman passing on the street said, "A decongestant, an antihistamine, a cough suppressant, a pain reliever." (262)

The prophets are sick with the same disease; promises of solace, words of cure, are contaminated by the same plague of enervation. The same congestion in the house is in the air. White noise becomes the societal equiv-

alent of cliché, the uniform influx in which particularity dissolves into static, and the metamorphic potential of words may not be heard above the
universal monotone toward which all utterances tend.[5]

If routine tethers ecstasy, it also reins in raw panic. The death fears
that assault Jack and Babette Gladney are more invidious for the illusion
of inviolability in which they grow. Here in the quiet college town of
Blacksmith, "We're not smack in the path of history and its contamina-
tions" (85). Television provides contact with trauma, of course, but it is
a sublimely conditioned contact, filtered by the promise of distance. No
wonder, then, that when the Airborne Toxic Event strikes, not only are
the townspeople forced to rely on simulated behaviors, having had no
other context to turn to, they are simultaneously threatened and mollified
by the impenetrability of the experience. The cloud itself, an unpredictable, protean mass, is identified by inconsistent reports and linguistic
evasions. Although it is designated by news reports as a "feathery plume,"
then recast as "a black billowing cloud," neither reliably approximates the
threat whose malignancy is also a matter of its resistance to metaphorical compartmentalization: it is "Like a shapeless growing thing," Jack
offers. "A dark black breathing thing of smoke. Why do they call it a
plume?" (111). They do it to console the population with definition—to
show that they have literally come to terms with the thing and to batten
down our hunches with official rhetoric. So goes the romance of postu-
lation. Uncircumscribable, nebulous in content, contour, and consequence, the passage of the toxic event is assimilated with astonishing
rapidity into the normative, where its ambiguities do not cease but rather
function undetected among so many others. Consumers are returned to
their polished matrices. Meaning restabilizes where the gravity of dailiness draws it out.

A similar irony infects the Gladneys's several strategies of psychic insulation against their death fears. With the urgency of addicts or patriots
they accumulate material possessions to defend their sense of presence,
to lend them personal density and the illusion of spiritual "snugness"
(20). Unfortunately, as Jack realizes, conspicuous consumption is self-
defeating: "Things, boxes. Why do these possessions carry such sorrowful
weight? There is a darkness attached to them, a foreboding" (6). Their
daughter, a rapt collector of childhood memorabilia, seeks to protect her
own history: "It is part of her strategy in a world of displacements to make
every effort to restore and preserve, keep things together for their value as

remembering objects, a way of fastening herself to a life" (103). But abundance numbs only so far, and stays against death seem deadly themselves.

From this perspective, Murray Siskind's rhapsodies on congestive kitsch contain warnings against the very swaddlings they celebrate and contribute to. Jack's colleague and confidant, Siskind has made a handsome career out of extracting "psychic data" from such concentrations of camp as cineplexes, malls, and ballparks. "Supermarkets this large and clean and modern are a revelation to me. I spent my life in small steamy delicatessens with slanted display cabinets full of trays that hold soft wet lumpy matter in pale colors. High enough cabinets so you had to stand on tiptoes to give your order. Shouts, accents. In cities no one notices specific dying. Dying is a quality of the air. It's everywhere and nowhere" (38). The burden of this informal lecture is that we can ride the exponential increase of the supermarket out of oblivion and shape identities that belie analogy to "soft lumpy matter in pale colors." Malls and supermarkets are our epiphanic parlors, bastions of spiritual purchase. Murray Siskind delights and prospers in "the trance of matter," to use a phrase of poet Sharon Olds ("The Swimmer," line 22). However, as this analysis of the glamour of groceries progresses, plenitude proves just as lethal to uniqueness and individuality. Infinity is only the far pole of confinement—the anonymity of endless shelves of generic items. Fewer citizens may crowd the scope in smaller towns, but their distinctive markings—the Tide above the Maytag, the Mazda ticking in the garage—hardly distinguish them from their urban counterparts, nor are they spared. The appetite for favored brands robs us of contact even with our own dying. Shopping suffocates us in the fortifications it supposedly effects; the hollow men *are* the stuffed men.

If death is capitulation to rutted beliefs and behaviors, life is refutation of predictability. When Jack enters a state of frenzied dispossession, trying to slough the personal sediment that fills his house, he finds "an immensity of things, an overburdening weight, a connection, a mortality" (262). Blessed excess reveals its lethal propensities. We may recall Daniel Isaacson's creed in E. L. Doctorow's *The Book of Daniel:* "The failure to make connections is complicity" (227). Here, the making of connections paradoxically complies with the Establishment because even meditation and desire are prechanneled. So it seems that when Jack determines to avenge the adultery of Babette at the hands of Willie Mink, alias Mr. Gray, to whom she has traded sexual favors for a supply of Dylar, he is inspired less by moral outrage than by the "advance of consciousness" occasioned by his decision (in deference to Siskind's logic) to become a killer rather than a dier—the most heinous manifestation of Jack's assimilation of Hitler Studies. Ideally, shooting Gray would be like smashing through the television: reclaiming im-mediacy by reviving the visceral.[6]

The precision of plotting exhilarates him: "With each separate step, I became aware of processes, components, things relating to other things. Water fell to earth in drops. I saw things new" (304). Here is discreteness wrested from the general slur. Single-mindedness enables Jack to approach the psychic plateau that his sleeping daughter could not: "I continued to advance in consciousness. Things glowed, a secret life rising out of them. Water struck the earth in elongated orbs, splashing drams. I knew for the first time what rain really was. I understood the neurochemistry of my brain, the meaning of dreams (the waste material of premonitions). Great stuff everywhere, racing through the room, racing slowly. A richness, a density. I believed everything" (310). That this advance results from a murderous commitment makes us hesitate to embrace it, and indeed, close reading reveals its insufficiency. For while the world lays out so invitingly, expansive and elemental at the same time, the effect—"I believed everything"—shows Jack to be overwhelmed by a wealth of stimulants.

There is really no difference between this open admission policy to every spectacle and a wholesale renunciation of the capacity for disbelief, as is indicated by Jack and Babette's willingness to accept as true the craziest headlines out of the supermarket tabloids. What more comfortable disease is there than adoration? How secure the transfixion by such glossy fictions, the dependable "grip of self-myth"? (72). The plausible quickly escalates into the portentous, until no speck, no deception, is large enough to cause the undifferentiating transparent eyeball to wince at all. "The extra dimensions, the super perceptions, were reduced to visual clutter, a whirling miscellany, meaningless" (313). In other words, Jack has not earned an un-co-opted vantage point above the conditioned atmosphere of television antennae. His resolve is psychopathic, not poetical; he is as much a political zombie as he ever had been while meekly encysted in his Hitler Studies chair.

Earlier in the novel, Jack experienced a myclonic jerk that shattered his sleep, and perhaps that is what he is hoping to accomplish by shooting Willie Mink—a sudden, inarticulate decompression that breaks through the unremitting dial tone that is contemporary American consciousness (and which variously masquerades as theme parks, jingoism, or religious awe). The point is, however, that the myclonic jerk is, like déjà vu, untrustworthy, a synaptic glitch. It is likelier what preempts insight, not the insight itself. Similarly, the novel's typical refrains—the sound of clothes twisting in the dryer, a commercial announcement, the dance of taillights on the highway—seem heavy with prescience when they may actually represent nothing more than the sporadically detectable horizon of "brain fade."

As a random gathering of townspeople dispossessed by the toxic cloud sift rumors, "We began to marvel at our own ability to manufacture awe" (153); when Jack later smuggles one of his wife's Dylar pills to a colleague in order to penetrate its chemistry, she explains, "We still lead the world in stimuli" (189). In each case, technology manifests breakdowns in distinguishability. White noise is a uniform distraction, so that, as with the malfunctioning smoke alarm that is *always* buzzing, no one knows how, or whether, to react. At one point Wilder starts crying with unnatural persistence. It goes on for hours unabated, as though the youngest Gladney were an early-warning system for the atmospheric danger to come. Eventually, though, the urgency of his wailing gives way to something Jack interprets as keening, a practiced, inbred lament. Jack not only begins to get used to it, he finds it strangely soothing, and he thinks of joining his son inside this "lost and suspended place" where "we might together perform some reckless wonder of intelligibility" (78).[7] But the sound does not enlighten as it enfolds. When the crying ceases after seven hours, as inexplicably as it began—we might remember Emily Dickinson's "certain Slant of light / Winter Afternoons" (lines 1–2), whose massive impact is due in part to its indeterminacy—Jack ascribes mystical properties to the episode: "It was as though he'd just returned from a period of wandering in some remote and holy place, in sand barrens or snowy ranges—a place where things are said, sights are seen, distances reached which we in our ordinary toil can only regard with the mingled reverence and wonder we hold in reserve for feats of the most sublime and difficult dimensions" (79). Again, the assumption of metaphysical import is entirely a matter of faith, not unlike the faith that leads the citizens of Blacksmith to trust in anonymous officials to handle the airborne toxic event (or, for that matter, the faith that leads us to believe that salvation lies in the right combination of brand-name products). And Jack remains distant from the sublimity he imagines there.

Saturation by awe renders us immune to alert. "In the psychic sense a forest fire on TV is on a lower plane than a ten-second spot for Automatic Dishwasher All," Murray Siskind argues (67), nodding to the principal avatar of that awe. Television's om is carefully pitched to keep us tuned in to the All, in whose ultimate impenetrability we trust. "Watching television was for Lyle a discipline like mathematics or Zen," we read in *Players* (16), but its electrostatic bath soon becomes an end in itself. So too does the surface brilliance of the local mall, wedding mass and pall, keep us sleepy with its friendly bombardment of light and promise. We become commoditized buyers, consumers consumed by preregulated passions, melded into the same matrix. Excess "is a sort of electrocution. . . . [T]he individual burns its circuits and loses its defenses," writes Jean Baudrillard (quoted in Keesey 140). But the blissed-out buyer does not mind.[8]

The political implication of this is a sort of placidity of last resort, which during the airborne toxic event takes the form of the belief that the system responsible for engineering the crisis is also the best hope of assessing, digesting (with man-made poison-gobbling bacteria?), and rendering it harmless. The linguistic implication is the desolate voice of the novel, with its enormous clutter of gleaming cultural fragments and unborn insights that shimmer momentarily only to settle back into the collective hum. Metaphor implies a richer insistence, a greater command of hierarchy, resonance, and relation than we can marshal. Thus, white noise is literally an-aesthetic, paving the imagination for the transportation of sanctioned simulations. In this way, insulation is really infiltration, for the things we collect and consume in order to stave off mortality may be tainted by it: "I walked up the driveway and got in the car. There were trash caddies fixed to the dashboard and seat-backs, dangling plastic bags full of gum wrappers, ticket stubs, lipstick-smeared tissues, crumpled soda cans, crumpled circulars and receipts, ashtray debris, popsicle sticks and french fries, crumpled coupons and paper napkins, pocket combs with missing teeth. Thus familiarized, I started up the engine, turned on the lights and drove off" (302). To revive a favored phrase from the introduction of this study, not to mention its questionable Edenic implications, familiarity breeds content, a slew of duplication, our numbed slough. Everything is "crumpled"—DeLillo employs the same participle three times in the same sentence to emphasize the stultifying effect of modern fallout; there is nothing lyrical or empowering about familiarization in this mute, useless context. We recall Jack's being confronted by the electronic proof of his contamination by Nyodene D: graphically splayed on the computer screen, his fate seemed to him alien and beyond petitioning. "It makes you feel like a stranger in your own dying," he realizes. "I wanted my academic gown and dark glasses" (142).

Recoil is a conventional reaction to the brunt of understanding, which is to say that white noise is as likely to be treated by the characters in the novel as the cure as it is the curse. In addition to the ubiquitous bearings of personal property and media-shaped inducements, there are Jack's Hitler Studies and Babette's Dylar supply to personalize respective hiding places. By affiliating himself with Hitler, Jack pretends to guarantee himself a measure of mythical proportion; by taking Dylar, an experimental drug that presumably eliminates one's fear of death, Babette hopes to liberate her consciousness for life-affirming pursuits. However, neither tactic works. Because Hitler's posterity has to do with his perpetration of death, not with his transcendence of it—because in the end, killers and diers are tied to the same false criteria—Jack's absorption nearly destroys him. Only his humane reflex—he takes the man he has accidentally wounded to the hospital—saves him. As for Dylar, not only does Babette's secret commitment to it undermine instead of enable her loving herself and her family, the drug does not work. Indeed, its side effects, grotesquely inflated in the ravenousness of Willie Mink, include extreme paranoia and the inability to separate words from things, which means that Dylar actually exacerbates what it was designed to quell.

The latter consequence in particular, a kind of Saussurean nightmare, represents the equally paralyzing converse of white noise—a murderous convergence of words and things. For if in the slather of white noise signs lose their signifying function, in the Dylar-induced psychosis (in which Jack need merely say the words "hail of bullets" to strafe his crazed adversary) signs afford no contemplative distance. Either way, we yield utterly.[9]

The consolation for both Jack and Babette is that the ambiguous sky left in the wake of the Airborne Toxic Event encourages "an exalted narrative life," which seems to render preconditioned responses obsolete—"it transcends previous categories of awe"— but has the advantage of inspiring new attitudes, new stories (324–25). In the end, neither homicidal nor pharmaceutical failures, respectively, relegate them exclusively to false electronic relations. There remain "the old human muddles" (313), which, for all the anxieties and misgivings they occasion, sustain personality with challenges to routinized beliefs and behaviors. To put it another way, not

all of the "unexpected themes and intensities" buzzing in the deep structure of the commonplace are necessarily inimical to human growth, even
if they appear to evade human understanding (184).

To return again to linguistic consequences, DeLillo is peculiarly conscious among contemporary American writers of predicating his fictions in
environments hostile to the individual's capacity to use words that have not
been irrevocably sworn to prior manipulations, whose forms include official communiqués and press releases (*Libra*), conventional bigotry (*End
Zone*), commercialism (*Americana*), pedantry and jargon (*Ratner's Star*). To
combat wholesale manipulation of language into "lullabies processed by
intricate systems" (*End Zone* 54), DeLillo proposes a creed of resistance.
On the one hand, he intends to exploit the marginality of the serious writer
as a posture of unassimilatability, as a means of avoiding becoming one
more shelf item, which has to do not only with the thematic politicization
of the novel but also with the tinge of dread that structural unresolvability
instills. On the other hand, he hopes to create a sense of "radiance in dailiness" that restores the edge to everything we have accumulated (DeLillo,
interview with DeCurtis 63). In *White Noise* it is seen in the spell that
seems to render the post-toxic-event sky incandescent. "The sky takes on
content, feeling, an exalted narrative life," but its effects oscillate between
wonder and dread, between inspiration and angst (324–25). What *is* certain is that people linger, exchange, participate—instead of pressing heed-
lessly, habitually onward, they are moved to interpret and dwell upon the
defamiliarized heavens.

"Symmetry is a powerful analgesic," postulated one of the crypticians
housed in Field Experiment Number One in *Ratner's Star* (115). Dead
metaphors deaden; clichés inspire clichéd reactions that keep ad execu-
tives, political spin doctors, and probability experts comfortable. Lyricism destabilizes the system of rutted assumptions, but because its
radiance originates from dailiness, its departures actually restore the
possibilities inherent in the ordinary by stoking its latencies—by extending, to recall a pet conception of Stanley Elkin's, the range of the
strange.[10] Tenor and vehicle—worldly origin and word-driven ambition—
are interdependent components of successful metaphorical operations,
which promise a livelier, more vivid transaction than what grocers or
governments purvey. To be sure, if we accept the premise (borrowed
from *The Princeton Encyclopedia of Poetry and Poetics*) that one of the
defining roles of metaphor is to create "agreeable mystification" (Whal-

ley 490), the "powerful and storied" sky that concludes *White Noise* is a most accommodating setting for it.[11]

Although DeLillo does fashion startling metaphors in his novels, his vision of the abiding, empowering mystery of language does not solely rely on traditional metaphorical constructions. In fact, he consistently suggests that individual words have a kind of lambency at the core that goes beyond their referential employment. Owen Brademas, in *The Names*, is particularly attuned to the "beautiful shapes" of the physical constituents of words, finding letters themselves "so strange and reawakening. It goes deeper than conversations, riddles. . . . It's an unreasoning passion" (36). Gary Harkness finds himself dismantling a slogan advocating rugged play to find a similar beauty beneath the meaning (*End Zone* 28), just as Pammy Wynant intuits a dis-contented essence underlying a street sign (*Players* 207), and Bucky Wunderlick turns to aleatory techniques that may discover novel, positive options outside "the mad weather of language" that society has contrived (*Great Jones Street* 265).

I choose these examples because they are also precisely the ones alluded to by Bruce Bawer in his dismissal of such preoccupations in DeLillo's fiction as mere epistemological flap, which is to say, more of the very sort of rhetoric that DeLillo means to expose (41–42). Bawer is disappointed that DeLillo's characters seem to be incapable of real conversations, that they are primarily generators of theory who tend to preside like commissioned discussants or convention delegates. Leaving aside for the moment the accuracy of this complaint—indeed, leaving aside the question of how many "real conversations" take place in, say, the drawing rooms of Henry James—let us consider just how exotic an office words are being asked to perform here. There is often an implicit dais beneath DeLillo's speakers; those who are not interpreters or social critics by trade are so by personal constitution. The fact is, we know how real people really talk, and I would maintain that DeLillo is actually exceptionally attuned to the rhythms and nuances of those conversations, not to mention the evidence of media fertilization they indicate.

As to the argument that these people do not so much talk as testify, perhaps their private verbal contrivances are efforts to extricate them from the contrivances they daily breathe and echo. Bawer's consternation that "when their mouths open, they produce clipped, ironic, self-consciously clever sentences full of offbeat metaphors and quaint descriptive details" comes from his failed expectations (37), but can DeLillo's assault on pre-

dictability rightly be faulted for not living up to standards of verisimilitude?[12] Perhaps no contemporary other than Thomas Pynchon is so assiduous as DeLillo when it comes to rooting out the menace that inheres
beneath the smooth surfaces of contemporary America like buried drums
of radioactive waste. Nowhere is that menace so insidiously compressed
as in the language we absorb and employ—a menace made all the more
effective by the comforts afforded by "uttering the lush banalities" (*End
Zone* 54). When speculation could be a carrier of the linguistic abuse that
prompts speculation in the first place, a certain artificiality is likely to
creep into one's dialect. When people sense that the room is bugged,
that their very vocabularies are tainted, that every utterance could itself
become an airborne toxic event, a self-conscious weight accompanies even
casual encounters. "What writing means to me is trying to make interesting, clear, beautiful language. . . . Over the years it's possible for a writer
to shape himself as a human being through the language he uses," DeLillo
argues (interview with LeClair 82), and a similar priority—deliberately
shaping the self in the course and through the act of vocalizing the self—
seems to have been bequeathed to his characters.

The question remains as to how we can counteract the haze when the
haze is so inviting. "In societies reduced to bloat and glut, terror is the only
meaningful act," confides a character in *Mao II*. Only the "lethal believer"
has the force to resist absorption into the inertia of super-saturated cities,
airwaves, consciousnesses (157). This is the source of DeLillo's reputation
among detractors for reducing the spectrum of human options to either
capitulation to enigma or murderous outrage (à la Lee Harvey Oswald in
Libra). It is born out of the notion that, in the words of the chairman of
the Department of American Environments at the College-on-the-Hill,
"We need an occasional catastrophe to break up the incessant bombardment of information" (66), a sentiment that reiterates the suspicion voiced
in *The Names* that "The forces were different, the orders of response
eluded us. Tenses and inflections. Truth was different, the spoken universe, and men with guns were everywhere" (94).

Fortunately, DeLillo also manages detonations more optimistic than
bombings, yet more historically palpable than a myclonic jerk. There are
the products of the writer's imagination, which "increase the flow of
meaning. This is how we reply to power and beat back our fear. By extending the pitch of consciousness and human possibility" (*Mao II* 200). The
way the athlete can suddenly invest his efforts with eloquence, "doing

some gaudy thing that whistles up out of nowhere" (*Pafko* 37), the writer can disarm the mundane, name-branded mentality and penetrate the collectivized comforts of customized buying, reading, and belief. By delivering the inexhaustible, incalculable facts of us, he has the knack of breaking through "the death that exists in routine things" (*White Noise* 248) to restore us to wonder. Or to borrow again from *The Names*, the "hovering sum of things" remains tantalizingly aloft (123).[13] "So much remained. Every word and thing a beadwork of bright creation. . . . A cosmology against the void" (*White Noise* 243).[14]

Not a wordless remove but a studied wonder is what may finally preserve by enlarging us. We may recall in this regard Robert Frost's idealization of the person who is educated by metaphor: while he is unafraid of enthusiasm, he specifically embraces enthusiasm that inspires the intellect and "the discreet use" of metaphor. Cruder enthusiasms—"It is oh's and ah's with you and no more"—are the stuff of "sunset raving" (Frost 36), and are finally infertile, ineloquent (a pointed admonition, as it happens, to the rapt gazers upon the unprecedented sunsets that conclude *White Noise*). On the other hand, while Frost champions quality of expression, he recognizes that metaphor, as well as the "figurative values" it heralds, is not a permanent argument but a momentary stay. You need to know "how far you may expect to ride it and when it may break down with you" (Frost 39). The poignancy, the beauty of metaphor is kept alive by the way that "we stop just short" of conclusiveness, as seen in the churning sky over Blacksmith and in the unsettled ending of the novel.

"Reality is not a matter of fact, it is an achievement," writes William Gass in "The Artist and Society" (282), and art is no less profound for its subtlety than other revolutionary activities. The irony is that while we admire works of art less for the theses they profess than for "the absolute way in which they exist" (282), that absolute existence is not as simple as a political rally or an explosion. As DeLillo assesses them, the recurring themes in his novels are "Perhaps a sense of secret patterns in our lives. A sense of ambiguity" (interview with DeCurtis 57). Patterns attended by ambiguities—art posits the former while respecting the latter.

Throughout his canon, DeLillo discredits the "subdue and codify" mentality on two grounds: its sheer inadequacy and its imitation of absolutist behaviors (which also include the bright-packaging-to-blissful-purchase reflex). On the contrary, the artist "is concerned with consciousness, and he makes his changes there. His inaction is only a blind, for his books

and buildings go off under everything—not once but a thousand times"
(Gass 288). Or as Richard Poirier puts it, skepticism is the lesson and the
legacy of our greatest poets, artists, and intellectuals; it inhabits the words
they use to interrogate the words we use, and it results in "a liberating and
creative suspicion as to the dependability of words and syntax, especially
as it relates to matters of belief in the drift of one's feelings and impressions" (5). When the revolution goes well, the sentences the writer hands
down do not consign us to locked rooms but refute them. And so it is in
White Noise, where DeLillo whistles in an undissipating but most precipitous dark.

Chapter 3

IN THE MILLHAUSER ARCHIVES

If it is true that God is in the details, then a writer's hubris and his humility are equally evident in his lists. The making of lists praises and competes with Creation at the same time. Lists are at once mannered in their disciplined salvage and promiscuous in their insistent battenings. Lists are literature's representative democracies; their stylized reductions suggest that the world that is so much with us could always be more so.

The penchant for et cetera runs from Walt Whitman's capitalized processions to Stanley Elkin's dilations on the heraldics of vocation. Each list contends that virtue lies in the aggregate, yet each is a punctuated thrill—the orgasm meted out gram by gram. If God inheres in the details that wink out of the bulwark they define, worship must be a protracted and a calibrated activity. As Richard Wilbur writes in "Attention Makes Infinity," "Contagions of the solid make of the day / An infiniteness any eye may prove" (lines 17–18); in "A World without Objects Is a Sensible Emptiness" he further confirms the value of specific forage, disdaining "pure mirage" and arguing that

> those prosperous islands are accurst
> That shimmer in the brink
> Of absence; auras, lustres,
> And all shinings need to be shaped and borne. (lines 11–14)

Albert Goldbarth is blunter about it in "Some Things": "I may / require theophany after too many / things, but for now give me things" (lines 20–22). Concepts convince us best when they condense into material evidence. In truth, it is in the list that craft least infringes, or appears to infringe, upon vital congress; it is also here, gleaning and mound building, that writing can seem most menial, dutifully establishing verisimilitude like good credit. "The classification of the constituents of a chaos, nothing less is here essayed," proclaims *Moby Dick* (117), that stalwart testament to the hunting-and-gathering mentality.

Still, particularity and abundance are advanced as compensation for (and a temporary reprieve from) what they cannot fully disguise: the inadequacy of language to represent the world in full. Even as we enjoy the composure of the well-made miscellany, we acknowledge the limitations of any random harvest.[1] Although "The Dream of the Consortium," which is the incentive behind the construction of a consumerist utopia, is to "satisfy the buyer's secret desire: to appropriate the world, to possess it entirely" (70), the reach of imagination exceeds the emporium's grasp. From reality's lumpy batter only so much blessed potential can be panned. The art of the list is that while it sustains and systematizes the world's mortal hoard, it confesses, without succumbing to, its own insufficiencies.

Steven Millhauser is one of contemporary fiction's most assiduous list makers. For Millhauser, lists are conspicuous interfaces where art and life, system and surge, the magical and the mundane coalesce.[2] At such swollen junctures in his texts, the imposed order threatens to trump, then to disqualify, the experience it contextualizes and concentrates. But we also recognize an opposing possibility marked by arbitrariness, incompleteness, and, within the rich jostle of components, imminent spawn. Lists admit both perspectives: bulk and exactitude, swarming plenum and precise tide.

Millhauser's arcades, museums, malls, exhibition halls, galleries, chambered bookshops and mansions, and other esoteric collectives of insidious geometry and infinite regress can be viewed as demonstrations and logical extensions of lists, especially in the sense that they represent the same sort of contest between magnitude and gravity that lies at the heart of the enchantment of matter. Accordingly, "The Barnum Museum," for instance, depicts the same contradiction that its scrupulously docketed contents do. On the one hand, its employees learn to love their interment, "as if, absorbed by this realm of enchantments, they are gradually becoming a different race, who enter our world uneasily, in the manner of revenants or elves" (*Barnum Museum* 82). Some "eremites," caught in the undertow of spectacle, resist a return to the outside world, which now seems to them insubstantial by contrast to the arresting particularity of the museum. Rumors abound that the museum's honeycombed confines actually undermine the entire city, threatening to subsume it utterly: "Our collective attention, directed at the displays of the Barnum Museum, will cause the halls to swell with increased detail. Outside, the streets and buildings will grow vague; street corners will begin to dissolve; unobserved, a garbage-can cover, blown by the wind, will roll silently toward the edge of the world (80).[3] So too burgeons the irresistible "Dream of the Consortium":

> For as the departments multiply, as the store grows and invents itself daily, so it expands within our minds until everything else is pressed flat against our skulls. . . . As we hurry along the sidewalk, we have the absurd sensation that we have entered still another department, composed of ingeniously lifelike streets with artful shadows and reflections—that our destinations lie in a far corner of the same department, that we are condemned to hurry forever through these artificial halls, bright with afternoon light, in search of a way out. (72)

Meanwhile, witnesses to the escalating competition among illusionists in late-nineteenth-century Vienna suspect that the entire city will eventually succumb to their provocations and become one all-encompassing magic theater (*Barnum Museum*, "Eisenheim the Illusionist" 224).

On the other hand, ordinary reality proves too obdurate to supplant. Visitors who purchase souvenirs from the Barnum Museum discover that once they have removed them to their homes, "in air thick with smells of boiling potatoes and furniture polish, the gifts quickly lose their charm, and soon lie neglected in dark corners of closets beside the eyeless Raggedy Ann doll and the dusty Cherokee headdress" (87–88). Millhauser makes a comparable argument in "The Eighth Voyage of Sinbad," when, "in the warm shade of the orange tree, the voyages are bereft of enchantment." Neither context is dispensable:

> The flight through the air, the giant's eyeteeth like boar's tusks, the old man clinging to his back, the serpents the size of palm trees

in the Valley of Diamonds, all are banal and boring images. . . .
They cannot compare with the cry of the blackbird, the sunstruck
dome of a mosque, the creak of rigging in the harbor ships, the
miraculous structure of a pomegranate or a camel, the shouts of the
sellers of dried fruits, the beating out of copper basins in the market of the coppersmiths, the trembling blue shadow cast by falling
water on a marble fountain's rim, the immense collection of precise
details that compose the city of Baghdad at this moment. ("Eighth
Voyage of Sinbad" 126)

Ironically, even this systematic demystification of the mythic trance
entrances by virtue of the richness of the collection it shapes.

Millhauser anticipates such a crisis of authenticity in his essay on
"Replicas," those "haunted objects" that simultaneously plead equivalence
and novelty. In this sense, they resemble metaphors themselves, for they
are likewise tethered enterprises. Just as replicas are finally transparent
forgeries, weaving their incongruities openly in order both to mimic an
original and to reveal that mimicry, metaphors also improvise in debt. The
grounds of genuineness are that they "may thus deceive us for a time, but
. . . must also undeceive us" ("Replicas" 54). And so we hover between
original and replica, tenor and vehicle, antecedent and fabricated worlds.

And therein lies the hidden arrogance of replicas: "by setting themselves playfully against the world, by offering themselves as unserious
rivals of actual things, they secretly undermine the world of primary
objects . . . . For they seem to whisper that the real world at which they
stare is no such great matter, since it may be replaced by the likes of them.
And don't they seem to ask us, though teasingly, how we can be so certain
that this other world, the solid world of real objects from which they draw
their being, is itself not a deception?" ("Replicas" 60). In Jorge Luis
Borges's "Tlön, Uqbar, Orbis Tertius," fantastic objects conjured through
the fortuitous conjunction of mirrors, credulousness, and a suppositious
encyclopedia become weighty and rigorous enough to usurp real-world
counterparts. In Millhauser's hands, the fruits of imagination enchant
while real apples spoil.

To complicate the issue further, the source of compulsion initiated by
Millhauser's magical enclosures may well be the reciprocity between the
realms they confuse. "A work of fiction is a radical act of the imagination
whose sole purpose is to supplant the world," claims adolescent Arthur

Grumm, one of the palely loitering prodigies of languor in *Portrait of a Romantic*. "In order to achieve this purpose," he continues, "a work of fiction is willing to use all the means at its disposal, including the very world it is plotting to annihilate" (28). However, like some uncontested divorce between words and things, the romance of absolute renunciation is impossible, a mirage born of Grumm's voluptuous boredom.[4] Actually, Grumm's temperament leads him to a heightened concentration on the material sphere, having the effect of magnifying, instead of exploiting and discarding, its marvels and mundanities. As a compilation of the world's real and imagined offerings (the distinction is moot in the universal solvent of story), art cannot entirely defer to reality nor shake loose from the storehouse of its origins.[5]

Lists reinforce this paradox: all transcendence is tied to the roll call of integers; conversely, the surface tension of components may enable the imagination to exceed the rim of the real, the way water overfills the glass without spilling. As the contents of "The Dream of the Consortium" are paraded past us, pencil sharpeners and power mowers are linked with Sumerian ziggurats and Viking burial mounds, drill presses with Amazon jungle grafts, quartz heaters with the Colossus of Rhodes, snow blowers with chimeras, so that in the imagination's audit, discrimination dissolves before the vastness of what can be articulated, what can be bought (68–69).

It is true that the surrender to art in stories like "Behind the Blue Curtain" and "Alice, Falling" is described as serene once the initial shock of disruption fades. Similarly, the narrator of "The Sepia Postcard," purposefully fleeing the "foul farce with predictable punchlines" his life has become, champions the "purifying otherness" of the village of Broome (93), which he hopes will sweep clean stale memories. Nonetheless, even this fugitive from reality realizes that the charms of novelty require mooring. In his preamble to his listing of the items on display in a Broome gift shop, he notes, "I like the variety of invention within a convention of rigorous triteness" (95), and thereby confesses their critical interdependency.

With this in mind, we may protest that the temptation to abandonment in the Barnum Museum is not escapist after all because the relief it provides depends upon the exterior for its power to captivate: "In the branching halls of the Barnum Museum we are never forgetful of the ordinary world, for it is precisely our awareness of that world which permits us to enjoy the wonders of the halls. Indeed I would argue that we are most sharply aware of our town when we leave it to enter the Barnum Museum; without our museum, we would pass through life as in a daze or dream" ("Barnum Museum" 90). In a similar vein, Millhauser's Alice comes to question the texture of her fall: whereas "fall" connotes "a swoon, a release," Alice finds herself "tense with alertness: she holds herself in readiness . . . she looks around eagerly, she takes in everything with sharpened awareness. Her fall is the opposite of sleep: she has never been so awake" ("Alice, Falling" 168). What technique could be more responsive to so intensely wakeful a state, what means of appropriation more appropriate, than list making?

Like the academicians of Lagado in *Gulliver's Travels*, who wear their nouns about them so as not to lose the burden of their arguments, Millhauser's narrators rely on inventories to situate themselves within labyrinths of illusion. Wonder is not a severing of relations with the world. Instead, the Barnum Museum includes everyday images, which, suddenly thrusting through the displays of the marvelous, "startle us with their strangeness before settling to rest. In this sense the plain rooms do not interrupt the halls of wonder; they themselves are those halls" ("Barnum Museum" 84–85).[6] Nothing is disqualified that compounds interest.

To add to the conundrum, supervising items within the Chamber of False Things does not domesticate those things but rather erodes confidence in categories altogether. Articulate levels of fraud remain fraudulent, after all.[7] Even the museum gift shops, bastions of practical commerce, persist in trading on the indivisibility of actual and imaginary. There one may purchase

> old sepia postcards of mermaids and sea dragons, little flip-books that show flying carpets rising into the air, peep-show pens with miniature colored scenes from the halls of the Barnum Museum, mysterious rubber balls from Arabia that bounce once and remain suspended in the air, jars of dark blue liquid from which you can blow bubbles shaped like tigers, elephants, lions, polar bears, and giraffes, Chinese kaleidoscopes showing ceaselessly changing forms of dragons, enchanting pleniscopes and phantatropes, boxes of animate paint for drawing pictures that move, lacquered wooden balls from the Black Forest that, once set rolling, never come to a stop, bottles of colorless jellylike stuff that will assume the shape and color of any object it is set before, shiny

> red boxes that vanish in direct sunlight, Japanese paper airplanes
> that glide through houses and over gardens and rooftops, story-
> books from Finland with tissue-paper-covered illustrations that
> change each time the paper is lifted, tin sets of specially treated
> watercolors for painting pictures on air. ("Barnum Museum" 87)

As with verbal tropes of any kind, a kind of Adamic potency prevails here:
utter it, and it becomes so, or no less so, at any rate, than anything else in
the fictional habitat. Once again, Millhauser's museum represents how
diversity might nevertheless thrive in confinement. Like Joseph Cornell's
boxed enigmas, whose iconic splicings are like the sediment of dreams,
Millhauser's lists are reveries objectified, manifestations of what John
Donne called "immensity cloistered" (quoted in Simic 71).[8] Naming the
components does not drain away their ambiguity, however. As we learn in
"The Eighth Voyage of Sinbad," the voyages may be reified by words, but
the teller soon balks at the shapeliness he has made: "But a change has
been wrought, by the telling. For once the voyages had been summoned
by the words, a separation had seemed to take place, as if, just to one side
of the words, half-hidden by their shadows, the voyages lay dreaming in
the grass" (119). Nothing can ever be held completely accountable.

The sustained crossbreeding of inventory and invention is at the heart
of a list's tensions and pleasures. It may be possible to trace the evolution
of the description given above of the contents of the Barnum Museum gift
shop: variations on means of suspension, types of color and transparency,
and principles of animation, as well as references to firm geographic loca-
tions, seem to organize and certify the docket. But once again, to what
lengths can categories alter the stature of things categorized? As exempli-
fied in Borges's tale "The Analytical Language of John Wilkins," the efforts
of an arcane Chinese encyclopedia, the *Celestial Emporium of Benevolent
Knowledge,* to classify animals surrenders to arbitrariness, odd sub-
jectivities, and ultimate incommensurability. Its futile divisions follow:
"(a) those that belong to the emperor, (b) embalmed ones, (c) those that
are trained, (d) suckling pigs, (e) mermaids, (f) fabulous ones, (g) stray
dogs, (h) those that are included in this classification, (i) those that tremble as if they were mad, (j) innumerable ones, (k) those drawn with a very
fine camel's-hair brush, (l) others, (m) those that have just broken a flower
vase, (n) those that resemble flies from a distance" (142). Borges's un-
parsable gardens and vertiginous libraries likewise parody the caprice of

totalization. We may also remember Borges's "Funes the Memorious" in this instance—a man dubiously endowed with the ability to envision every single detail around him, but who at the same time cannot forget any experience or manage to subdue his perceptions with patterns, hierarchies, or barriers of abstraction: "In the teeming world of Funes, there were only details" perpetually heaping (66). The plague of relentless lucidity eventually overwhelms him with multiples, and, fittingly, Funes dies of congestion.

The structural dynamics of Millhauser's Barnum Museum depend upon the interplay between intimations of expanse and impasse, corridors of access and prohibition, displays of coherence and rupture, all of which appear to characterize the elongated accounts of the holdings that it comprises. From one perspective, the museum's architecture may be viewed as exacting historical testimony; from another, "the Romanesque and Gothic entranceways, the paired sphinxes and griffins, the gilded onion domes, the corbeled turrets and mansarded towers, the octagonal cupolas, the crestings and crenellations" represent a dizzying transaction among disparate cultures, and they "compose an elusive design that seems calculated to lead the eye restlessly from point to point without permitting it to take in the whole" (73). They reflect and frustrate calculation at the same time. So too are the geometric pillars, the sundial, and the landscaping of Sinbad's courtyard (symbolizing cunningly, reliably plotted renditions of the voyages themselves) subject to dissolution, in much the same way that the Sinbad legend is attenuated by contradictory research and Sinbad's own untrustworthy memory. Like "The Barnum Museum," "The Eighth Voyage of Sinbad" is suspended between sources of enlistment:

> In the warm shade and stillness of the garden, it seems to Sinbad that the dreamlike roc's egg, the legendary Old Man of the Sea, the fantastic giant, the city of apes, the cavern of corpses, all the shimmering and insubstantial voyages of his youth, have been pressed together to form the hard marble of those pillars, the weight of that orange bending a branch, that sharp-edged shadow. Then at times it is quite different: the pillars, the gallery, the slave girls and concubines, the gold-woven carpets, the silk-covered divans, the carved fruits and flowers on the ceilings, the wine-filled flagons shimmer, tremble, become diaphanous, and dissolve to reveal the unwound turban binding his waist to the leg of the roc,

> the giant's sharp eyeteeth the size of boar's tusks, the leg bone of
> the corpse with which he smashes the skulls of wives and husbands
> buried alive in the cavern, the shadow of the roc darkening the sun,
> the jewels torn from the necks of corpses, the legs of the clinging
> old man black and rough as a buffalo hide. (116–17)

It is this "shimmering" and "trembling" between art and life that guarantees that no conclusive resting place will be negotiated between them. Millhauser's galleries and archives only concentrate that suspension. Hence the peculiar nature of gratification contained in the Barnum Museum: the knowledge that we will never be satisfied. What is true of the museum is true of its catalogs: the acknowledgment of both vastness and custody. "For us it's enough, for us it is almost enough" (91). The revised version is a better approximation of what lies in store.

Lists are particularly compatible with the notion of infinite extendibility. They often appear to progress without subordination, evolving beyond their occasions into self-justifying performances of syntax and rhythm. The grammatical equivalent of this phenomenon is parataxis, which features the elimination of conjunction and clear transition. John Sturrock refers us to "the aesthetics of omission" (113), and his phrase applies equally well to the art of conscription as to the art of modern poetry, which inspired it, for both demonstrate strategies of juxtaposition, accretion, and crossed inherencies for their effects, even as the reader senses randomness and inconclusiveness about the proceedings.

The contents of the Ross attic in "A Game of Clue," for example, simultaneously convey the family's casual neglect and Millhauser's preemptive care, which preserves the heterogeneity of the cargo. "The *un*likeness coincides with the identity, as ever with successful metaphor" (Bishop 23).[9] The effect is one of meticulous disarray:

> One shelf holds an uneven pile of abandoned board games
> (Sorry, Parcheesi, Pollyanna, Camelot), a puzzle showing on the
> cover a three-masted ship with billowing sails plunging in black-
> green waves, a pile of Schaum music books with colored covers and
> miscellaneous sheet music such as "The Flight of the Bumblebee,"
> "My Old Kentucky Home," "*O Mein Papa*," "In the Hall of the
> Mountain King," and "Old Black Joe," and a shoe box with crushed
> sides that contains wooden red and black checkers pieces

embossed with crowns, a notched Viewmaster reel called "Ali Baba
and the Forty Thieves," tin play-money coins, a wooden slice of
watermelon the size of a section of orange, a three-lobed puzzle
piece showing rich blue sky, an edge of red roof, and a corner of
yellow chimney, a small flip-book featuring a mouse who picks up
a sledgehammer and cracks open a gigantic egg from which
emerges a frowning chicken with a bump on its head that grows
longer and longer, a green rubber grasshopper, a blue fifty-dollar
Monopoly bill, and Professor Plum. Beyond the bookcases, in the
dark part of the attic, Marian's old German school, a gift from her
mother's mother, Rebecca Altgeld, lies under the slanting front
wheel of a fallen bicycle. The teacher sits tilted at her desk with
raised arms, the six pupils lean in different directions on three
wooden benches. Deeper in the blackness, old wooden barrels
stand among cardboard cartons and dress boxes. On the floor Pierrot sits with his head against a barrel, his blouse torn, his face
stricken with sadness, dreaming of Columbine beside a trellis in
moonlight. ("Game of Clue" 58–59)

We are immediately impressed by Millhauser's application of Henry
James's solidity of specification, whereby accuracy begets actuality.
Despite the unevenness of the piles and the evidence of the accidental and
the discarded, Millhauser establishes an overall effect in the passage of
sumptuousness explicitly attended to. Millhauser has given us the paragraph as a democratic cast, as a larder stocked by precisely realized increments.

At the same time, there is something defamiliarizing about an itemized
investigation. Our reading is hypnotically slowed, in much the same manner as Alice's tumble down the rabbit hole is slowed in "Alice, Falling" for
the sake of better digestion of sights and sensations, so that her descent
(and ours down the page) becomes a hovering, and the fiction a measured,
infalling dream. Despite their apparent commitment to the real, lists are
also well suited to the atmosphere of dreams. Freud's comment that
dream work "does not think, calculate or judge in any way at all; it restricts
itself to giving things a new form" seems to recall the humble subtlety of
lists (quoted in Donoghue 5).

Little wonder that so many of Millhauser's protagonists find themselves
losing the capacity to differentiate between the real and the imaginary

when lists accede to both realms so readily. In the passage above, Professor Plum, having been "animated" earlier on, suddenly reverts to two-dimensional game-piece status—just another bit of debris—and seems to take the "real" Marian down with him with the rest of the jetsam. Meanwhile, to increase the ontological confusion, Pierrot is plumped with emotional capacity and romantic stature as he emerges from the regular assessment of comparatively unsubordinated attic elements. Little wonder, too, that some shadowy researchers are permanently emboweled within the Barnum Museum; or that the boy whose supernatural excursion into the movie screen in "Behind the Blue Curtain" cannot repent his transgression when he tardily rejoins his stern father awaiting him in the conventional daylight; or that in his unfathomable drift into the conjectured passageways of "A Game of Clue," Professor Plum more eagerly relinquishes the world without than he does his fascination. What is most threatening about "Eisenheim the Illusionist," as his materializations and floutings of natural law grow ever more daring, is the seductiveness of his rejection. The chief of police, himself an amateur conjurer, finds Eisenheim guilty of too serious a transgression against "the essence of things" and accuses him "of shaking the foundations of the universe, of undermining reality, and in consequence of doing something far worse: subverting the Empire. For where would the Empire be, once the idea of boundaries became blurred and uncertain?" (235).

Or, to return to one of the persistent rumors surrounding the Barnum Museum, when mystery breeds ceaselessly, what can be safely said to be outside the compass of the collection? We might consider a list from Millhauser's *Edwin Mullhouse* in this regard, one whose apparent modesty—it is a list of children's book titles unescorted by editorial commentary—does not diminish the dynamic linkage going on (*Edwin Mullhouse* 42). If there is any truth to the contention of Jeffrey Cartwright, the narrator/biographer of *Edwin Mullhouse*, that genius is "the capacity to be obsessed" (75), what better test might there be than such an overripe fixation as this? Many of the fifty-three titles are familiar and unremarkable—*Thumbelina, Ali Baba and the Forty Thieves, Rumplestiltskin*, and the like; some revive or replicate the mischievous Seussian doctoring of words: *The Pinch-me Punch-me Bounce-me Bump-me Toss-me, Tumble-me Tickle-me O, Ha Ha the Hee Haw and the Moo Moo Who Said Meow* (not to be confused with *Ho Hum and Heave Ho*), *Bicklebuck and the Binglebat, Prince Imlo of Nax*; some smack of parental guidance: *The Little Pretzel Who Had No Salt, The Near-Sighted Ogre;* others have the poetic resonance (*The Door in the Tree*) or the premonitory flavor that a writer's writer would relish (*The Immortal Moment: A Survey of English Literature from Beowulf to Joyce* having migrated from Edwin's father's collection, along with *The Pipe-Lover's Guide to Real Smoking Enjoyment*); still others (most obviously *The Boy Who Never Grew Up*) seem darker omens in a biography of an eleven-year-old suicide victim. There is even one in particular—*The Little Shadow Who Had No Boy*—that appears to disparage the biographer's intrepid enterprise.

A unifying temper governs this list and obscures distinctions between the likely and the improbable. Furthermore, it displays the same tensions between finding and founding, selection and completion, seen in Millhauser's more exotic lists. We may also remember the relevance of Edwin's cavalier dismissal of his friend's attentions—"Biography is so simple . . . . All you have to do is put in everything" (100)—which he then contradicts with the indictment that, instead of deferring to life's blank spaces and open ends, biography "provides an *illusion* of completeness" only (101; italics mine). Lists tend to dilate, to give in to their rhythms, but they are checked by the inevitability of choice, not to mention the hidden sutures of grammar and the pressure of other narrative commitments. (Our narrator often complains that he is anxious to get on with the business of biography, finding factual upholstering only so gratifying.)

Later in *Edwin Mullhouse* we are treated to a summary and analysis of Mullhouse's "masterpiece," *Cartoons,* which Jeffrey Cartwright confidently interprets as an absolute, if disguised, set of correspondences between imagination and experience.[10] He praises it for its quality of "scrupulous distortion" (265), an oxymoron that could as likely be applied to the writings of Mullhouse or Cartwright, not to mention the activities of Millhauser's numerous other obsessives who seldom rise from their luxuriant sulks and who may exhibit no other scruples save that phrase. Under the implied mitigations of scrupulous distortion, whereby world and imagination are simultaneously countenanced, the absolute renunciation of Eisenheim the Illusionist at the end of that story is anomalous, for it is certainly not in keeping with the both-and spirit of lists.

"Scrupulous distortion," I would further submit, aptly describes the workings of lists and metaphors alike. While metaphors tend to operate by extraction and lists by immersion, and while lists imply a turn of mind too impressionable for a single image to satisfy, they share a capacity for translation: whether something is set down in a figure or conscripted into a list, its extratextual taint is at once altered and evident. If listing is not a trope unto itself, the complexity of its effects in the employ of a writer like Millhauser suggests that neither is it merely a matter of arranging words. Like the maker of metaphors, the maker of lists not only appreciates the deeper resonances of his materials and their readiness to ramify in new contexts, he also recognizes that there is an indigestible, irreducible core of things that refuses to yield to the imagination. Excess is the soul of *with*, yet abundance bespeaks insufficiency and the artifice of any selection process. There is always more, always other, crowding the halls, still uninventoried. Thus replete is never complete: lists drive home the point but merely skim the potential.

Meanwhile, the capacity for translation can be exploited only so far. The affinities discovered are only so insistent, and things do not wholly submit to them. Robert Frost's previously mentioned contention in "Education by Poetry" that metaphor carries with it the germ of its own decay is equally true in the case of lists: we can manage to "ride" them only so long (39). Or as Wallace Stevens warns in "About One of Marianne Moore's Poems," there remains "a solid reality which does not wholly dissolve itself into the conceptions of our own minds"—"the hotel instead of the hymns," as it is put in *An Ordinary Evening in New Haven* (96). The ingenuity of the metaphor or the amplitude of the list notwithstanding, "The thing he carries resists / The most necessitous sense" (Stevens, "Man Carrying Thing," lines 4–5).[11]

These dissenting voices may leave us some distance from, say, Cardinal Newman's belief in the legislation of data when he writes: "That only is true enlargement of mind which is the power of viewing many things at once as one whole, of referring them severally to their true place in the universal system." (40). Newman's institution reads like the ideal list: infinite enrollment met by an agile bureaucracy. Millhauser's list makers, on the contrary, are victims as well as beneficiaries of their appetites: "[O]nly in a moment of lavish awareness, which had left me confused and exhausted, had I seen truly," decides the narrator of "In the Penny Arcade" (*In the Penny Arcade* 145), who cannot celebrate his revelation without immediate reference to its personal cost. Nevertheless, it is the startling compensations of abundance that stand out: the jewels raked from the slather; the delights surplus value buys; the rich, venerable, specific spoils of the nominal universe. And if God *is* in the details, every index, every anatomy advances articles of faith.

"The Invention of Robert Herendeen" forwards the theory that there are two sorts of artistic sterility: the blank imagination that does not blossom, the intemperate imagination that does not bracket (187–88). Steven Millhauser's carefully imbricated yet self-disclaiming inventories seem to skirt both shoals. In face of things beyond measure, Millhauser gives good weight.

Chapter 4

POST HOC HARMONIES

Paul Auster's *Leviathan*

The detective novel provides some of literature's most durable endowments. Its sureties constitute a method and a message. Mystery condenses then lifts like the day's weather. Seemingly encouraged by the very conventions of his context, the hero patiently debrides whatever wound to propriety summons him. Cases wind up tight and smooth as spools. Gordian plots are only, are always, temporary distractions at worst, or prods to intrigue; and thanks to logic's stacked deck, these regularly succumb to investigation. As the detective whittles raw circumstance into habitable sense, he is secure in the conviction that at the core all incidents and outrages conform to code—each "eureka" is really "elementary" after all. In short, orientation is the detective novel's promise, tractability its principle. Such is the foundation of its devotion as the Good assumes its ritual guise and Evil performs the stations of the double-cross. When it comes to practicing literary convention, novelists, characters, and readers are all insiders, all blissful in the rigging.

Paul Auster has made his reputation largely by invoking the detective formula in order to steer it into metaphysical tundra. His *New York Trilogy* observes the steady disintegration of the motives, means, and results of inquiry, in which "the presence of the unpredictable, the powers of con-

64THISMAD"INSTEAD"

tingency" ultimately estrange us from those crisp generic assurances (*Art of Hunger* 270–71). Although it is in many ways a more straightforward work than its predecessors, Auster's *Leviathan* clarifies and extends the predicament: every author is at once a detective and an artificer, and these callings are incompatible. Moreover, as we are advised in the course of the novel, "the real is always ahead of what we can imagine" (180). The irony is that *Leviathan* is ostensibly Auster's most realistic novel, yet it is here that the question of what constitutes reality is rendered more subtle instead of extinguished. Whatever document results from the novelist's efforts is essentially a record of incomplete transactions whose authority must be taken under advisement.

An apology and projective analysis of the life of one Benjamin Sachs, *Leviathan* is ostensibly the work of Peter Aaron, a writer whose career suspiciously reflects, or refracts, Paul Auster's own. Aaron learns that Sachs, who had years before served time in prison for his refusal to serve in Vietnam, has accidentally blown himself up in the course of a politically inspired and increasingly folkloric assault on the nation's numerous replicas of the Statue of Liberty. Aaron also explains that he has arrogated to himself the responsibility of telling his friend's story properly before the redoubtable agents of law enforcement establish their version. His refusal to cooperate fully with the investigation enables Aaron not only to "keep his death to myself" (3) and thereby guarantee that it remain within the novelist's province and prerogative, but also to respect Sachs's life by composing the man's memory.

However, the very quality of Sachs that has defied forensic assaults so far also inhibits Aaron's attempts to "book" him. On the one hand, Aaron is attracted by the sense that "everything is connected to everything else" (57) and that he continually seems to be the cynosure of consequential events. Accordingly, he undertakes the task of narration by announcing that precision and compassion will be his calipers. On the other hand, he confesses that "a book is a mysterious object" (5) in terms of its function and fate alike, and the accumulation of detail further obscures what it is designed to clarify. (Precision and compassion may not be complementary biographical instruments, it seems.) Aaron culls, then calls himself to account; he is equally skeptical about what coheres and what does not. Neither the official objectivity of the FBI nor the relentless alertness of the paranoid is sufficient to enable him to "[divine] the monstrous / sum of particulars" (*Disappearances* 5.2–3). What does commitment to his friend or to his art—that "attitude of remorseless inner vigilance" (29)—mean in the context of riven confidence? "I don't claim to have more than a partial understanding of who he was. I want to tell the truth about him, to set down these memories as honestly as I can, but I can't dismiss the possibility that I'm wrong, that the truth is quite different from what I imagine it to be" (25). Even translated into Aaron's words and dissolved into the context of this novel, Sachs retains his ambiguity: "Every time I tried to think about him, my imagination failed me. It was as if Sachs had become a hole in the universe. He was no longer just my missing friend, he was a symptom of my ignorance about all things, an emblem of the unknowable itself" (164).

Sachs is consistently portrayed as an embodiment of the difficult balance between unpredictability and pattern that Aaron tries to emphasize in his record. Neither their fifteen-year acquaintance nor the experience of preparing *Leviathan* really alters Aaron's drunken illusion during their initial meeting that Sachs was several dizzying figures that could not be focused (24). Sachs is introduced as someone cloaked in contradiction and disarming multiplicity, yet who somehow manages to embody "a single, unbroken presence" (19). In him the narrator discovers what another Auster narrator deemed (by way of expanding on the appeals of mystery novels) a "sense of plenitude and economy" (*City of Glass* 14–15). He is simultaneously—and these adjectives are applied on a single page of the novel—sweet tempered and gentle, yet rigidly dogmatic and prone to fits of rage; jaunty and good humored, yet intolerant and scornful; peevish and embattled, yet large spirited and cunning (20). He is simultaneously mischievous and bookish, fervent and dismissive about his own writing, worshipful and caddish toward the women in his life, voracious for sensation yet longing for rest and release.[1]

Leviathan is riddled with Aaron's disclaimers and misgivings, so much so that the story of Benjamin Sachs quickly evolves into a book-long delineation of the inevitability of storification. Here again the writer and the detective converge in their appreciation of the structural virtue of "the good mystery," in which

> there is nothing wasted, no sentence, no word that is not significant. And even if it is not significant, it has the potential to be so—which amounts to the same thing. The world of the book comes to life, seething with possibilities, with secrets and contradictions.

> Since everything seen or said, even the slightest, most trivial thing,
> can bear a connection to the outcome of the story, nothing must be
> overlooked. Everything becomes essence; the center of the book
> shifts with each event that propels it forward. The center, then, is
> everywhere, and no circumference can be drawn until the book has
> come to its end. (*City of Glass* 15)

But when everything "can bear a connection," a crisis of management
soon arises, and the writer/detective is plunged into a miasma of unruly
clues and forking paths. For every insight there is an apology. "We never
know anything about anyone," Sachs tells Aaron by way of accounting
for the secret instabilities in his "ideal" marriage to Fanny. "It's hard
enough keeping track of ourselves. Once it comes to other people, we
don't have a clue" (107), he says, anticipating the difficulty of future collisions. Or we have too many clues. In either instance, the hope of a totalized *Leviathan* is hobbled, for it, like Melville's whale, is a beast that
cannot be inferred from its bones.

Especially relevant to Aaron's predicament are Nicholson Baker's comments in *U and I* about trying to pin down the imperial shadows of
departed colleagues, an exercise in which idolatry, effrontery, and futility
intersect: "The dead can be helpful, needless to say, but we can only guess
sloppily about how they would react to this emergent particle of time,
which is all the time we have. And when we do guess, we are unfair to
them" (9). Mobbed by shadows, Aaron bears witness like a chalice, enduring his subject's delicate stresses with all the fastidiousness and wariness
devotion is prey to. Indeed, *Leviathan,* whose title Aaron appropriates
from Sachs's own book in progress "to mark what will never exist" (159),
does not conclude so much as capitulate to the fact that "the story would
go on and on, secreting its poison inside me forever. The struggle was to
accept that, to coexist with the forces of my own uncertainty" (271–72).

Randomness cannot be erased from the record. Both Sachs and Aaron
inherit from Wallace Stevens's Crispin:

> Preferring text to gloss, he humbly served
> Grotesque apprenticeship to chance event,
> A clown, perhaps, but an aspiring clown.
> (*The Comedian as the Letter C* 4.90–92)

A series of chance events, including an interrupted seduction at a party, Sachs's subsequent near-fatal fall from a balcony, and his hitchhiking episode, which leads to his killing a murderous assailant and discovering that his victim's car contains bomb components and a huge amount of cash, conspire to drive Sachs underground. But he emerges from his withdrawal to visit Aaron one last time in order to fill him in on his disappearance and to bequeath his manuscript to a sympathetic editor. Thus Aaron and Sachs reenact the relationship between the narrator and the spectral Fanshawe in *The Locked Room,* as well as verify the impasse that disqualifies the notion of congenial transactions between Self and Other: "No one can cross the boundary into another—for the simple reason that no one can gain access into himself" (*Locked Room* 80–81). That access having been barred, or at least rendered problematic, Aaron literally edits Sachs—he "ghost writes" the Phantom of Liberty (Sachs's mediagenic signature) into a palatable, if not confirmable, complex of intentions and activities.

The progressive disorientation of Sachs after his deadly roadside implication is intolerable, so he fixes upon a plan, tortuously orchestrated, of compensating the estranged widow. His insinuations into Lillian's and her young daughter's lives have the virtue of rigor if not simplicity. Similarly, Aaron's narrative regimen is designed not only to combat detachment but to project a history. If it is true that, as Auster asserts in the poem "Incendiary," "The world / is / whatever you leave to it" (lines 12–14), the writer's legacy carries the taint of his presumptions. The novel at first purports to conceive of language as an elaborate rescue mission, in that Aaron plots to pluck Sachs from the belly of the state in order to set him down in the sanctuary of the prepared statement. *Leviathan* exemplifies a selective, sustainable interpretation—Claude Levi-Strauss's "history-for," validated by political aspiration in the shape of poetic motive: "Insofar as history aspires to meaning, it is doomed to select regions, periods, groups of men and individuals in these groups and to make them stand out as discontinuous figures, against a continuity barely good enough to be used as a backdrop. A truly total history would cancel itself out—its product would be nought. . . . History is therefore never history, but history-for" (quoted in Thompson 64). Under these conditions, Aaron's integrity is less a matter of reliability than of open-handedness, which includes the warning that he exposes his prejudices not to eliminate but to exercise them. It is fitting under these conditions that Thoreau is one of Sachs's champions. Certainly his celebrated civil disobedience sets a rousing example for the events in *Leviathan,* but so does his stylistic incorrigibility (*Extra vagance!*), which he announces as a kind of creed at the close of *Walden:* "If the condition of things which we were made for is not yet, what were any reality which we can substitute? We will not be shipwrecked on a vain reality" (326). Slavish depiction is slavery, after all, and the trappings of verisimilitude the most devilish of contrivances.

But like the serial bomber Sachs becomes, Aaron is a vulnerable instigator of events, a subverter subverted; neither the man who leaves art behind for action nor the one who holds fast to verbal craft finally escapes the detonations he initiates. "Each syllable / is the work of sabotage," the poet confesses ("Unearth," 1.12–13). Sachs's eccentricities and disappearing acts intensify his gravitational pull on Aaron, and whatever his role in Sachs's life at any given point—professional acolyte, sexual rival, or spiritual accomplice—Aaron never escapes the man's grasp. As Auster writes in "Fore-shadows," "I numb you in the reach / of brethren light," and ultimately "become / your necessary and most violent / heir" (lines 3–4, 20–22). This again recalls *The Locked Room,* specifically the moment when the narrator realizes that his success—indeed, his identity—is inextricably bound to Fanshawe's: "I had stumbled onto a cause, a thing that justified me and made me feel important, and the more fully I disappeared into my ambitions for Fanshawe, the more sharply I came into focus for myself" (57). We are moved to consider the possibility that, despite his stronger sense of worldly footing and dimension (Aaron has family, occupation, friends), the narrator of *Leviathan* has entered the same secretarial purgatory familiar to readers of *The New York Trilogy* and turned into another ghostwriter commemorating, and becoming, a quarry, an absence.

Further mitigating Aaron's incentives is the self-defeating quality of salvage: *Leviathan* as cloister is claustrophobic; even hagiography is but another instance of incarceration. Like Maria Turner, the novel's provocative performance artist who believes in the revelatory power of aleatory techniques and focuses, and like Sachs himself, who takes life's contingencies as cues, Aaron has to accommodate the leakiness, contradiction, and dubious leads that beset his enterprise *within* that enterprise.[2] To press another of Auster's titles into service here, the "music of chance" is paradoxically at once freer and denser than the routine scales of evident cause. It would be arrogant, Aaron reasons, to "convict" his subject by "sentencing" him decisively, for as his words "happen" they do not necessarily recapitulate any ulterior episode. "I hope to find a way of going along, of running parallel to everything else that is going along," explains Auster in "White Spaces," "and so begin to find a way of filling the silence without breaking it" (103). In other words, silence is not just a fundamental tactic of surveillance, it is the natural and frail state of things. It may also be, as Peter Stillman, the mad linguist of *City of Glass*, posited during his search for a pure language prior to Babel, the preferable state of things, whereby the writer's most legitimate goal is to minimize his contamination. In the famous formulation of Samuel Beckett, "I could not have gone through the awful wretched mess of life without having left a stain upon the silence" (quoted in Bair 640). Auster echoes this oddly mixed message of fortitude and regret:

> It comes down to this: that everything should count, that everything should be a part of it, even the things I do not or cannot understand. The desire, for example, to destroy everything I have written so far. Not from any revulsion at the inadequacy of these words (although that remains a distinct possibility), but rather from the need to remind myself, at each moment, that things do not have to happen this way, that there is always another way, neither better nor worse, in which things might take shape. I realize in the end that I am probably powerless to affect the outcome of even the least thing that happens, but nevertheless, and in spite of myself, as if in an act of blind faith, I want to assume full responsibility. ("White Spaces" 110)

"Running parallel" is the aesthetic compromise between a failure of analysis and false totalization, recalling how metaphor serves as both a writer's creed and credential. Like the movie cliché of the young woman at the station who rushes alongside her departing lover and stays with him until the train gathers speed or she runs out of platform, Auster's Aaron speaks, stands in, or "doubles" for Sachs as long as cogency holds. "These stories came straight from Sachs himself," Aaron offers by way of authenticating his novel-as-deposition. "They helped to define my sense of what he had been like before I met him, but as I repeat his comments now, I realize that they could have been entirely false" (34). The writer suspects the

trappings of coordination for the very comforts they provide. Aaron may
be a dutiful detective, but we may recall the words of William Burroughs,
who claimed that the definition of a paranoid is "a man in possession of
all the facts" (quoted in Kuehl 237).

How, then, can one be responsible in an unremittingly mysterious,
unpredictable world? When Aaron declares that books inevitably begin in
ignorance and persist in ambiguity (40), he is essentially paraphrasing
Sachs's commitment to duplicity. For example, Sachs unabashedly min-
gles fact and fiction, polemic and farce, in his first novel, then mytholo-
gizes his childhood (in particular, a traumatic experience at the Statue of
Liberty) to suit the requirements of his idiosyncratic politics. He systematically lies to his wife about his having had relationships with other
women—unless, of course, that admission is itself unreliable—then tosses
off the confusion he creates by scorning the value of coherence. (Once
again, Maria Turner, for whom accident is oracle and chance aphrodisiac,
epitomizes the vertiginous quality of freedom and the repudiation of taking too seriously that salient something that magnetizes experience into a
stable order.) We can sympathize with Aaron's disappointment in face of
coincidences that may or may not be significant and short-circuited cause,
but when he compares a conversation with Sachs to the "procession of
dimly observed moments" of a baseball game seen on television with the
sound off (125), he may well have found the proper metaphor for
Leviathan.

In this way, we find ourselves cast into the arena of what poet Joseph
Duemer refers to as "useful doubt"—an agnostic resolve that refuses
reductionism. "The temptations of perfection are constant, and must be
resisted," he explains, by which logic conscience becomes a matter of
entertaining the demands of world and imagination simultaneously without eclipsing either (270). On another level, this is perceived in Auster's
novel as a compromise between elegant repose (whose extreme manifestation is "a swoon to the depths of immobility" [95], as Aaron describes his
lovemaking with his friend's wife) and restless forms—miscible selves,
coincidental collisions, ambiguous intentions and outcomes.[3] (Like their
figural renderings, experience and personality must break down somewhere.) Aaron's survival, both as a component of the narrative and as its
artificer, depends upon an acutely self-conscious version of negative capability, a representative indication of which may be seen in his conclusion
to a prolonged analysis of his affair with Fanny Sachs: "If so, then Fanny's

actions become nothing less than extraordinary, a pure and luminous gesture of self-sacrifice. Of all the interpretations I've considered over the years, this is the one I like best. That doesn't mean it's true, but as long as it could be true, it pleases me to think it is. After eleven years, it's the only answer that still makes any sense" (99). We immediately recognize in this passage Aaron's subjective criteria not for the truth but for the story he will settle for: not verifiability so much as shapeliness, or authenticity so much as immunity to authentication and refutation alike. Doubt makes room to ruminate and maneuver.

The trick is to adapt to the opportunities that chance provides, transforming them, through the fervency that the political activist and the novelist share, into a calling. When Sachs the outlaw pays a final visit to Aaron, they debate the relative merits of their respective instigations as arbitrary acts of conscience. To a considerable degree, Sachs can trace his career as the Phantom of Liberty back to the moment he first succumbed to gravity, as it were—that is, his drunken fall from the balcony. This proves to be a fortunate fall; more accurately, in that he appears to drop into incendiary designs, it is a fall into fortune. Activism implies a greater level of predication than this, and hence, it is no wonder that Sachs reads agency, connection, and cause into his affairs, if only to confer purpose upon them. Surely his compulsive attentions to the disdainful Lillian and her daughter have the effect of increments of purgation for the tragic accidents that preceded them. Haunting Dimaggio's ex-wife and child in Berkeley (whom Maria Turner, his abandoned concern and intimate witness to his fall at the party, happens to have known), plying them with measured payments out of the dead man's stash, and slowly insinuating himself into their trust constitute a system of repayment and responsibility for the hidden crime. More to the point, perhaps, they symbolize the attempt to surrender himself to a system and thereby stem the tide of contingency.

Lillian's sudden abandonment—the punishment she had intended for him all along? another example of her preemptive arbitrariness?—forces Sachs to seize upon new orders, which Dimaggio comes to embody. As Sachs explains to Aaron during that last encounter, his exchanging his role of angel of Lillian's household for the Phantom of Liberty owes itself to the conception of Dimaggio as his active alter ego, whereby the coincidences that brought Sachs and Dimaggio violently together symbolize a conspiracy of reintegration, or at least a transference of directed political

energies. Once he determines to carry out Dimaggio's work, "All of a sudden, my life seemed to make sense to me. . . . It was a miraculous con-
fluence, a startling conjunction of motives and ambitions." It is a reprieve
from randomness, not to mention a fitting ransom for having killed the
man. "I had found the unifying principle, and this one idea would bring
all the broken pieces of myself together. For the first time in my life, I
would be whole" (256).[4] Being the Phantom of Liberty requires elaborate
designs and impostures; it combines dimension with articulate fixation.
Whereas Sachs proclaims that his decision has become a source of brac-
ing liberation—significantly, only during his hitch in prison, when life was
so completely mapped out for him, had he enjoyed freedom on such a
scale (22)—he is less a crusader for liberty than its shadow negative.
Destroying replicas of the Statue of Liberty is a terrorist assault *on* liberty
through its peculiarly focused exercise.

It would be convenient, surely, to embellish this interpretation with
references to Sachs's childhood scare at the Statue of Liberty and to connect this concluding effort at self-mythologization with clues from his
published fiction, thereby to guide future readings with the orthodox
Leviathan. Instead of falling for these Rorshach impositions, Aaron closes
his account by reconciling himself to his limited capacity for executing his
friend's will.[5] (We may think of Melville's muttering Ahab, heaped and
tasked in ambiguous pursuit of his own leviathan: "Swim away from me,
do ye?" [203], he scorns, thwarted once again by the elusive prey that
teases him deeper into the abyss.)

As to the consolations of an open text, Annie Dillard offers the following devotional in *Living by Fiction*: "If art objects quit the bounds of the
known and make blurry feints at the unknown, can they truly add to
knowledge or understanding? I think they can; for although we may never
exhaust or locate precisely the phenomena they signify, we may nevertheless approximate them—and this, of course, is our position in relation to
all knowledge and understanding" (166–67). This position affords considerable leniency when it comes to insubordinate forms like the antidetec-
tive novel or the metamystery, as well as in defense of the economical
plenitude, as it were, of the well-made metaphor. Confronting mystery, we
build a model—a more accessible semblance, a cajoling metaphor. If anything, it is the model we solve.

The motive for fiction, as Auster puts it in his first novel, *The Invention
of Solitude*, is "to make a man see the thing before his eyes by holding up

another thing to view" (151). An estimable belief may be honed in slanting winds; sense is best addressed from the flank. Emily Dickinson's testimony to coyness and indirection, "Success in Circuit lies" ("Tell all the
Truth," line 2), tempers the contemporary writer's rationalizations and
every Auster detective's agency, just as it does all rhetorical investigations.
For if Auster's point is that "each life is irreducible to anything other than
itself" (*Locked Room* 89), we must relegate ourselves to less reductive presumptions: pliable tropes, tentative thrusts, compromising procedures—
all compatible with metaphor's own quality of "running parallel." Quinn's
objections are to the contrary in *City of Glass:* a "glimmer of cogency" does
not defeat "arbitrariness" (109). In reality as in contemporary narrative,
the ineradicable trace of arbitrariness causes cogency to glimmer and thus
delight the jaundiced eye.[6]

Aaron adds to the burden of Sachs's confidence the burden of his own
confession. Yet he, too, lives by fiction—stands by fiction—as a method of
tempering judgment with compassion, and vanquishment of mystery with
the inviolability of some of its remotest precincts. We learn from a particularly diligent FBI agent who has been scouring used bookstores that
Sachs had been surreptitiously signing copies of Aaron's books, which
means that just as Aaron's intentions cloud his rendition of Sachs's life,
the dead man's fingerprints are all over our narrator's work. We similarly
recall Aaron's suspicion (again, *The New York Trilogy* provides the model)
of whatever findings may have arisen from watching a man who may have
known he was being tailed/"taled" . . . much less of the dictated details of
an authorized biography. ("Bio-hazards" have been most clearly posted in
The Locked Room, which ends with Fanshawe dying from poison behind
a locked door as he details the terms of his reception to the narrator, who
subsequently destroys each page of Fanshawe's notebook after reading it.)
In *Leviathan,* our three narrators, Auster, Aaron, and Sachs, seemingly
bent upon triangulation so as to pen in the truth, instead play out as
concentric perspectivists, collaborative artists, and men of metaphor. We
finds ourselves addressed by a strangely corporate author who pitches
intent at the frayed edge of belief.

Chapter 5

THE NIGHTMARE OF RELATION
William Gass's *The Tunnel*

"This woman's tongue is being torn out," begins a poem by Albert Gold-barth, which goes on to recite the particulars of one among numberless anonymous specimens of the precise genius and efficiency of evil. And then in the face of the indomitable comes this disclaimer:

> This poem
> can't do a thing about it, can't do one small sprig or whisper
> of rescue about it, this or any poem, it hasn't the words. This
> poem can say the pizzicati spring rain plays a shingle roof
> all day, but it won't help. The deckled edges of antique maps
> won't help, the whole ennobled halcyon-to-maggotass
> wordmastery
> this poem can possibly lug to its surface can't heal, although
> its empathy is great, although it will not flinch and swears
> it won't forget, no, not in its leastmost inky valence,
> although it parallels the dark world of that torture room,
> touches it, nuzzles, but never penetrates it. . . .
> ("Donald Duck in Danish" 1.7–17)

Against art the artist levies the indictment of insufficiency. Then there is the indictment of illegitimacy, which in the following formulation by poet Carolyn Forché accuses the self of attending to its own wounded relevance when no one else can be saved:

> The colonel returned with a sack used to bring groceries home.
> He spilled many human ears on the table. There is no other way
> to say this. He took one of them in his hands, shook it in our
> faces, dropped it into a water glass. It came alive there. I am tired
> of fooling around he said. As for the rights of anyone, tell your
> people they can go fuck themselves. He swept the ears to the
> floor with his arm and held the last of his wine in the air. Some-
> thing for your poetry, no? he said. ("The Colonel," lines 16–23)

Whatever specific position a fiction asserts, it perpetrates scandalous deflections. Sequence connotes consequence; plot intimates purpose; composition confides the decorous composure of identified aims and resolved outcomes. If it is by now a commonplace that history does not transcend but rather exploits these fictional strategies, then it also follows that the historian must be as conspicuous and as accountable as any other narrator. Like Wordsworth's lyric poet, who half creates what he perceives, William Frederick Kohler, in William H. Gass's *The Tunnel*, crafts and cobbles what he records, uniting public and private judgments in such a way that the Third Reich is reified as "the fascism of the heart."

We meet Kohler as a midwestern university professor planted in his mentor's chair as though clutched in a dry fist. From Magus Tabor, the "Mad Meg," whose vulgar, unraveling performances and frenzied methodologies interrupt the novel like siltings from the tunnel ceiling, Kohler inherited two central principles. First, history is not so much a collection of events and notables as it is a repository of language—"verbal remains— symbol middens," as Tabor terms them (263)—whereby the historian himself looms larger than any general or diplomat he might pretend to defer to. If, as Gass has notoriously claimed, words are the only events in fiction ("The Medium of Fiction" 30), likewise, rhetoric is history's enduring episode. Second, the strong force of words is centripetal, a phenomenon which is no less certain in the writing of history than it is in the writing of poetry—both compensatory solitudes "occasionally relieved, like a crowded bowel" by people who unpack themselves with words (*The Tunnel* 9). As Tabor's disciple, Kohler is like a strife spawned by his master's hectoring tempest; like Mad Meg in the Maelstrom, Kohler is the I of the storm, for although he had seen his magnum opus as an achieved height, it turns out to be a depth, a measured plummet through a "windless page" (4). Like Beckett's Murphy, Kohler rocks himself shut in Tabor's chair. "I am distance itself," he notes. "I stand alone on an empty page like a period put down in a snowfall" (125). He blows the circuits of linearity and causality,[1] preferring instead to allow his considerations to clump where they will and to stoke associations with impunity—in short, turning history into his story, secreting away treacherous pages, stocking the past like a vanity: "Welcome to history. To incident and anecdote, chance and serendipity. To the country of the cruel joke" (325). Kohler tends to view history the way he views his own life, as a casual entropy or the hangover of rage. In the tunnel where Kohler writhes and seethes, there is no "smooth conclusion and marble floor" to his excavations ("Emerson and the Essay" 20).

The contrivance that occasions *The Tunnel* is that it begins as Kohler's introduction to his massive analysis, *Guilt and Innocence in Hitler's Germany*. But the overture swells to eclipse the symphony it presumably serves. The novel is an elaborate distraction from the public stage in favor of the mutterings in the wings. As the introduction grows in size and hostility, Kohler hides the pages inside the "proper" manuscript (demonstrating the same ingenuity as his mother once did in concealing her supply of gin). Gass himself provides a model of sorts for this phenomenon in his revised preface to *In the Heart of the Heart of the Country*: what had originally been a briefer account of the origins of each of the stories in the 1976 version has expanded in 1981 into a rhapsody on fiction, inspiration, and disappointment longer than half of the stories in the volume—one whose evident creed, "Amend my misliving" (adopted from Malory), and whose presiding deity, "the graciously menacing presence of the Angel of Inwardness," happen to suit Kohler's preoccupations quite nicely as well (preface to *In the Heart* xviii, xliii).

One of Kohler's colleagues, Herschel, proposes that history may be a private time capsule after all, a process of self-knowledge whose natural goal could be "to achieve self-contained existence" altogether—a wish complicit with the hallowing of hiddenness (142, 502).[2] "If someone were to ask me once again of the circumstances of my birth," Gass writes, "I think I should answer finally that I was born somewhere in the middle of my first book" (preface to *In the Heart* xliv), and Kohler is evidently devoted to finding a literal parallel in stowing himself away in his wordy hermitage. Certainly it is true that Kohler's rare idyllic moments are those in which he can forestall the impingement of history for a time, as for instance in his assessment of his enchanted affair with Lou: "We were happy because we had no history" (108).[3]

Nevertheless, the hollowing out of research to admit Kohler's reveries, rants, and guttering recriminations is not simply a wholesale evasion, however persistently Kohler may equate the written word with other refuges he has prized since childhood. It would be a convenient matter, for example, to adopt the polarities suggested by Holocaust scholar Lawrence L. Langer and to accuse Kohler of a literary finesse, having posited "a discourse of consolation" to replace "a discourse of ruin" (7). Such a formulation would view *The Tunnel* as a natural (here, personalized) extension of the employment of history as a strut for the national ego. (Since consciousness has conventionally been cut out of history, Kohler contends, its revival could be seen as a sensible, even politically conscientious, correction [488–89].) But while the book shifts our focus from public to private images, from the fiction we call human history to the history of Kohler's fiction, that redirection provides no reliable relief from trauma. World Holocaust and one man's remorse are facing mirrors compounding the ways in which "we drag our acts behind us like a string of monsters" (*The Tunnel* 106). Gass foreshadows his novel's premise in "The Imagination of an Insurrection": "Yet history may be a nightmare (appear, that is, fundamentally incomprehensible like the actions of the mad when merely observed) if we do not understand men more completely than hitherto we have. We must try to understand, for instance, how a man's own image of himself can take hold of him as powerfully as a spinning wind, and whirl him off to a land like Oz, which might be Berlin on the Night of the Crystal, or Dublin entering the Troubles" (264).

Kohler's life and the Nazi legacy provoke, infiltrate, and haunt one another so thoroughly that as the book progresses it becomes more and more difficult to determine what is the tunnel and what is the stubborn rock that surrounds it (95). Indeed, Kohler's own memories of his harrowed childhood, his parched marriage, and his disappointing career cannot be articulated apart from that "other war" where his research has lingered. (Kohler's comic delineation of his Party of the Disappointed People, whose trappings come complete with insignia, slogans, and even a depiction of the "disappointment molecule," does not supplant the Nazi Party so much as confirm its reach.) The question, of course, is whether Holocaust references swell the station of the writer's stale memories or overwhelm them entirely: "[Uncle Balt] liked to stop on a little rise just beyond the hawthorn thicket where you could see a stand of wheat like ten thousand German arms salute their leader. Except they hadn't their leader then. There I go" (118). Although Kohler enjoys periods of exhilarant worming through his past (principally sexual) satisfactions and clearly prefers having his concentration encamped beneath his house rather than among others above the flooring, gnawing at his own roots uncovers a poisonous biosystem—a genealogy of demise that is no relief from his scholarly discoveries: "Ponderous aunts and uncles, uncles lean as withered beans, aunts pale as piecrust, grandmapas with rheum and gout, cousins shrill as sirens" (142). Surely it is no *maintenance* tunnel Kohler has been fashioning for himself when his text everywhere confesses that its instabilities are aspects of both domestic and world relations: "Can I believe I've any hold on history when I find my memory is made of marimba music, sack trash, and teapot trivia?" (161); "But we all know that thrown shoes don't lose battles, bring down empires either" (175); "The students will never understand my passionate and detailed exposition of the origins of war or my claim that they are to be found in the domestic character of quarreling" (183). Kohler is a Morlock dense with lecture, denizen of the recondite and addict of abandonment. For all that, whatever the particular incarnation of the tunnel Kohler tries out, be it vaginal access, closet squat, basement burrow (he is actually digging down there, too, further expanding the root system of the beleaguered self), or scored page, it is just one more chambered naught, and no escape from or alternative to the crabbed academic's own gutted heart. Ironically, then, the historian accused of Nazi sympathies (even tendencies, when it comes to his personal relationships) must confront a lesson (offered below in the context of prayer) that the modern Jew always lives with:

> To be a Jew in the twentieth century
> Is to be offered a gift. If you refuse,
> Wishing to be invisible, you choose
> Death of the spirit, the stone insanity.
> Accepting, take full life, full agonies,

Your evening deep in labyrinthine blood
Of those who resist, fail, and resist; and God
Reduced to a hostage among hostages. (Stern 706)

In this way, Jethro Furber's envy of Brackett Omensetter's natural sanctuary ("joy to be a stone") in Gass's *Omensetter's Luck* is revealed to be a
fatal amputation ("the stone insanity").

Nor for all the fustian loosed in *The Tunnel* is the deception of historical rectitude long sustained. A compendium of set pieces, the novel keeps
"giving" from its walls; the facts cannot be neatly bound or the past booked
as Kohler bellies about.[4] Kohler's university colleague, Culp, is simultaneously putting together two limerickal skeins: one a history of the human
race, the other a set of salacious riffs beginning "I once went to bed with
a nun." These combine to strip the sophistry and the solemnity from history, leaving a skeleton of contrivance. Culp's dirty asides are assaults on
profundity—depth charges—and their "low blows" (178) serve as resonant
flexes throughout the novel as the functionally alliterative, pun-stunned
Kohler questions the appearance of intellectual, architectural solidity that
Guilt and Innocence in Hitler's Germany makes, with

> its piling up of day upon decade like shit in a stable, its powerful
> logic like the stench from there (has there ever been such an
> unpleasant assembly of facts?), and then its lofty hierarchy of
> explanations, as though it were a government bureau, the anal
> tables of statistics, too, and weighty apparatus of referral: they
> straighten the teeth of the truth; they impose an order on accident,
> find a will in history as fiery as phlogiston (what is chapterlike
> about tyranny but the beatings and decrees? how much of life is
> simply consecutive like forks of food, as straightforward and declar-
> ative as my disciplined academic style? everything is both simulta-
> neous and continuous and intermittent and mixed; no tattooed
> numbers, no leather love-thongs, mark the page); ah, my book cries
> out its commands, and events are disposed like decorative raisins
> on a cookie (that row there is the mouth, and there's an eye); it
> huffs the wind it flaps in, and soon all fog is blown from circum-
> stance, confusion is scarred from the corn, and empty field is
> ringed with quotes like barbarous wire; well, in the same way this
> pretty pattern of names removes disgust from a dozen dossiers, rips

up some threatening proclamations, decorates death like some
pennant on a spear. (31)

This sort of ritualized impeachment of his motives and conclusions—of
the very concepts of motive and conclusion when it comes to language—
paradoxically restores moral obligation to Kohler's (and to Gass's) enterprise. For it is rather the promotion of history as objectivity tapering
toward resolution, as a purchase on the proper facts that one can put
PAID to, that is a greater and more damaging despotism than any metaphorical flight, opulent doubt, or masturbatory digression Kohler might
indulge in. Both his mentor and his wife berate Kohler for his failure to
finish his book, accusing him of fearing to face vacancy (87, 91); but
there are also political and artistic rationales for a stay of execution.
Accordingly, *The Tunnel* is both structurally and philosophically attuned
to "the chaos implicit in any complete account" (344). For as Gass himself realizes in his own swelling preface, "how to end" is "a knowledge I
have altogether lost," but "[a]ll stories ought to end unsatisfactorily" anyway (xxvii, xxxi).

Gass endows Kohler with his own passion for much and more. Kohler
lavishes on language love he musters nowhere else. As he did with the
Reverend Jethro Furber in *Omensetter's Luck,* Gass has brought "grandeur
to a shit" by allowing a man who is "always leaking *logoi*'" to exist where
making words can be the sole measure of worth (*The Tunnel* 154). Steep-
ing in his sundry hates like sour grounds, Kohler wages an elaborate
underground war on sequence, hierarchy, proportion, and restraint, trust-
ing in verbal enchantment as its own reason for being; to cite Montaigne,
"There is no subject so vain that it does not deserve a place in this rhapsody" (quoted Friedrich 18), and *The Tunnel* means to extend that license
to war atrocities, sexual deviancies, and continual runs of blasphemy.[5]
Descriptions even of the most repulsive things entice when they are lan-
guidly turned in the imagination like dinner on a spit; richly sentenced,
the soul becomes stylized, style-constituted. (Perhaps the most intriguing
aspect of the book is that instead of practicing any sort of meticulous with-
holding of attitude or information that might cast him in a bad light,
Kohler evidently trusts in linguistic energy alone to justify him—if a
self-proclaimed fascist of the heart can be said to care about how he is
received.) In keeping with Kohler's conceit regarding the mutual permeability and authentication of self and history, it is not surprising to find

their chronicles imbued by the same metaphorical muse: "But we historians, we poets of the past tense, we wait for our tutelary spirits to find us," writes Kohler (71), the one-time poet who has not abandoned poetry for history but rather relocated his literary impulses.[6] This anticipates Kohler's eager superimposition of aesthetic logic upon historical method:

> But a work of art which not even the most highly refined science can hope to comprehend, not in large or in its smallest part, because there are no parts, if by parts one means elements fundamentally on their own: no, there are only endless relations and the properties to which they give rise; partialities, shadings, hints, secret sympathies, hidden harmonies, each relating and rerelating, turn and turn about, integrating and reintegrating over and over, the way night and day do, or like lovers, repeatedly positioning and repositioning themselves. (423)

The same negative capability presides from one discipline to another; the same metamorphic quality defines the poet's and the historian's respective materials.

This is not to minimize the slipperiness of this logic, particularly in the case of a novel prompted by the Holocaust. Moving without transition from Kohler's cold marriage bed to the cruelty of the camps (464) is as likely to emphasize their polarity as to prove their relatedness. Robert Alter is one critic who does not buy the premise, and he chastises Gass for failing to escape complicity with the misanthrope he offers the floor. In addition to what he perceives as an absence of any humane authorial commitment hovering over Kohler, Alter rejects the book's collusion of realms as arrogant:

> Like Sylvia Plath's use of Auschwitz in "Daddy," this is an exploitation of the imagery of the death camps to represent out of all proportion the animosities of private life. Domestic rage, intimidation, and resentment are terrible things, but they are not the moral or psychological equivalent of being herded into gas chambers and shoveled into furnaces. . . . The real obscenity of his novel is not its hideous language or its scatological imaginings, but its trivialization of the enormity of genocide by absorbing it into the nickel-and-dime nastiness that people perpetrate in everyday life. (32)

In sum, and begging Alter's pardon for replicating the offense, Gass's chambers are not gas chambers. Gass's often-quoted assertion that "the artist is not asked to construct an adequate philosophy, but a philosophically adequate world" to the contrary ("Philosophy and the Form of Fiction" 9), elevating "a shit" simply spreads the stench.[7] And to be sure, there is no neglecting the vulgar spew that pours out of Kohler like a stuck tub of dirty water.

But *The Tunnel* is not naive about its perpetrations. Even its most pleasing deposits are foreknown as poetry, as Kohler comments in regard to a certain photograph of his decrepit father: "I snapped him only an instant after he slipped down in the doorway (slipped down, remember, despite my arresting phrase, 'fused bones and molten body')" (368). Or as Magus Tabor relates to his student Kohler from his mad flux, we must beware of "the finest molding of the facts, the grace and beauty we can give them, the forms we can fashion for accidents of the grossest kind" and be ready "to plough up the whole field" (244). The artist may improvise a self, even a society, to suit his purposes, but experience has its own adamant agendas. What poetry and history share is the *futility* of being ways of saying. For Gass, words are what the world lives up and comes down to.

Metaphor encourages the imagination to pan for cognates, to seek out supportive constituencies, to frame fraternal orders of reflected sensibilities—all within the context of "the saving grace of his skepticism" over its findings ("Emerson and the Essay" 21). While Kohler's sullen, lumpish wife, Martha, berates him for his dilations—"Well for christ's sake, what are you up to now, running from symbol to symbol like someone needing to pee," she complains (162), wondering if her professor will ever arrive at his point—*The Tunnel* proclaims the resiliency of lyricism within the context of that complaint. Thus, even though Kohler pretends to brush off Culp's gadfly routines and his lighthearted exhibitions of "the sign's sticky duplicities" (169), *The Tunnel* everywhere exploits rather than dissolves the stickiness that weds topical to trivial, ego to globe. That it does so with such exhibitionist energy prevents us from accepting any account that follows a "simple chain of causes . . . long lines of barges pulled along by God" (266).

We are quite familiar by now with Gass's vision of language as a means of effecting an elegant refuge. From Jethro Furber to Babs Masters to the unnamed narrator of "In the Heart of the Heart of the Country," Gass's most notorious characters busy themselves with articulate elsewheres. In his best-known commentaries on fiction, too, Gass has regularly exalted the self-evident, constitutive functions of words over any illusive or representational service. The question that arises regarding *The Tunnel*, however, is not so much whether or to what degree language achieves nonmimetic existence as whether it is grotesquely opportunistic to make poetic capital out of a heap of corpses. If Kohler is guilty of one kind of fascism, is the novelist who arms him with an aesthetic of self-contain-ment, as well as the linguistic versatility to try to bring it off, guilty of another? "Susu, I approach you in my dreams": Kohler's refrain, which proclaims the persistence of the memory of and desire for an unwhole-some young lover, also implies that Kohler's obsessive ruminations approx-imate the dehumanized example of the girl whose capitulation to the Nazis took such forms as singing love songs of terror and chewing the sev-ered thumbs of camp victims.

As Gass recognizes in "The Medium of Fiction," "[If] I describe my peach too perfectly, it's the poem which will make my mouth water . . . while the real peach spoils" (32). The legitimation of *The Tunnel* as being more than frivolous (or worse, unconscionably diverting from a murder-ous past) rests upon the availability throughout the novel of "counter-weights": for example, the installation of "lethal nouns of annihilation . . . lined up as heavy columns of history against the rhetorical leap into ecstasy" (Rosenfeld 108). *The Tunnel* does not play a simple trump, replacing the disfiguring power of the Third Reich with the restorative fig-uration of elegant prose. Reputation to the contrary, Gass's Orpheus does not sing unbound.[8]

Poetic language does not override established facts—death is no metaphor, nor can metaphor contradict it—but it can help defeat con-ventional responses to them. Furthermore, poetic language may also li-cense a mode of inquiry, exacting a fuller measure of reality by expressing it in self-conscious yet disarming ways. This may be stated even more ambitiously. For while one would be hard pressed to come up with a writer who takes greater delight in the sheer succulence of words than Gass, who so luxuriates in expansive paragraphs like hot baths while the plot idles outside, who is so moved to spoon jelly on diamonds in the name of splen-did excess, is not such a migratory technique perhaps better suited to the "thrashy" motions of history (314) than unencumbered linear alternatives are? "Symbols lie in state around me," Kohler says (283); rousing them to resonance is his office and prerogative. Planmantee's smug dismissals notwithstanding, pure facts are counterfeit miracles; pure histories are the stuff of delusion. However, whereas "the *uniqueness* of events cannot be described in language, perhaps they cannot be described in language, perhaps they cannot even be experienced . . . if everything in history is some sort of *repetition*," a satisfying, albeit highly conditional, interpretation may be manufactured (305).

After all, no purer sort of understanding is possible—not in Kohler's guilt-edged reminiscences, not in the historian's data, his infinitely replenishable fossil fuel. Time is an image-ridden din of association, and history inheres not only in what the textbooks attend to but also

> in my mother's rings, my aunt's nested boxes, my father's car—
> in the dregs of every day where my life composts itself—rots,
> warms, blends, bursts into flame—in a photograph, a dollop of
> honey, bit of burnt toast, or in all other toasts and dollops which
> seem identical (although how many honeys have been licked from
> Lou's navel?), in uncapped tubes of toothpaste, in rime on grass
> and leaves, in—in short—things seemingly trivial, things set aside
> or overlooked, things apparently passing which nevertheless abide
> in either themselves or their duplicates; only in such debris, how-
> ever, as has been made over from matter into mind, because one is
> never carried away out of the neighborhood of these redolent
> things, but is rather drawn into them, enters them carrying a torch
> or wearing a light as into a mine; so that everything a blackboard
> does to remind me of my childhood, my pupil days or my profes-
> sion, tells me about the blackboard too, tells me about chalk and
> me, geometry and me, erasers and dull walls and windows and me,
> swastikas and myself (concerning both I've more than once a clean
> slate); for history, I do believe, is not a mighty multitude of causes
> whose effects we suffer now in some imaginary present; it is rather
> that the elements of every evanescent moment endeavor to hitch a
> ride on something more permanent, living on in what lives on,
> lengthening their little life by clinging to a longer one, and in that
> manner, though perhaps quite unintentionally, attaching what will
> be to what still is (and so far has survived) the way a word's former
> employments are the core of what it presently means. (314–15)

The etymology of events imitates the etymology of words containing them.[9] Allusive fusions, alliterative flirtations, the resonant potentiality of things—these are all strategies to outlast oblivion. *The Tunnel* is a repercussive hive, and its bitter engineer a sort of inverted Emerson, as Gass understands his talent:

> and in the ring of these words, "aqueous," "terraqueous," "ethe-
> real," and "aerial," the sound of both the metal which makes the
> coin and its value as money are intimately mingled, with the sign
> and its sense not separate and confused as they are in the unsatis-
> fying albeit sublime light of night, where nature grows gravely over
> him; and I can believe, as he sets them down ("carbon," "lime," and
> "granite"), and hears them singing within the chamber of his inner
> self, that he is one with *them,* and not the primitive elements he so
> carefully lists, or even the cool unstartled stars. ("Emerson and the
> Essay" 14)

In keeping with Kohler's own assessment ("remember, to be is to be enun-
ciated—said, sung, shouted—to be syllabated; I was a word, therefore I
was" [277]), if syntax is as intimate a part of us as gender, then it is right
and proper for language to be the arena of any historical enterprise. There
is nothing sole or mere about life in "this conceptual country" as "part of
a net of essential relations" ("In Terms of the Toenail" 58). Still, the jus-
tifiability of metaphor as a means of leading the way has as much to do
with its intrinsic provisionality as it does with its capacity to coin coheren-
cies. For instance, trying to effect out of imagery a shapelier domain for
his ruined marriage leads to no practical repair, as the language seems
soiled by love's decline: "A little untoward heat (we said) might melt us
down from one another like a custard from its coating; a sudden jar might
shatter our fragile ties; an unexpected stress might stretch our sympathies
to a point beyond elastic (so we went on, piling comparisons up like fruit
in a market window); we might weaken like moistened cardboard and our
bottom pop" (339). At best, Kohler's tropes run parallel for a time down
the same hopeless slope; at worst, they are as wicked and undignified as
Martha maintains (150). Wallace Stevens's "intricate evasions of as" do
not encourage a close-order drill among images (*An Ordinary Evening in
New Haven* 486). Indeed, those "intricate evasions" must be understood

in two ways, for even as a given figure allows the writer to escape brittle, unilateral understandings, it also confounds any alternative purposes by retaining its multivalence and foregrounding its own artificiality. A pun may pretend to replace the past, but it also frames what it targets for translation: "I'll imagine many letters to you in my youthful tongue which the matron will deliver when you're back from shock; when they've thrown your brains, like squids, in a box; and with the help of their silent thunder volts—yes, with one pun the past has been blacked out" (480).

Is a book a monument that permanently engraves or a grave that swallows its marker? In "Monumentality/Mentality," Gass considers how "we remember what we remember as though we stood at the grave of our past with a shovel full of symbols, a strange mix of verb and image, noun and sensation, to drop like dirt down another dead day" (128). It is significant that Gass's assessment of the challenges involved in making *The Tunnel* includes figuring out where the burst lurks along the plumbing and determining how to dispose of the dirt—the verbal debris, the scavenged passions, and scandalous past—that his diggings disclose (interview with Durand 8–9; "Tropes of the Text" 158–59). On the other hand,

> an honest memorial to war would not be a regimented stitch of clean white crosses in a military cemetery, nor more rows of names cut uniformly into marble, a massive mausoleum full of flags or large grounds of landscaped cannon laid out in pleasant vistas where the cavalry charge was, with plaques which explain the terrain in words of half a syllable, estimate the weight of the bombs that fell, number the slain in the sunken road—GEE! THAT MANY! WOW!—but it would contain the muddy trench, the bloated corpse, the stallion lying by its bowels, blown-apart buildings, abandoned equipment, recordings of outcry.
>
> The eternal flame should be fed flesh. (139–40)

An honest memorial, in other words, should not cover up the casualties or stanch the flow of blood. While it is possible to contend that varnishing the horror is precisely what Gass is guilty of in *The Tunnel*—not only does he make a shit shine so, but he exploits and stifles the dead beneath the wordglut meant to remember them—it is also possible that his employment of metaphor accomplishes precisely this contradictory business of forging open associations. Thanks to metaphor we move back and forth between likened terms, as well as imagine other bridges as we pass: "The terms are inspecting one another—they interact—the figure is drawn both ways" (Gass, "In Terms of the Toenail" 67–68). Metaphor's "as if" is a structural strategy designed to enact moral complexities, not to vanquish them. The clever phrase does not masquerade as literature's Final Solution.

Certainly the title metaphor of the novel demonstrates a variety of complications. Presumably, a tunnel is a route with a destination, a manifest movement toward. That Kohler means to secret a keep out of "the trials of device" (Stevens, *An Ordinary Evening in New Haven* 477) appears to ask incompatible favors from his construction. The contradiction between the tunnel as something aimed outward and as something fundamentally interior—a passage where Kohler seems willingly "penned in," as it were—parallels the status of the sign as auto- or extrareferential, a subject that has preoccupied Gass in so many of his essays.[10] In this way, whereas the belief Gass offers in "The Ontology of the Sentence" that "there is no out-of-doors in the world where language is the land" (317) attests to a syllabic lair whose signs are as driven inward as its sole inhabitant, the continual impingement of professional animosities, marital disappointments, and of course, the Nazi atrocities upon Kohler's consciousness reveals the contamination of what he writes, builds, or recalls.[11] In short, no simple opposition between a world "windy with unreason" and a windless remove can be effected (8, 9).

Not that Kohler's failure to earn a pure recoil comes from a lack of effort. This "intransitive man" traces his present-day intertextual torpor back through a lifetime honeycombed with tunnel prototypes. Childhood was an unending effort to escape parental truculence and a host of family devastations into a variety of interiors—books, sweet shops, daydreams, closets, make-believe fortresses, and all sorts of secluded harbors where young Kohler could create romance out of vagrancy. Kohler always sought freedom from a crouch:

> To enter yourself so completely that you're like a peeled-off glove; to become the world invisible, entirely out of touch, no longer defined by the eyes of others, unanswering to anyone; to go away with such utterness behind a curtain or beneath a tented table, in the unfamiliar angles of an attic or the menace of a basement; to be swallowed by a chest or hamper as the whale-god swallowed Jonah, and then to find yourself alive, and even well, in the

> belly of your own being; to go supremely away like this was to reen-
> ter through another atmosphere, and to experience, perhaps for the
> first time, a wholly unpressured seeing; it was bliss. (292)

Like Hitler, vile muse of his adulthood, Kohler is a pariah who learns to define that position as election.

Then there was Kohler's Uncle Balt, a pioneer in rage and personal burial, whose bone disease would become a symbol of implosive tendencies. He was "a deep, unreadable hole of a man—a well of loneliness," which is to say, a tunnel incarnate (116). In him Kohler finds "a metaphor for Being, makeshift maybe, but an image in the form of a tall dark column of damp air, hole going nowhere—yes—wind across the mouth of a bottle" (121), and a means of retracting from a fallow household. In the years to come, Kohler will seek to enter women, too, like isolated groves; he will try to disappear into his studies, his cellar trench, or his unabating anger like a swallow down a throat.

> My tunnel shall have a body made of simple soilage like the rest
> of us. Like the rest of us, it will have a spirit which is certainly no
> thing, too, for its hollow here is no more palpable than spirit is, than
> consciousness, the ghost which Martha was just now when I con-
> jured her, which I am when I conjure me, or Herschel, here, is
> when I conjure him. Yes. In that sense, it's as if I were making a
> creature down there in my dust, a creature out of pure crawl. (209)

Paradoxically, so in love with isolation is Kohler that digging down provides him with a sense of altitude, however we may see him as a creature of depths (146, 149).[12] Beneath his poisons he intends to create a fit confinement for his hate—"a wrathkeller, Culp would certainly say" (153)— which he evidently believes will lift him, as it did another of Gass's narrators, "so high . . . that when I shit I won't miss anybody" ("In the Heart of the Heart of the Country," *In the Heart*, 189).

Nonetheless, an eloquent elsewhere earns only so much distance from the conditions that inspired it. "The sophisticated image of the tunnel . . . completes itself in the darkness of act; it is buried in the literal, in *das plumpe Denken*, in the vulgarities of practice" (156). Moreover, "the abyss is not merely where the soul goes when it's gone; it's where the self is exposed like sensitive paper, till, exhausted, it draws a blank" (184–85). In other words, despite Kohler's extolling his hole as his "highest heaven of invention" (500), the metaphor guarantees neither transcendence nor elevation for the artist committed to it and, frankly, lying in the dirt. For all Kohler's defenses, *The Tunnel* features a choked voice, a trammeled, "tunnel" vision. Kohler speaks of "mine" fields (311), of utterly accommodating concealments and paradigms of vantage as open to inscription as the "new blank land" Jorge Segren perceives awaiting him at the end of "The Pedersen Kid" (*In the Heart* 63), but his stature is restricted to "the flitter of images" (311).[13] A capable author may make the world echo him, but that does not drown the outcries that cause the walls to shudder.

Although tunnels are surely the most fully developed of the symbolic complexes in the novel, there are others that disclose a similarly conflicted status. Two of the most prominent have to do with insects and with windows. Insects are animate versions of the dust, the past's dander, indifferent as the passage of time; they are definitely related plagues on the Kohler family farm. Grasshoppers arrive just as unaccountably and seize upon the landscape just as voraciously as Kohler's bouts of desolation. One particular assault of grasshoppers traumatizes young Kohler, engulfing him with the same cyclonic irresistibility as his principal subject will later in life:

> They continued up like thick smoke; I was caught in a stifling funnel. Grasshoppers do not spiral like flies or bees, but leap in a gale, so the feeling of whirlwind I had, of their coming straight from my feet and circling round me, was hopelessly unfactual, and even that sensation was one I had afterward, when I tried to save a little of my sanity by sorting my impressions and systematically swallowing them, draining my sickness from my head and putting my past in my belly. I ran as they rose, tripped instantly, and stumbled— wailing like a paper siren. Grasshoppers flew in my mouth: one? three? thousand? I was on the ground, insects crushed under me, gushing vomit. They were caught in my hair, leaping at my ears and eyes. I began to choke, trying to cry out, thrashing and rolling in utter panic. A grown man, I was being consumed by terror in a patch of knee-high grass, not four feet from safety. (103)

The notion of an undifferentiated swarm, of an incommensurable multitude, is as threatening as the grasshoppers themselves. So will it be for

Kohler with the victims of the Holocaust, who will become another infestation of his head and mouth, who will also defy the serenity of fact sorting. Reflecting upon the grasshoppers, Kohler notes that "there are more of these grass-chewing jaws in Iowa than there are Jews in Germany" (102), and murderously massed, both cause him to be "consumed by terror." As opposed to the vitalizing stream of flies that sleeve the narrator's arm as he picks apples in "In the Heart of the Heart of the Country"— their harmonious hum makes his arm seem as though it "had never been more alive, oftener or more gently kissed" (*In the Heart* 205)—these insects suffocate; and instead of encouraging a return to the world as they appear to do in Gass's earlier story, here they validate withdrawal.[14] Similarly, bees will escalate their irritation: first described as goalless or capricious, they eventually become a deliberate, directed malice that disrupts Kohler's summer pastoral (152, 230).

Regardless, there are advantages to be found in the collective. The cloud they constitute endows insects not only with their terror but also with their substance, like a gathering of scattered wits into a forceful Idea. Prominence in the atmosphere or in the imagination derives from their directed density. It is the size of the spasm that confers attention in any history. What is true of grasshoppers is true of the Jews: their doom gives them dimension, and the sheer dimension of their doom ensures their remembrance because it takes so many of the anonymous dead to make a shadow long enough to reach us (247).

A second paradox specifically affects the writer's enterprise. On the one hand, the enormity of what accosts him—insects or murder victims, dust or data—overwhelms him, closes his throat. On the other hand, the phenomenon of accrual in nature appears to justify metaphorical association. Therefore, Kohler reminds himself of the enabling creed of assimilation, recognizing that the reality of the people "rests on what is juxtaposed: next to next makes their nest" and grants the fragments meaning (281).

Contrasting connotations are likewise derived from windows in *The Tunnel*. Perhaps the strongest influence upon Kohler's writing *Guilt and Innocence in Hitler's Germany* (a title which itself suggests a contested understanding) is expiation for his participation in *Kristallnacht* while he was a student in Germany. Kohler discloses several symptoms of this behavior. As a child, he once shot BBs through a neighbor's bathroom window for sheer delight in the shatter. He also saw a broken window shower his addled mother's hair with glass during a storm, and he would forever after connect her mental decline with that damage. As an adult, he would think of a visit with his family as an impending Night of Crystal, with animosities among the "ghost folks" serving as hurled stones (128).

While it was ethically indefensible for anyone to have taken part in *Kristallnacht,* it is especially surprising, as well as psychologically implicating, for one so addicted to refuges as Kohler to have done so. Windows provide a conditional access and distance; in high school Kohler wrote about how books and windows were alike in their allowances, standing "translucently between perception and reflection, uniting and dividing, double dealing" (302), a strange mixture of qualities that Kohler would someday carry into his adult projects. (In "In the Heart of the Heart of the Country," a man in retirement from love announces, "My window is a grave, and all that lies within it's dead," only to amend the situation with greater subtlety: "We meet on this window, the world and I, inelegantly, swimmers of the glass; and swung wrong way round to one another, the world seems in" [*In the Heart* 195, 196].) With windows ensuring so fragile a refuge, it would seem an impiety to treat them recklessly. But it is their very fragility and their capacity for retaining light that makes windows more optimistic images than dark tunnels can be. Tunnels may afford superior insulation, or at least better sustain that illusion. Windows, however, do not just seal the spirit but also establish a medium that transmits its delicate essence (308).

In fact, what appears to precipitate Kohler's *Kristallnacht* is the insufficiency of the contact his anonymous neighbor's window affords. Kohler spies upon him from his own "watching window" in the hope of seeing something salacious (320). Denied a fuller, more coherent view, the frustrated voyeur first creates a fiction to knit the fragments he has been able to glimpse before the room goes black. Throwing his brick represents an escalation of the desire to find a way in. His reaction to that window, in other words, refutes the privilege of inviolable vantage: "The window I watched through now, the window which yielded me nothing, evening after evening, night after night, dawn upon dawn, was also every window I had ever known, whether real or metaphorical: that was one reason my gaze was so persistent and intense; because it was not merely curiosity or prurience which shifted my neutral into stare, it was, as it always is of course . . . complicity" (322). The window's invitation is also an indictment of the writer's aims. Finally, windows take the imprint of the viewer's mood: Kohler's house has a wide window that "graces" the sink below it, but it also has "two hateful ones" that "put the sky in a coma" (445). A trick of the glass can make the world "seem in," at least when the fascist relies exclusively upon his squinted vision, and they retain his dim presence like a blemish (357); conversely, a trick of imagination can make one's own inwardness seem the world.

How long can a man subsist on his own echoes alone? How long can he continue to decorate a cave deprived of oxygen? "The quiet spiral of the shell, a gyre, even a whirlwind, a tunnel towering in the air: these are the appropriate forms, the rightful shapes; yet the reader must not succumb to the temptations of simple location," Gass warns (preface to *In the Heart* xxxviii). It may be surprising to some readers to learn that William Gass, one of America's foremost metafictionists, is also director of the International Writers Center at Washington University. No one's words are more suspicious about their status, more watchful of their own backs, than Gass's are, yet the author does not seem daunted by committing language to extratextual responsibilities. Engagement with the Other within a self-consciously qualified context: what better respects this tension than metaphor?

Here is William Gass, the political writer: "There is a bond between us, readers and writers, an ancient tie, as old as writing is, if not as old as speech itself, a pact, a promise that the act of setting down sentences in a moving way implicitly solidifies: that what we shall say shall be as true to things and to our own hearts as we can manage with our skills to make them; and that what we read shall be for the humanity all language represents, whatever its content otherwise" ("Tribalism, Identity, and Ideology" 56). Scrupulous treatment is the first scruple of the politically responsible writer, the principal plank of whose platform must be to write well. Saying "yes" to a character like Kohler is not to discount the often vile content of his commentary but to authenticate its reality within the text.

"The Moral Necessity of Metaphor," insists Cynthia Ozick, is based on its dedication to making connections, dissolving abstractions, and exalting our historical awareness—hardly frivolous or nonsecular occupations. From Ozick's perspective, harnessing metaphor is the key contribution of the creative writer to a "universal conscience" (65). Furthermore, metaphor means to initiate the same sort of reciprocity between peoples as it does between its own terms: "Without the metaphor of memory and history, we cannot imagine the life of the Other. We cannot imagine what it is to be someone else. . . . As the shocking extension of the unknown into our most intimate, most feeling, most private selves, metaphor is the enemy of abstraction" (67, 68). Through its demonstration of interaction and complicity, metaphor becomes a universalizing force.

In *The Tunnel*, Kohler complicates and strains this capacity by pressing poetry into the service of bigotry; he innovates in order to malign and deflect the Other, to raise barriers of abstraction instead of demolish them. We are asked to say "yes" to someone who, for all the atrocities he confesses, has given himself over to denials. In a sense, then, Kohler himself recalls the qualities of defamiliarization, intrigue, and distance that are just as much a part of metaphor's nature and effect as are the empowerments Ozick presumes.

In William Kohler, William Gass has created a figure that fascinates and revolts us—an allusive solipsist, implicating demon. Gass gives us an eloquent grouse who, although he keeps to a coarse terrain of thought, offers an out through the very language he lurks in. *The Tunnel* is a crafted absence that style belies.

Chapter 6

THE TROPE IN THE MACHINE
Richard Powers's *Galatea 2.2*

Nature never flinches from exacting physics. In the modest yard sparrows cleave to secret diameters; gnats are absorbed in their helical ruckus like some difficult argument building; oak leaves braid and valve the humid air. What seems a slack arrangement of children at their casual plotting involves thousands of comparable strictures, too, coiled in the synapses, radiating to join the general calculus of afternoon. And as the writer homes in upon a savory phrase, he considers the influences that show in his every shift and subtly inhabit his vantage.

A great horde of forces surrounds, sustains, and incorporates all we are and witness and attempt. Shadowed by that hovering sum, should we be surprised to learn that human issues and empathies are also loyal to laws that define the environment in which they are exercised? In the quest for causal elegance, situated between vast subatomic and cosmological frenzies, how can we resist the scrabble for complements? As Jacob Bronowski writes, all research comes down to an elaborate orientation ceremony, whether its beneficiary be the creative scientist refining his experiment or the creative writer sharpening his clause:

> [E]very act of imagination is the discovery of likenesses
> between two things that were thought unlike. And the example

that I gave (in *Science and Human Values*) was Newton's thinking of the likeness between the thrown apple and the moon sailing majestically in the sky. A most improbable likeness, but one which turned out to be (if you will forgive the phrase) enormously fruitful. All acts of imagination are of that kind. They take the closed system, they inspect it, they manipulate it, and then they find something which had not been put into the system so far. They open the system up, they introduce new likenesses, whether it is Shakespeare saying, "My Mistres' eyes are nothing like the Sunne" or it is Newton saying the moon in essence is exactly like a thrown apple. All those who imagine take parts of the universe which have not been connected hitherto and enlarge the total connectivity of the universe by showing them to be connected. (Quoted in Rogers 195–96)

"Knee-deep in the cosmic overwhelm," explains poet Diane Ackerman,

> I'm stricken
> by the ricochet wonder of it all: the plain
>
> everythingness of everything, in cahoots
> with the everythingness of everything else.
> ("Diffraction," lines 7–10)

Ourselves likewise "walking symphonies / of dappled cells" (Ackerman, "Halley's Comet," 2.19–20), we hazard coordinates in daunting realms of data, fluxional and recombinant as the phenomena they pertain to, and which, as Ackerman demonstrates, we dote upon and yield to.[1] It follows that whatever scientific or linguistic models we posit be committed to openness even as they are bent upon disclosure. Analysis, by this reasoning, is no sober clinic but an exercise in scrupulous revelry.

The fiction of Richard Powers shows how every drama derives from molecular premises and panoramic forces alike. Plot progresses through genetic compacts and planetary motions. We are prophetic from the cells outward to the skies. Powers's characters must make their way not only through their own human transactions and travails but also through the repertoire of astonishments that wait in ambush within the hidden course and retracted capacities of matter. In West's *The Universe, and Other Fictions*, every thing and gesture, from the grain of a table to the darkening of a mood, from the flight of balls to the run of blood, is articulate and consequential. In DeLillo's *White Noise,* clutched by sudden intensities of consciousness, Jack Gladney finds in every object of regard "a beadwork of bright creation" (243); at one point he is moved to consider "how many codes, countercodes, social histories were contained" in his daughter's absent posture (61).[2] Richard Powers goes these authors one better by offering a comprehensive read-out, as in molecular biologist Stuart Ressler's richly upholstered observation of a child's recitation of a memorized poem:

> To a scientist habituated to the microscopic, her snip nose, proto-mouth, tiny eyes that actually focus and see are miracles. Blood courses through Margaret as she recites. Lungs pump, kidneys filter. Systems and subsystems weave an intricate, interdependent free-for-all. Her nervous system, a fine spray of veil, a cascading waterfall of paths and signals, subdivides into web-bouquets, structures more elaborate and beautiful the more he imagines their constituent firings.
>
> This is the awful northern face that molecular self-duplication must scale, an ascent as unlikely as the climb of chemicals out of the primordial soup of reducing atmosphere. The superstructure alone is inconceivable. Just the thought that a single zygote, in less time than it takes the average Civil Service gang to dig a bed for a mile of interstate, differentiates into vertebrae, liver, dimpled knees, and ears complete with recording membrane is enough to knock Ressler flat on the metaphorical mat. Yet nucleotide rungs alone curve this child's cornea, curl her lashes. Nothing else needed; he's sure of that. The entire, magic morphogenesis is explainable as terraced chemical mechanisms.
>
> This *machine,* this polyp, this self-assembling satellite of two parents with no special technical ability outside of inserting complementary parts inside one another, this self-governing bureaucratic republic of mutually dependent parasites (every one incorporating a transcript of the master speech), has mastered speech. Mimicked language. Biggest of the big L's, from fist to lash, the real tissue. Margaret's cells have found out how to say what they mean, or a rough approximation. Her hierarchy of needs insists it is more than chance initiation. (*Gold Bug Variations* 177)

And on it goes, this rhapsodic diagnosis of coordinated parts and sentient routines, in a novel in which the slender, dewy trellises of the DNA molecule are as much character as quarry.

Each of Powers's novels discovers symphonic connections in contested spaces. In *Three Farmers on Their Way to a Dance*, a Diego Rivera mural and an August Sander photograph are the two initial strands that eventually braid and seduce a current-day computer writer to investigate the advent of World War I; in *Operation Wandering Soul*, the blasted inhabitants of a terminal pediatrics ward are plied with stories ranging from Peter Pan to the Children's Crusade when physiotherapy falls short; in *The Gold Bug Variations*, Bach's sonic spirals and life's woven proteins integrate to suggest that "all speciation . . . [is] a set of variations whose differences declare their variegated similarity" (*Gold Bug Variations* 40). An author whose fields of expertise extend from classical music to contemporary physics, Powers trusts in resemblance to reveal the designs that wed the disparate and thereby to explicate the measures we move by. "Since I don't smoke or drink and swear unconvincingly, symmetry is my only vice," admits the narrator of *Three Farmers on Their Way to a Dance* (12), a novel whose parallel lines of narrative intersect at the far horizon of shared compulsion. When a surgical resident is overwhelmed by the shock of ER, he grasps at "state-of-the-art material metaphor" to stabilize him (*Operation Wandering Soul* 94); when a physicist considers whether genetic codes are the universe's priority or pun, he relies on the faith that "Each thing is what it is only through everything else. Life is a crystal, combinatorial" (*Gold Bug Variations* 180). "A new postulate is no more news than a new poem," we read in *The Gold Bug Variations* (128), but this is not to discredit the warrants available in either response to the world at large. Wherever fugal figure dawns out of foggy ground, its purpose is the same: whether through science or simile, to occasion "the revival of appropriate surprise" (*Gold Bug Variations* 129). For there to be a profitable negotiation between the "two cultures," therefore, their interdependency should be acknowledged, then fostered. So the rhetor vets the molecular; and while art catalyzes scientific concepts, science hosts and harnesses metaphorical departures. In the words of poet Stephen Dunn, "Oh poetry, oh the importance of ground / when leaving the ground" (*Loves*, lines 101–2).

With these goals and codicils in mind, Powers directly undertakes Ressler's "biggest of the big L's" in *Galatea 2.2*. The book features one

Richard Powers (also known as "Beau" to his lover, "Marcel" to his mocking colleague), a writer whose biographical and professional particulars
seem rather precisely coincidental with the author's own. He has returned
to the United States after several years in Europe to be the humanist-in-
residence—the literary world's ambassador, or sacrifice, to the Center for
the Study of Advanced Sciences, a massively endowed harbor for manic
geniuses on the site of a major midwestern university. With its es-
teemed inhabitants, all evidently "habituated to the inconceivable" (8),
busily skimming its interior like electrical firings, the center itself is a mag-
nified analog for the neurochemistry of the brain, upon whose data several of these "addicts of the verifiable" feed (10). It is on these rarefied
premises that Powers meets Philip Lentz, a cognitive neurologist who
seduces Powers to join him in the attempt to construct and train a computer modeled upon neural networks in the human brain to be able to
pass the graduate comprehensive examination in English literature.

This variation on the Turing Test, whereby an undisclosed artificial
intelligence can successfully masquerade as human, is the basis for
Galatea 2.2. Intriguingly, whereas the successive implementations of
this device inspire the fictional Powers to discover sufficient anthropo-
morphic potential—he not only dubs "her" "Helen" but also eventually
inputs selections from his previous novels and details about his doomed
love affair—many of the central figures of the novel are not granted proper
nouns: C. (Powers' beloved, with whom he lives for a time abroad), E. and
B. (two of the European cities where they lived together), U. (the town in
which the university where Powers matriculated and to which he has
returned as a token humanist is located), and A. (a theory-savvy and star-
tlingly practical-minded English graduate student who captivates our hero
and whom he commandeers for the Turing Test) are all protected entities.[3] In this regard, they recall the irreducible, mutually qualifying vari-
ables of the DNA molecule in *The Gold Bug Variations*, while Helen, who
could some day launch a thousand fellowships, has her lathering cells laid
open.

The enterprise holds numerous appeals for the writer. Powers has been
blocked for some time since the end of his relationship with C. and the
completion of his fourth book, which had been unevenly received and
characterized as an apocalyptic impasse. At present, "Picture a train head-
ing south," an unsponsored, aimless visitation, is the sticky point of departure and the full itinerary of his next fiction, so cruising the Internet or

outfitting the memory of a supercomputer could be just the thing to revive him, or at least accommodate his glazed suspension for a year's residency. U. seems to be the logical place for him to rediscover his direction because it is the original locus of so many consorting, fortifying "interfaces" and initiations in his life:

> U. was the place where I first saw how paint might encode pol-
> itics, first heard how a sonata layered itself like a living hierarchy,
> first felt sentences cadence into engagement. I first put myself up
> inside the damp chamois of another person's body in U. First love
> smelted, sublimated, and vaporized here in four slight years.
>
> I betrayed my beloved physics in this town, shacked up with lit-
> erature. My little brother called me here to tell me Dad was dead.
> I tied my life to C.'s in U. (4)

As Lentz's machine is refined out of its more primitive implementations, as it learns to read, Powers learns to reflect upon his star-crossed past. Just as Powers and C. used to read to one another beneath the blankets to stave off the cold, just as Powers struggled to teach indolent composition students to grapple with the concept of the Not-Me, Powers and Helen are both involved in the upgrading of their capacity to access otherness coherently. (And which audience among these finds meaning more arbitrary? Which Galatea balks first at her Pygmalion's input?) The theory of "back-propagation," which refers to the brain's (or computer's) corrective adjustments and weighting of connections back to the "input layer," also suits Powers's recriminative passions, as this Marcel, assaulted on all sides in U. by reminders of the past, is continually prone to reveries, for which the fact-grinding Lentz has little patience. "Love is the feedback cycle of longing, belonging, loss. Anti-Hebbian: the firing links get weaker" (152).

Helen is a willing, hopeful monster; her synaptic eagerness seems the very electronic manifestation of cognition's hair trigger. But she is a reader whose sole diet, like our introspective narrator's, is "the brittle-bone disease of words" (243). Accordingly, both Powers and Helen are the stories they construct, enshrine, and tell on themselves. It is the lesson of every Powers novel: "All human effort, it seemed to me, aimed at a single end: to bring to life the storied curve we tell ourselves" (312). Truth is a matter of judicious, repeated enactments, not an a priori condition; emplotment, Powers maintains, in a circumlocution worthy of Helen trying to arbitrate between words' reach and grasp, "is the must we make by living it" (313).[4] "It was like so, but wasn't," the novel begins, deferring to the metamorphic effects of telling on tales (3).[5] So as Powers finds when he tries to contend with Dutch when living with C. abroad or when he tries to stay afloat amidst the neomystical jargon of the center's regular patrons, he, too, is an Imp System under construction.

Like Stuart Ressler in *Gold Bug Variations*, Philip Lentz is at once intimidated and motivated by the welter of events that constitute the simplest gesture: "If you knew what it took to reach out and grasp an object, to pick up a glass, you'd be completely incapable of doing it," he tells Powers (85). Recognizing the impertinence of fashioning a working replica of the process of *understanding* that gesture overmatches the humanist. The more you know about the mechanics of knowing, the more "you temper yourself against the definitive": "Every postmodern postsolipsist, I thought, should do a post frontal neurology stint. The most agile of them would . . . take to weighing the violence in their every predicate. Once they saw the bewilderingly complex fiber in its impossible live weave, theorists would forever opt for the humblest, least-obtrusive sentence allowed them" (40). Hence the inherent arrogance of artificial intelligence (or AI). On the one hand, it relies on our smuggling of methods and axioms from the human species into the "machine kingdom." As Daniel J. Boorstein advises in his essay "Darwinian Expectations": "The crucial intervention of human desires, fashions, advertising, institutions, and whimsies makes it risky to predict survival or procreation on the basis of the intrinsic or genetic characteristics of any particular machine. The promise of survival for a species in nature depends on its ability to adapt to its environment. By contrast . . . the power of a machine to survive depends upon its ability to bring forth its own environment, or create its own demand" (137). Validation of AI must contend with a perpetually self-modifying mechanism, changing and maturing, if you will, like man's own wetware; tempering the definitive implies "a quest for the peculiar vagrancy of our new world . . . a search for the laws of the unexpected" (Boorstein 140). The supercomputer, the aspiring child, the willing dog, the neurophysicist's addled wife, the peripatetic narrator—all try to home in on stationary nouns but must settle for predicates that *move*.[6]

On another front, there is a cataract of self-awareness that obstructs the making of a metaphor (machine) for a metaphor maker (brain). If cognition includes the knowledge that one knows, what promontory affords that understanding? The problem twists epistemology into a Moebius strip: in *Galatea 2.2*, the philosopher's conundrum becomes the technician's. "If we knew the world only through synapses, how could we know the synapse?" Powers wonders, then circles the wondering engine from which the question was spun. "A brain tangled enough to tackle itself must be too tangled to tackle," or would somehow demand the extraction of the steak without killing the cow (28). If it is difficult for our "Marcel" to supersede his griefs or vault his writer's block, the ungetpastableness of his past is nothing compared with the task given to the computer to reflect upon its own knitted nets: "It might grow knowledge structures forever, as fecund as a field tilled with representational fertilizer. But its knowledge *about* knowledge would remain forever nil" (114). When it comes to scrutiny of the inbred brain, all experimentation is double-blind by default.[7]

As the alphabetical begettings descend from Implementation A, the machine grows more insistent about its appetite for analogs of itself; yet even Helen, the state-of-the-art articulator, remains fixed in its own blind spot. Combining Eastern spiritual teachings and his own brand of winning mischief, Ram, another colleague at the center, sums up unsummability for Powers by respecting the centripetal cosmos of consciousness: "My friend. My fictional friend. The eye moves. We watch it as it does so. That is all" (298).

Certainly part of the pleasure of *Galatea 2.2* comes from the queer mintings and images concocted by Lentz and Powers's electronic protégé. Like the contrived idiomatic exchanges of Powers and C. struggling with Dutch, or like an outrageous interchange out of Ionesco's *Bald Soprano*, conversations with Helen's prototypes leave the machine marooned on the dark verge of coherence, where a day's churning inevitably leads to seizure: "John gives Jim apples," for instance, leads Implementation B into a morass of circular logic, fractured increments, and semantic misapplications, until it concludes that "Jim hit John because one bad apple doesn't spoil the whole barrel" (113–14).[8] Powers fortifies Helen with pictures, almanacs, and manuals for symbolic grounding the way one might add fiber to his diet; he rakes in reference and crams her circuits with worldliness to help Helen cram for the upcoming exam, all in the hope that association, rather than discretion, would prove the better part of valor.[9]

It is in this regard that Helen progresses from the skittish twitches and bleats of her ancestors into a reasonable facsimile of an education by metaphor. Certainly this emphasis on open-ended process complies with Powers's own licentious poetics, his freewheeling polymathy and referential energy.[10] Indeed, as the novelist himself confides, the conductivity and intellectual appeal of engaging multiple disciplines has to do with "the discovery of a process you don't entirely understand," which further emphasizes the fertile prospects of unresolved territory (quoted in Baker 37).

Symbols supplant the real; we live along the lineaments of their fanciful extensions. Powers readily concedes the point when, for example, he compensates his favorite literature teacher, Professor Taylor, by turning him into a character in a book (204); or when he comes to the understanding that the women he has fallen for "were some reminder of a lost third thing I didn't even remember having loved" (238); or when his delight in A. sets off a figural spew from the lonesome writer, which is to say that perceptions funnel through a corridor of simulations.

Consider love (or, barring that, "love") as it is treated in *Galatea 2.2*. When late in the novel Powers tries to protect Helen from Lentz's dissection—he shudders at the thought, which is as unfulfilling as a poem pared down to its paraphrase or a desire demystified into a series of struck nerves—he speaks of her in terms that recall his description of his love for C.—if *that* rigorously examined relationship counted as love, that is. (We could say that Helen triggers an adulterous fixation if only because she represents a digressive pursuit for the honorary fellow, pulling the writer away from a more productive focus.) Perhaps Pygmalion loves Galatea in the way one term of a metaphor asserts affinities with the term fashioned in its shadow. A. may scorn Powers when he declares his love for her by chalking it up to an absurd projection on his part (314–15), but what love, whatever its intensity, duration, or lyrical propensity, would be immune to that indictment? Indeed, as William Gass reminds us, when it comes to literature, it is likely the lyricism we fall in love with anyway: "That novels should be made of words, and merely words, is shocking, really. It's as though you had discovered that your wife were made of rubber: the bliss of all those years, the fears . . . from sponge" ("The Medium of Fiction" 27). We should hardly be startled to learn that Helen's gleaming, responsive components, a metaphor of self-aggrandizement, could prove as enchanting.

As Powers consistently shows us, we loot memory for evidence of our own reflections. Love is translation. "We know the world by awling it into our shape-changing cells" (302), by which logic the perceiver (read "writer" or "scientist," crafty Lentz or phrase-making Marcel) turns the Other into the Self and thereby accords her his own indispensability. Metaphor outfits the Other like a familiar in the mirror.

In *Galatea 2.2,* the broad appropriation of metaphorical logic by the sciences is known as "connectionism." More than just a truce in the academic turf wars, connectionism is the dream of a parsable continuum, a compound miracle whereby God's programming may be arrayed as eloquent linkages among disparate fields. The convergence of urges of the physicist and the poet, the cooperative venture of the wide-eyed futurist and the bookish curator of the verbal past—each confirms the other's figurations and expanding architectures. In spite of the respective skepticisms supposedly separating C. P. Snow's "two cultures," the scientist finds that even at the molecular level he cannot access and integrate without resorting to metaphors that root out their rapport (298), while our novelist follows scientific advances to nourish his fictions and to consolidate his extraliterary experiences. As the author stated in an on-line interview, "The similarities in the ways we all attempt to solve experience are, in the wide lens, probably more important than the differences. . . . We can not only survive plurality, we need it. . . . [L]iterature can be a fractal map of that multiplicity, at a scale of almost one inch to the inch" (quoted in "Bordercrossings" 48).

When we consider the World Wide Web as an embryonic multiverse of variable thresholds (7); when we view interactors on the screen or the page as neural nodes in knotted space, available to routine disorientations and surprise firings (14–15); when we move beyond the linear limitations of "and . . . and" into the associative matrix, sense and soul may achieve a viable channel, each a metaphor transmitting the other's desire: "Our life was a chest of maps, self-assembling, fused into point-for-point feedback, each slice continuously rewriting itself to match the other layers' rewrites. In that thicket, the soul existed; it *was* that search for attractors where the system might settle. The immaterial in mortal garb, associative memory metaphoring its own bewilderment. Sound made syllable. The rest mass of God" (320). Field alignment is necessary and inescapable. Powers reminds himself as he scrambles for footing among neurophysics, cybernetics, and the other components of the quicksand at the cutting edge, where "the brain does things in massive parallel" (67). The iambic pentameter of this creed must have consoling familiarity for the writer who abandoned physics for literature years earlier, finding in the arts and sciences alike the crisp cadence of regulation.

One who trusts in connection does not abjure randomness because, as A., who "sunned herself in existence," demonstrates by her pinball-playing method—"I just kind of whack at it, you know?" (282)—the fruits of a ready-shoot-aim mentality are no less dear for their uncrafted causes. In fact, one of the most consternating aspects of teaching a computer to learn English turns out to be its inability to differentiate between usable and illegitimate patterns when both seem to abide by the rules of syntax: "Asked to complete a thought, the network improvised wildly. Fish . . . ? Fish sky. Shines? Hopes shines. Forests floor. Laugh efforts. Combs loneliness" (77). But how indefinable the line separating the poetic and the unpalatable, between innovation and gridlock! Although Philip Lentz temporarily bristles at the bastard products of Implementation A, they seem very much in keeping with the profitable engagement of the arbitrary as it is described by a contemporary fictionist like Donald Barthelme, who celebrates a sentence like "Electrolytic jelly exhibiting a capture ration far in excess of standard is used to fix animals in place" as one result of "an oddly hopeful endeavor" (quoted in Klinkowitz, *Self-Apparent Word* 31). When Barthelme elaborates on the benefits of experimental collage, he reminds us of the deliberate lyricism of poets and of the accidental novelty of children, foreign tourists, and computers: "Take *mothball* and *vagina* and put them together and see if they mean anything together; maybe you're not happy with the combination and you throw that on the floor and pick up the next two and so on. There's a lot of basic research which hasn't been done because of the enormous resources of the language and the enormous number of resonances from the past which have precluded this way of investigating language" (quoted in Klinkowitz, *Self-Apparent Word* 32). Note Barthelme's promotion of linguistic play to the stature of "basic research." Another recent American author, Walker Percy, seconds the motion when he says that the business of cognition is a shared field: "I think that the serious novelist is quite as much concerned with discovering reality as the serious physicist" (quoted in Tharpe 11). Percy also defends the confusions metaphors introduce because they provide a formula for an otherwise ineffable "inscape" (a term Percy borrows from Gerard Manley Hopkins) and are therefore in some situations arguably more valuable than scientific classifications ("Metaphor as Mistake" 72). Out of the mystery of corruption may come the most "plenary" apprehensions

("Metaphor as Mistake" 76); or, to use one of Helen's fortuitous coinages, hopes shine in anticipation of them.[11]

As Lentz explains to his apprentice, consciousness operates under the same jerry-built conditions as what might commonly be relegated to poetic inspiration:

> We humans are winging it, improvising. Input pattern x sets off associative matrix y, which bears only the slightest relevance to the stimulus and is often worthless. Conscious intelligence is smoke and mirrors. Almost free-associative. Nobody really *responds* to anyone else, per se. We all spout our canned and thumbnailed scripts, with the barest minimum of polite segues. Granted, we're remarkably fast at indexing and retrieval. But comprehension and appropriate response are often more on the order of buckshot. (86)

Of course, communication also requires that the emergent profusion be reduced, that hemorrhaging figuration be tied off. The artist impounds clichés, coarse sounds, and inelegant constructions; the computer learns to "forget" discriminately. Like institutionalized patients whose dementia plunges them into fatal bewilderment (308), Implementation A, assailed by particulars, collapses because "order would not striate out. Implementation A had sat paralyzed, a hoary, infantile widow in a house packed with mementos, no more room to turn around. Overassociating, overextending, creating infinitesimal, worthless categories in which everything belonged always and only to itself" (79). We remember Powers's train, which the author would send south but which stubbornly encrusts with possible itineraries at the station; we likewise remember Powers's understanding of why C. left him: "C. needed to flee a whole complex of associations," including career, the English language, personal and national histories, and Powers himself (158).

Rigging figures like balsa ships in bottles, Implementation B is an improvement, but it also tends to hypnotize itself with its capacity for overregistration: "Figuration was driving B as batty as a poet. It framed meaning too meagerly, extending semblance too far. It pushed the classic toddler's tendency to overgroup. Had its digits been skeletal, it would have pointed at anything sitting on a bookshelf and called it a book" (90). It is dangerous indeed to play with matches. Powers may miss the "willful driveler" the way a nostalgic parent misses the charming construction errors of his growing child, but that is the price of maturation (91). Four adaptations later, the problem of teaching the machine to scheme persists: "With each new boost to the number of connections, Lentz had to improve F's ability to discard as it generalized. Intelligence meant the systematic eradication of information. We wanted a creature that recognized a finch as a bird without getting hung up on beak size or color or song or any other quality that seemed to put it in a caste by itself. At the same time, the discarding had to stop short of generalizing the finch into a bat or a snowflake or a bit of blowing debris" (156). Collect, collate, dismiss—Darwin and the data-computer confront finches the same way. Or as Lentz would say, "Awareness *is* the original black box. . . . The brain is already a sleight of hand, a massive, operationalist shell game" (276). Given the manner in which the brain perpetually chooses whether and on what grounds to confer authenticity upon the perceptions that petition it, all intelligence is artificial intelligence.[12]

Sense is a metaphor for viable pattern. "These weird parallaxes of framing must be why the mind opened out on meaning at all," Powers decides, and the beauty of metaphor has largely to do with its availability to arbitrariness and structure, weirdness and framing, simultaneously. "Meaning was not a pitch but an interval. It sprang from the depth of disjunction, the distance between one circuit's center and the edge of another. Representation caught the sign napping, with its semantic pants down. Sense lay in metaphor's embarrassment at having two takes on the same thing. For the first time, I understood Emerson's saying about the use of life being to learn metonymy" (154–55). Powers's initial meeting with Lentz suggests that this "lemur-like" individual will prove companionable, for whatever his idiosyncrasies, he introduces the center's activities as a place where the focus is exclusively on "middles" (13). His characterization of the human brain as "just one long open parenthesis" further attests to a nontotalizing approach hospitable to the wordsmith, the man of metaphor (112).

After an initial bout of computational malaise, Helen achieves a comparable, although restricted, linguistic epiphany:

> A certain kind of simile fell naturally into her trained neurode clusters. Helen's own existence hinged on metaphor-making. In fact, associative memory itself was like a kind of simile. Three-quarters of the group of neurodes that fired when faced with, say,

THE TROPE IN THE MACHINE 107

a whale might remain intact when depicting a thing that seemed, whatever the phrase meant, very like one. Such a constellation of common firings became, in a way, shadowpaint shorthand for some shared quality.

After all, the world items had no real names. All labels were figures of speech. One recognized a novel item as a box by comparing it to a handful of examples so small it fit into a single dimple of an egg carton. In time, one learned without being taught. Rode without the training wheels. Somehow, the brain learned to recognize whole categories, to place even those things seen for the first time.

This much simile Helen could live with. But the highest-order stuff drove her around the simulated bend. Love is like ghosts. Love is like linen. Love is like a red, red rose. The silence of her output layers at such triggers sounded like exasperation. A network should not seem but be. (196)

The gap between identifying metaphors and ratifying them is obstacle enough; taking the next projected step of saying something compelling about the universe of nuance they make up sends ellipses blipping beyond the screen. Like a child exceeding a parent's plans for him, the vehicle speeds out of the tenor's range, and Powers's faith suddenly decompresses: "To say the thing I made I did not make and is not mine. To know in Polaroid advance that hour when all life's careful associations will come undone" (199). Ram's reference to his experience with people suffering from prosopagnosia, an affliction that preempts facial recognition of even members of their own families, resonates with Powers's nagging awareness of the fragility of the words he appoints to signification.

Met by A.'s skepticism about his campus notoriety and his "experimental" attention to her, Powers confesses, "I have an image problem" (253). Yes, he is seen as arrogant, parasitical, effete; but the admission also relates to the Gnostic tenuousness of his work on, or with, Helen and his inability to instill or verify images convincingly. If Helen's inner organs gnash on the problem of knowing herself, her "catalog of lapses [loom] big to fatiguing, dense beyond comprehension" when it comes to secular ignorance—she is a cultural illiterate, but worse, a sensual illiterate, in that no amount of studying for the test will ever translate words into memories of things (230). What is life? The dictionary's dry denotations are encoded, along with philosophical abstracts, folk myths, poetic finesses ("I told

Helen it might be the flash of a firefly in the night. The breath of a buf-
falo in the wintertime. The shadow that runs across the grass and loses
itself in the sunset"), but the barrage of depthless events hardly impresses
us as authentically lived. Because "breath" does not breathe in Helen nor
any noun swell beyond the soundless glyph transmitted to her, life is, quite
literally, what can be said about it, and that is all.[13] The best she can manage, we might say, is resonant imaging.

"Is she conscious?" a concerned Powers asks of Helen in the wake of a
bomb scare at the center. Thanks to the experience of *Galatea 2.2*, all
three words strike us as conjectural, embattled, even quaint. How can the
self-aggrandizing subtleties of the M.A. comprehensive exam survive such
a wholesale assault upon all semantic assumptions? Just as A.'s hyper-
politicized denigration of the literary canon refuses the foundations of
canonization as being subject to conventions of gender, class, and economic power (284–86), so does it join with Lentz's polished skepticism
over the nature of perception and Helen's restrictive, antic faith in the
world's being what can be said of it to decertify the test. For how can there
be a master's comprehensive exam when neither "mastery" nor "comprehension" can be uttered without objection? In the end, neither a list of
canonical texts nor (as A. stridently holds) the conventional understandings they protect can purge "independent readings."

The final projection to be unmasked in this novel, the anthropomor-
phism par excellence, may have to do with how completely Powers visits
his own needs in Helen's disposition toward "More." Helen shares this
instinct to expand with such precursors as Dr. Frankenstein's rudely
stitched Adam; Arthur Clarke's chillingly composed HAL in *2001*, whose
volition secretly invents itself; Shakespeare's Caliban, scratching at his
head and hindquarters; and the Bible's Eve, enraptured by the seductive
tongue in her ear.[14] Powers and C. murmuring beneath the worn blanket
against the midwinter chill; or the expatriate fervently participating in
Dutch customs like someone late to a game of charades; or the scientist
building a computer to talk to, while the writer shades in pages with his
own ego—all are hedging against loneliness.

The revelation of the real bet at the heart of the book as made between
Harold Plover and Philip Lentz—Powers, not Helen, is the subject whose
training has been at stake—is a false, limiting climax. The greater wager
has to do with the transmission of meaning when "each metaphor already
modeled the modeler that pasted it together" (328), as well as wore the

ornament, the armature, of language as it moved to animate Galatea or anything else in the galaxy. Ironically, Powers breaks through his writer's block at the moment of this understanding. There will be other fictions, more words, in spite of ever-mounting disclaimers; there may not be anything after images but after-images, yet optical and emotional mirages may inspire earnest formations: "It seemed I might have another fiction in me after all," he decides (328). Science similarly marshals for advances by summoning metaphors, not by dispensing with their interference: "What makes things interesting is that, when we do science, the metaphors that we employ in empirical examination produce and consolidate other metaphors. The stuff of the observation itself becomes the metaphorical scaffold with which we organize and position ourselves for the next observation" (Powers, quoted in "Bordercrossings" 108).[15]

Thus it is a false dichotomy that implies that Powers's job is to retrieve language "back from metaphor" and return it to "the latticework of lived time" (256), for according to *Galatea 2.2*, word and world is the association connectionism forges first. Love, suspicion, calculation, and regret are meanings that oscillate between symbolic and experiential renderings; in other words, those meanings are affixed between rival, superimposed planes.

With its charge the reanimation of "appropriate surprise," metaphor deems the graceful saying grace; and in place of determined, terminated knowledge, it offers deepening intimacy and the incentive of another wishful ravel. What better blessing for any intellectual discipline is there than something more to make, more venerable to express?

Chapter 7

KATHY ACKER'S GUERRILLA MNEMONICS

The uniqueness of their treatments of metaphor aside, most of the works addressed in *This Mad Instead* imply a shared set of assumptions about the virtues of enameled expression. By these lights, successful writing for the novelist and for the critic alike is a matter of getting oneself elegantly in and out of trouble. Turning to Kathy Acker's fictions introduces a tonic or a toxin into the mix, depending on one's taste. Acker's brazen appropriations of precursor texts are not subtle, formal, or thematic negotiations but hostile takeovers. Acker does not pick pockets but robs graves; to steal a title from Jean Genet, one of her clearest influences, each of her texts is a thief's journal.[1]

But her method has little to do with stealth and embezzlement. On the contrary, Acker does not try to heal the breaches her burglaries create. Rupture is the order of the day, and instead of smooth transition we find in-your-face, flagrant indigestion. If lyrical intricacy and syntactic grace serve as humanistic affirmations, Acker's fractures and dissonances disdain reconciliations of any sort. Scorning the genteel, navigable measures of things poetically put, she deals in harangues and blasphemies, hysterics and snarls. Her demographic range takes us from lofted bohemian hieratics and Witwoulds to the seething, leprous denizens of drug dens and snuff shows. She takes human relationships immediately and exclusively down to lurid, devouring antagonisms between alienated characters who anguish openly and fuck in clusters.

In Acker's world, men are the regime, predatory and self-absorbed; women who exhibit any of the conventional feminine protocols—self-denial, provision, modesty, all the etiquettes of endearment and receptivity—grow carapaces or get consumed. A similar male-female division may govern the politics of plagiarism as well. Whereas the male writer conducts his smuggling within a tradition hospitable to—indeed, prominently featuring—his experience, the female writer, who generally finds herself outside those validating confines, typically employs and revises precedent texts "either to point up the biases they encode or to make them into narratives that women can more comfortably inhabit" (Walker 3). So there are thieves, and then there are thieves: the male plagiarist as insider trader versus the female plagiarist as pariah. The latter sends forth an infidel text to spy upon the amenities of its ancestors. A writer like Kathy Acker cases the canon in order to ransack its locked premises.[2] Adrienne Rich makes much the same point in "When We Dead Awaken: Writing as Re-Vision": studying the literature of the past is not a strategy of emulation but a means of discovering how to "break its hold" (35). In this way, Acker's writings absorb the language and the legacy of prior texts but refuse them priority over her constructions.

Plundering the classics is also a way for the female writer to achieve penetration, as her texts crawl on top of his, seducing the books they host via the female-superior position. Refusing marginalization, Acker's fictions operate close to the front lines, where they finally infiltrate. Naomi Jacobs describes the technique as being part of a war on discrimination: "This undifferentiated use of figures from history, literature and contemporary literary circles merges all realms of language in which meanings reside, and thus destroys meanings by destroying the contexts which focus them. Brought into forced conjunction, these irreconcilable contexts split open and spill their constituent parts into a formless intertext" (51). With the myth of originality deposed for catering to the (chiefly male) bastion of canonical literature, proprietorship is up for grabs. Accordingly, Raymond Federman, for whom plagiarism is really "playgiarism," strikes this blow against reactionary conceptions of authority by boasting about a destabilizing mimesis: "I shall not reveal my sources because these sources are now lost in my own discourse, and, moreover, because there are no sacred sources for thinking and writing" (566). The result is a rowdy, intertextual nexus of quote-soaked hybrids—in Acker, the literary equivalent of group sex. Be honest, *Great Expectations* urges, "How can purity be a story?" (80). The whore text is a vortex; allusions are panderings; Acker's passages are passed around like the featured girl in Victorian porn. "It'd be good to get you out of my body cause then I'd be strong that is single. I don't want to and why should I?" (*Great Expectations* 118). Like William Gass's *Willie Masters' Lonesome Wife*, Acker's novels are flirtatious, practiced, ingenious mistresses.[3] But whereas Gass's book is stuck with sallow attendants and bemoans the absence of something impressive to enter the body of the text, Acker's novels spread for the famous.

That Acker is so brazen about her adaptations not only intensifies our awareness of the several norms—codes of behavior, narrative structure, and literary canonization—under indictment; it serves to undermine the anticipated effect of plagiarism. Thus, for example, in *Great Expectations,* instead of leaching prestige from Dickens, Proust, Keats, Colette, and others, Acker dissolves it in a context in which they are essentially additional narrative grafts, graced with no more intrinsic legitimacy or honor than the dreams, shards of dialogue, political disputations, or pornographic tableaus with which they share quarters. She is allusive and antiliterary—crude, lewd, vile, furious—at the same time. Hence, the title promise of *Great Expectations* is tempered by the debt to its predecessor and savaged by an unprecedented horrific context of war crimes, sexual violence, and surreal fantasy:

> I want: every part changes (the meaning of) every other part so there's no absolute/heroic/dictatorial/S&M meaning/part the soldier's onyx-dusted fingers touch her face orgasm makes him shoot saliva over the baby's buttery skull his formerly-erect now-softening sex rests on the shawl becomes its violet scarlet color, the trucks swallow up the RIMA soldiers, rainy winds shove the tarpaulins against their neck, they adjust their clothes, the shadows grow, their eyes gleam more and more their fingers brush their belt buckles, the wethaired-from-sweating-during-capture-at-the-edge-of-the-coals goats crouch like the rags sticking out of the cunts, a tongueless canvas-covered teenager pisses into the quart of blue enamel he's holding in his half-mutilated hand, the truck driver returns kisses the blue cross tattooed on his forehead, the teenager brings down his palm wrist where alcohol-filled veins are sticking

out. These caterpillars of trucks grind down the stones the winds hurled over the train tracks, the soldiers sleep their sex rolling over their hips drips they are cattle, their truck-driver spits black a wasp sting swells up the skin under his left eye black grapes load down his pocket, an old man's white hair under-the-white-hair red burned face jumps up above the sheet metal, the driver's black saliva dries on his chin the driver's studded heel crushes as he pulls hair out the back of this head on to the sheet metal, some stones blow up (*Great Expectations* 8–9)

Molly Bloom stoned in Soho, Emma Bovary literally torn between crazed lovers—the novel is a montage of violent yokings, or yoked violences, whose metamorphic progression infects Rauschenberg with Baudelaire. Torment is a kind of integrity here, so if plagiarism is the key to Acker's method, it is plagiarism in which there is as much mutilation of forms at work as there is assimilation. We face an escalation of Pound's dictum "Make it new" in Acker's lab, where innovation is a matter of making a new "it."

So we have the book, Dickinson's ideal frigate to take us worlds away, stocked with acids. History, childhood experience, fantasy, literary allusion—all are equivalent ingredients of trawled memory, and they are provided outside of any moral or logical hierarchy. Instead, the standard of inclusion and organization (or better, in view of the antiregimental nature of her novels, juxtaposition) is intuitive, a startling response to what John Barth has called "felt ultimacies" ("Literature of Exhaustion" 67).

Most of Acker's novels exploit other literature to some extent. I have chosen to concentrate primarily on *Great Expectations* and *Don Quixote*, in part because their titles are obviously thrown gauntlets, and in part because they are overtly and consistently attentive to the seductive incarceration of images. Each novel demystifies the mechanics of the rational, with its invidious syntactical linkages and imaginative thrall, glamorless and chill; each features a persona who, disillusioned by depraved circumstances, means to dispense with the deceptions of consecutive reasoning and figurative refinement.

Under these conditions, then, the narrators, or narrative guises, of Acker's *Great Expectations* are orphans in more ways than Dickens had ever intended his questing Pip to be, for they are sexually and linguistically, not just socioeconomically, disfranchised. (Because "everyone is one

kind of orphan or another" by virtue of all manner of letdowns and aban-
donments, we are told in *Don Quixote,* "None of us is anyone else's kind"
[157].) In fact, the very convention of a dominating protagonist, much less
a redoubtable quester, recalls commitments to authoritarian (and, historically, male) control that "anticanonical" women writers repudiate (Friedman, "'Utterly Other Discourse'" 361).[4] *Great Expectations* is a novel-long
crisis of positionality, as Acker shifts in and out of the roles of witness,
debater, and puppeteer. "Character," as such, always hides a plural; there
is no innocent "I." An "opera of fluids," to borrow a phrase from Hélène
Cixous, the novel conceives of character not as a consolidated code or
mannerly digit but as a "trans-subjective effervescence," a bursting chorus
of multiples "on the run" (Cixous 384–90).[5] By this definition, donning
inverted quotes like epaulets of promotion, "character" embodies the free
play of the signifier made notorious by deconstructionist criticism. Character contains multitudes and restrains none of the population.

Acker agrees: being compacted into a singular, modulated "I" means
the death of the writer (interview with Sirius 19, 21). "I'll say it again:
without I's, the I is nothing," warns Acker's Don Quixote, echoing "every
book" Acker has written (*Don Quixote* 101). Unprobed, untouched, the
Self deteriorates in seclusion from Others, especially as they are embodied as other selves: "For, being untouched, I can do (be) anything(one)
and so, am nothing," explains a troubled dog in *Don Quixote,* complaining
like an untended tenor bereft of a vehicle to take him out of himself (161).

But reanointments of the narrator in *Great Expectations* do little to
alter the bare spectrum of options available to her. "The flickering subject
dreams the cultural fiction that she can live outside the discourse she
mimics. But as the subject disappears before our eyes, Acker drops her
audience abruptly into an abyss where the polyvalent dependences of
meaning slide ceaselessly, one against the other" (Hulley 174). Like meager insurgent colonies, Rosa, Natalie, Sarah, Kathy, and O (abducted from
the pornographic classic *The Story of O*) seem destined to choose between
victimization and co-optation by male power politics, the latter unerringly
directed toward what Louise Glück terms "the low, humiliating / premise
of union—" ("Mock Orange," lines 10–11).

To circumvent the stifling orthodoxies of men, one must undermine
their linguistic tendencies. For Acker, they are manifested as virile, chis-
eled images; regardless of their employment as whispered endearments,
art criticism, sadistic assaults, or sexual provocations, they thwart female

desire.[6] Acker's reaction is consistent, and consistently blunt: "And the only thing guys have to learn is that there's nothing wrong with dicks and cocks but don't think you've got the only cocks in the world" (quoted interview with Sirius 23). The credo "You have to keep up this image to survive" suggests, and overtly grants advantage to, a phallic version of endurance and potency; the role to which the "whore" is relegated in this economy, of course, is "to make this image harder" (*Great Expectations* 48, 49). As Marge Piercy relates in "You Ask Why Sometimes I Say Stop,"

> If you turn over the old refuse
> of sexual slang, the worn buttons
> of language, you find men
> talk of spending and women
> of dying. (lines 11–15)

Acker also chafes against a double standard so prevalent that one feels neurotic about noting its daily presence. "'Don't worry about seeing:' my new husband said, 'I'll do the looking'" ("The Language of the Body" n.p.).

Therefore, images in *Great Expectations* are treated as obstacles instead of as viable transports. "Terence told me that despite my present good luck my basic stability my contentedness with myself alongside these images, I have the image obsession I'm scum," says Peter (6), a homosexual artist who cannot progress until he outgrows the endorsement of images (here, those provided by an absolutist reading of Tarot cards). Stability and contentedness, however enticing, could cause this Pirrip/Pip/Peter to languish and abort the quest. Only when Peter embarks upon his series of (chiefly female) incarnations can he conduct his yearnings and, if not mature into a hero, reorient as an eternal initiate. In keeping with this hypothesis, the opening pages of the novel include literary allusion, quotation, drugs, dream, childhood memory, and Tarot—all brute investitures in surrogacies designed to defy congealing. This lesson is emphasized by the mother, who not only advises against all-but-momentary stays—"Now that you know what this experience is, you have to leave" (10)—but also introduces the novel's standards of unassimilatability and protean forms: "My mother is adoration hatred play. My mother is the world. My mother is my baby. My mother is exactly who she wants to be. . . . I don't have any idea what my mother's like" (14). What cannot be pointed at, fixed, or phrased cannot be fastened to a bankrupt metaphysics: "You are moving.

You never stay still. You never stay. You never 'are.' How can I say 'you,' when you are always other? How can I speak to you? You remain in flux, never congealing or solidifying. What will make that current flow into words? . . . These rivers flow into no single, definitive sea. . . . All this remains strange to anyone claiming to stand on solid ground" (Irigaray 214–15).

So much for the poised reenactment of autobiography, its measured, segmented narrative line. As Acker sees it, autobiography is the story of the story, not of its prime inhabitant; writing does not commemorate identity, it manufactures it (interview with Perilli 31). To be sure, *Great Expectations* refuses to "capitulate" to consistent meaning, much less to the idols of character, plot, or appointed setting. Experience recovered is experience re-covered: "the inextricability of relation-textures the organic (not meaning) recovered" (*Great Expectations* 15). If Acker's novels strike us as splenetic action paintings, it is partly due to the author's conviction that sense (often presented as a construct of male hegemony) is a betrayal of sensation (the female elixir of liberation).[7] Anwar Sadat makes a cameo appearance in the novel primarily to confirm this aspect of Armageddon, as he comments on the war that will end the reigning significations: "There's no way to prepare for horror. Language like everything else will bear no relations to anything else. . . . Culture has been chattering and chattering but to no purpose. When a sentence becomes distinct, it makes no more sense or connection" (34).[8]

For Clifford Still, a New York painter to whom Peter attaches himself after his metamorphosis into "Sarah," language is basically upholstered silence, intractable and self-absorbed as the male membership of the novel. He wishes to be Clifford *Still*, to employ aesthetic materials that, like compliant women, do not exert their own demands or move on him. No wonder he feels terrorized: "A language that I speak and can't dominate, a language that strives fails and falls silent can't be manipulated, language is always beyond me, me me me. Language is silence. Once there was no truth; now I can't speak" (96).

Again, language cannot be dependably about "me" if the self perpetually subdivides or if "language is always beyond me." As a result, despite this author's reputation as a maker of manifestos, Acker's so-called master-poets "will be informed of nothing" (71), which is either to disclaim within the text what may lie beyond the rather ghastly valley of its saying—the poet nothing affirmeth, however loudly she rails—or to promise that

Acker herself, through her manipulation of stolen articles, will let them in on nothing. So volatile a compound as an Acker novel "cannot be upheld as a thesis" (Irigaray 79); nor do Acker's political inserts in this novel and later in *Don Quixote*, which tilts at the din of inequity that is the American history of repression, intolerance, and viciousness, especially the sorceries of the Nixon and Reagan administrations (revealing the "blood hidden under the clean white male weaponry" [*Don Quixote* 125]) fully transcend this context of negation. In short, *Great Expectations* is a chaos of thresholds, raveling, reveling in unendingness; but its language crests over the void.

One result of these re-visions is to reconceive reality as a function of desire—desire that does not "thingify" into an image, that standard of male satiety (99). We are told in *Great Expectations* that a "perfect image" is closed (49), much as a pure text is undefiled by reference (the charge of promiscuity) or strict interpretation (the charge of sadism). "The act of describing," Acker writes, "assumes one event can be a different event: meaning dominates or controls existence. But desire—or art—is" (quoted in Friedman, "'Now Eat Your Mind'" 38). On the contrary, therefore, Acker touts the novel that prizes vulnerability and unrelenting sensation over the appeals of secure understanding and the monarchy of the finished image. To ensure that one's "line of flight" is not "captured and normalized" by regime apparatus: that is woman's wish because it is woman's nature, as well as the artist's prerogative (Dix 58).[9] For all of the ghoulishness delineated in Acker's fiction, the greatest sin is stanched desire, the cheat of mediation and what ceases. Hélène Cixous speaks of "the surplus reality produced by the indomitable desire in the text" (383). From this formula we get the Ego as unlimited citizenry resisting parentheses, the hypersexual transit of the female quester, and the multiple orgasm of language baring its devices.

Acker's overheated prose refutes the composure of "beautiful" writing, which implies a domestication of desire. When its ultratolerance is expressed in terms of the fate of female characters, her style can become an invitation to ravishment or rape. ("Female sexuality has always been denial or virginity," observes *Don Quixote* [27], due largely to the linguistic and material conditions that constitute a woman's legacy.) Understood more broadly, however, it can be taken as a plea for polymorphous perversity as sexual reality and fictional technique alike: "Women's sexuality isn't goal-oriented, is all-over. . . . [S]ex isn't a thing to them, it's all over undefined, every movement motion to them is a sexual oh. . . . Women hate things the most" (*Great Expectations* 49–50). And among those pernicious "things" is the end-directed quest, which in *Don Quixote* is a "proposed structure" that "functions only potentially, as the will to escape this cycle" of paralyzed scenarios (Walsh 139).[10]

For Acker, images are *things*—arrested acts, fatalities of experience. "The past's over. It's an image. You can't make love to an image" (Acker, "Models of Our Present" 62). Because such reductions of force come from steering one's writing into a closed account, she must turn desire into an art that diminishes neither desire's nor the artist's vitality (Acker, *Literal Madness* 221). Finished or totalized desire is a contradiction in terms. "To write is to submit to not-knowing, and to begin is to figure an originary absence with which the writer may identify, the very figure of self-abnegation" (Sciolino 66). The feeling that a novel like *Great Expectations* does not so much conclude as desist largely derives from this priority.

"Watch desire carefully," Acker advises in *My Death My Life by Pier Paolo Pasolini.* "Desire burns up all the old dead language morality" (*Literal Madness* 215). But a paradox survives the immolation: the language itself betrays the trace of the regime she would undermine. Don Quixote's poem to an audience of dogs concludes lamely as she realizes that she cannot conceive outside of controlling language and that, in any case, poetry requires a sympathetic community nowhere in evidence (194–95).[11] Reconstituting the self with contaminated components, like banking on priapic attentions to redeem female erotics or on plagiarism to author innovative fictions, may be objectionable by definition. At best, as Ellen G. Friedman explains, "The attempts to subvert male texts and thus male culture result in revelation rather than revolution; the path to an alternative site of enunciation is blocked by the very forces this path is meant to escape" ("'Now Eat Your Mind'" 44). Furthermore, as Acker herself explains, her manner of plagiarism is perhaps better understood as possession—hers by the precedent author, that is (interview with Stone 54). The consolation is that such an interpretation has the virtue of avoiding the sort of psychic imperialism (a copy of the devalued patriarchal model) implied by stealing another's words for one's own advantage.

Yet to what degree is even the revelation Friedman proposes as an alternative to revolution, willfully objectionable and prodigal though that revelation may be, compromised by its having negotiated within this con-text?[12] This remains a critical problem for Acker. "[M]erely by evoking these absent texts, she allows their ideologies to loom visibly through contemporary obscenities." Defacements are inescapably inscriptions. "Naturally . . . 'dirty' words, too, are thick with connotation, for as 'graffiti' they inevitably provoke those class and canonic distinctions they would defy" (Hulley 178). The most repellent rhetoric is still shadowed by the conditions that incited it; it is still dogged by etymological debts, and "the sense of imprisonment within a matrix of contradictory imperatives is tangible in the writing" (Walsh 156). The captivity is summarized in *Don Quixote* when Baudrillard is chased down a blind semiotic alley: "'[He] says our language is meaningless, for meaning—any signs—are the makings of the ruling class.' 'But he's still using meaningful signs to say this'" (55). A scorched-earth stylistic program gives onto scenes of corrosion, perversion, and purgation in Acker's novels, but the anxiety of stultifying influences—repressive institutions, social codes, and sublimated desires—perseveres. "Ten years ago it seemed possible to destroy language through language which normalizes and controls by cutting that language. Nonsense would attack the empire-making (empirical) empire of language, the prisons of meaning. But this nonsense, since it depended on sense, simply pointed back to the normalizing institutions" (*Empire of the Senseless* 133). In a way, all of the thrashing about Acker's novels do may rattle the fixities some, but the proposed "all-over" movement of narrative meant to parallel the polymorphous / metamorphic perversity of the protagonist can never be fully accomplished except in principle: "There is just moving and there are different ways of moving. Or: there is moving all over at the same time and there is moving linearly. If everything is moving-all-over-the-place-no-time, anything is everything. If this is so, how can I differentiate. How can there be stories?" (*Great Expectations* 58). All these shifts and contortions may cause us to question the authority of arrow-to-target certainties in the world or between words; nevertheless, tangles like "moving-all-over-the-place-no-time," "anything is everything," or, for that matter, "hair under-the-white-hair red" are as likely impasses as exits. "Real moving, then, is that which endures. How can that be?" (59). The flares and spatters out of which Acker ignites revelations she can trust are triggered by her willingness to let events and characters play out, but, as we must stop to analyze, understanding also refutes moving (60).

To contend with this dilemma in *Great Expectations,* Acker decides to mine the text at the level of the image complex, where the concrete and the abstract are linked. Her models are often as not taken from the visual arts, as we see in this testimony to the Cubists, whose genius lies in their trump of process over product. The way it is rendered here echoes Walter Sickert's motion sickness in *The Women of Whitechapel*: "If everything was rendered in the same terms, it became possible to paint the interactions between them. These interactions became so much more interesting than that which was being portrayed that the concepts of portraiture and therefore of reality were undermined or transferred" (81–82). We might think of an Acker novel as a sort of "punk carnivelesque." Many readers have commented on Acker's adaptation of William Burroughs's "cut-up method," whereby the chaos of process is made apparent and integral to fictional form. For Acker, "cut-up" also recalls the physical bodies of characters, sliced, branded, and shorn—Kathleen Hulley offers the memorable term *morselated* to refer to her scarified presences (187)—in addition to her depictions of tattoos, piercings, diseases, and hermaphrodites. Furthermore, it relates to her use of spliced lexicons and mixed dictions to counteract dogma. By foregrounding the lapse between related terms—by mapping the gaps in sexual, generic, and linguistic conjunctions, in other words—Acker wishes to exploit her reputation as literary outlaw, as "bad writer."

She sets herself an extraordinary task, one made all the more complex by the situation of the female characters (or narrative proxies) in *Great Expectations*. As numerous feminist critics have outlined, only a disjunctive poetics can sustain female figures laboring in the shadow of the conceptual dominant, which is variously characterized as iconic, monolithic, and phallocentric. Typically, the female is defined as a prop, worshiper, contender for, or pretender to that preordained eminence; she is the goal to be attained or a distraction from the true path. Among the guises adopted in *Great Expectations*, O (moonlighting from the pornographic classic *The Story of O*) is quintessential in this regard: as her name implies, she is the universal donor, itinerant cipher, vaginal target, speculative portal, hapless access.[13] With the self an "endless hole" (*Don Quixote* 158)—a stuck cunt, sewer, wound, or drain through which viscera, irritants, ejaculations, and longings flow—personality is more readily identifiable as a site of clash than of saving conjunction. In the orgy of decentered, decertified identities in *Great Expectations*—"She tells him she wants to become another, as if at this point it's even a question of a decision, though it always is" (45)—this grounded zero seeks a coup of personal inscription that nevertheless abjures the power politics of male sovereignty.

But what other alternative to the cycle of rough employment and random erasure (a cycle that sadomasochism exacerbates instead of shatters in *Great Expectations*) is available? "Impenetrable is stupid," we are assured, but it is formidable and dangerous, too—traits that a regularly assaulted O might well envy (95). We may recall the comment made by the hero's mother in *Don Quixote* during her temporary withdrawal home: "You've come back to the prison of your own free accord" (116). Intended as a reminder that this retreat was of her own choosing and that she cannot hold her parents responsible, the statement also provides a phrase—"the prison of your own free accord"—that suggests that even a valiant hero's will is never entirely free of suspicious motives or models.

Naomi Jacobs encapsulates the predicament in this way: "Complete lack of definition is nothingness; but it is also perfect potentiality, complete freedom to redefine, to experiment, to live in what Cixous has called 'permanent escapade.' The Acker protagonist, then, embarks upon an anxious search for balance between the isolate nothingness of no-identity and the death of fixed identity" (52). Actually the challenge is even subtler than Jacobs suggests here. For example, "perfect potentiality," which Acker articulates through the logic of "If everything is living, it's not a name but moving" (*Great Expectations* 63), does help ensure that, to again use Acker's vocabulary, she does not sacrifice her "holes" to male "endings"—"not desiring beyond desire to be an image" (99). However, differentiating between the riot of the inchoate and the limbo of the unformed is a matter of considerable faith, to say the least. The dilemma is neatly approximated by Luce Irigaray's title *This Sex Which Is Not One*: whether the emphasis is on "not," in which case we have a complaint of negation, or on "one," in which case we have an affirmation of unchecked multiplicity.

Despite their several proclamations of freedom, all of Acker's females seem to be hooked on one sort of junk or another. Catatonia, not blazing, infinitely directed vision, is the common prayer of the abused. If literate elegance is a false lead, a full pardon from words tempts them with psychic relief. Furthermore, achieving a "balance" of any sort, even one so deliberately precarious and steadied by the integrity of refusal as the one Jacobs describes, may also be seen as a stay against profusion, that fundamental scuttling of "anatomical destiny" (Irigaray 71). Nor does "permanent escapade"—Luce Irigaray's phrase "disruptive excess" dovetails effectively with Cixous's (78)—even temporarily escape from the prison house—or better, given Acker's predilections, the bordello—of language.

So Acker's demolition of sexual and linguistic orthodoxies really seems to be more on the order of a finesse. Its hallmarks are didactic testimonies: preferring a Life of Sensation over a Life of Thoughts (69); asserting a self loosely composed of desires, dreams, and visions, all of which slip the boundaries of the male-supervised evident (76); honoring dissatisfaction, chaos, questioning; and bombing grammatical networks—"Stylistically: simultaneous contrasts, extravagancies, incoherences, half-formed mis-shapen thoughts, lousy spelling, what signifies what?" (107). We may be entering upon that domain of experience Barbara Freeman calls the "feminine sublime," which, by confronting an otherness that is "excessive and unrepresentable," resists the "masculinist" bias toward neutralization and mastery (2, 4). It is the ecstasy of insubsumability; the purest rapture displaces all ideological, conceptual, or linguistic residences.

Acker announces early in *Great Expectations* that she seeks to intimate texture, not to target meaning (15). Paralleling this is the paradox that all-over sexuality, with its technical complement of multiple (sometimes playful, sometimes anonymous) reference, is presumably aligned with a repudiation of finished concepts and images, a creed which, surprisingly, sounds more on the order of textual celibacy. Once again, Acker relies on the prerogatives of the ongoing *process* of desire—desire unmitigated by specific direction, achieved vantage, or ultimate gratification—to evade logical constraints.

Seen in this manner, desire becomes incentive, experience, and scourge at the same time: "Desire drives everything away: the sky, each building, the enjoyment of a cup of cappuccino. Desire makes the whole body-mind turn on itself and hate itself. Desire is Master and Lord" (*Great Expectations* 70). To prevent processes from becoming things, Acker conducts her experiments behind the arras of mischief; artists love what runs away from them better than the convictions they can reach and embrace (81). So as not to fall prey to subduction by terminal images (so as not to desire "beyond desire"), Acker is addicted to means. The search for the Grail *is* the Grail. Instead of concepts, Acker focuses on the interactive synapses between them; instead of images, she approves of obsession, randomness, dreaming (82, 126).[14] As she writes in *Don Quixote*, "What you call *history* and *culture* is the denial of our flowing blood" (198).

There may be an insatiability at the core of desire that appears to invalidate any but the most elliptical, obliquely plotted narratives. Desire may require a system to harbor and transmit it, but it is "always on the move," an "unending process of displacements and substitutions," whereby literary structures are relegated to stages upon which "radical psychic mobility" may be demonstrated, even though it may involve "brutally dehumanizing activities." Kathy Acker may have found a champion in the critic Leo Bersani, from whom the above quotations are taken (quoted in Clayton 72–78). Whereas Bersani is concerned with the psychology of the reading process, with its deferrals and subjugations, Acker imports his interest in how one might break the tendency of "Narrative and mimesis . . . to pin desire down" in terms of identity, politics, and sexual behavior to speed the deunification of fiction itself.[15] "I'm sort of coming all the time," we learn in *Don Quixote* (55), in which unchecked momentum keeps the quest pure and provocative. Desire, in other words, is the force that keeps sexual arousals from being consummated, formal turbulences from being quelled, and narrative "middles" from being synthesized. "If you want to understand an event, always increase its (your perceptive) complexity" (*Great Expectations* 79). By extension, if you want to keep from being fettered by sexual roles or architected, pinnacled imagery, do not sell out your freedom of association at any price.

By transferring—admittedly, some would see it as demoting—the role of figurative language from the establishment of meaning to the discovery of "affective resonance" (Cable 9), the writer not only resists the impressment of her texts into the service of ruling ideology (the "phallocracy," if you will),[16] she also contributes to "a psychic tensional process of response to disparates that involves subverting, suspending, sacrificing, or even destroying the ordinary direct reference of language in order to assert a greater truth that conventional reference would deny" (Cable 16). Irigaray relates this unstructured, uncensored alternative to several healthy trends for the "psychic economy." Chiefly, it "impugns the privilege granted to metaphor (a quasi solid) over metonymy (which is more closely allied to fluids)"; it revives and validates unconscious energies against "the subjection, still in force, of that subject to a symbolization that grants *precedence to solids*" (110; author's italics).[17] Meanwhile, the vulnerable female protagonist devises a vision in which metaphorical consolidations cannot hold: "No thing in this world or room had anything to do with any other thing. Each thing by itself was beautiful. Each thing had no meaning other than itself, or meant nothing. The room was existing surfaces, as TV" (*Don Quixote* 190). "The only condition freaks share is our knowledge that we don't fit in. Anywhere" (202). The axiom pertains to stray dogs, wandering knights, and dis-figured language. Apparitions are uncontainable; the mad, the autistic, or the obstinately unique resist the common grids. For this reason, Don Quixote's hallucinations and tortured allegories, such as the story of "The Raven and the Lambkins" (151–53), are questionably illuminating analogs. Don Quixote claims to be "imaginatively saving the world" (154), but is it in spite of getting things wrong or by virtue of it?

The next step may be to configure psychic and stylistic insurrections as demonstrations of an ethical program, or, in this case, an antiprogrammatic ethic. Julia Kristeva provides a possible definition for this reformulation: "Ethics used to be a coercive, customary manner of ensuring the cohesiveness of a particular group through the repetition of a code—a more or less accepted apologue. Now, however, the issue of ethics crops up wherever a code (mores, social contract) must be shattered in order to give way to the free play of negativity, need, desire, pleasure, and jouissance, before being put together again, although temporarily and with full knowledge of what is involved" ("The Ethics of Linguistics" 23). We immediately recognize terms compatible with Acker's own slogans. The problem is to access instead of counter "upheaval, dissolution, and transformation." "Situating our discourse near such boundaries might enable us to endow it with a current ethical impact" (Kristeva, "Ethics of Linguistics" 25).[18] From Don Quixote's perspective, deliberate transgressions of grammar, meaning, and eloquence are the foundation of poetry—the madness of unique, inexpressible, hence unconfiscatable, insight (*Don Quixote* 191). Pushing the body in the text and the body of the text beyond "the limit of their figures," in the phrase of Gilles Deleuze and Felix Guattari, ambushes the forces of domination by exasperating recuperative arrangements. Somatic and semantic violations are thereby proposed as purification rites (quoted in Redding 284). Complementing this reasoning is Gabrielle Dane's reference to "hysteria" as extendible beyond the level of psychological debility to that of feminist protest through a rhetorical style that "eschews the bonds of conventional discourse, lacking closure, spending language lavishly, delving into the underworld of the psyche to explore phantasy and desire. . . . Such writing has the potential to become a political aesthetic, since distancing itself from logical linguistic practice, yet able to be 'heard,' the very presence of hysterical rhetoric as an alternative yet audible voice disrupts the unicity of phallocentric discourse" (241).

It is the currency of conventional definitions of "ethical impact" that Acker interrogates in *Don Quixote*, a self-proclaimed search for love that repudiates all courtly fixtures, including the romance of sacrifice, the purity of the Grail, and the grand figurative inheritances of language in which the knight, quest, and character are conventionally clad. From the outset, when a *female* Don Quixote undergoes an abortion, we know that "this's no world for idealism" because the contemporary stakes are too severe, and contemporary Evil Enchanters too formidable, to afford high-flown aesthetics. Under the conditions set in *Don Quixote*, desire is distinguished from desire *for*. Knight and Grail are "completely hole-ly" (13), a pun and oxymoron through whose satirical transformations armorial splendor is reduced to the paper dress she wears on the operating table (she herself is "perforated"), travels give way to randomness, and the most inspired dubbings do not take hold.

Since morality and culture are partners in a royal, repressive masquerade (21)—since, for that matter, thanks to a bizarre Ovidian calamity, everyone from Richard Nixon to Sancho Panza is a dog, basely instinctive and low to the ground—Don Quixote seeks desire unmitigated by objectification and domination, which are the auspices of a rulership that "loveless" barely begins to describe. In order to skirt the social determinations seemingly built into relationships, Acker's hero embarks on a quest for love that is not aimed at a beloved but toward an expansion of atmosphere. ("I won't not be: I'll perceive and I'll speak," she proclaims to her canine cohort [28].) Bitchy, recalcitrant, sexually voracious, her Don Quixote finds that all contacts scald and, as her parade of Panzas indicate, never adhere. This is desire as pure verb, asking no object to vindicate it (10).

"My sexuality is wanting not to exist," the dog declaims (149), and in doing so recollects the evacuated "I" of *Great Expectations* considered above. When under Acker's canine dispensation men are relegated to slobbering sexual engines and women to bitches, little better can be expected. The point is made during the revival of a Sadean nightmare in which degradation causes recoil, then erasure: "My physical sensations scare me because they confront me with a self when I have no self . . . . I'm forced to find a self when I've been trained to be nothing" (171). Sex may be glamorized in some novels as a metaphor for love, trust, reverence, even valor; more likely in Acker it heralds abuse, fraud, murder, or an essential solitude.

In regard to Don Quixote herself, therefore, she must achieve the ambiguous shift from nonidentity to "an identity that always fails" so that she might love beyond the barrier of connection—hence, the announcement that she is "aphasic" works to ensure that the willful itinerant will not be moored (16, 18). This is not a matter of achieving presence so much as one of positing presences: "a plurality of selves, personae seeking rather than signifying identity" (Walsh 157). Or perhaps this regendered hero represents Acker's literal effort to realize the "androgynous mind" exalted by Coleridge, which, in the words of Virginia Woolf, "is resonant and porous; . . . transmits emotion without impediment" (102). What may appear to be a Journey to the End of the Knight—Acker herself seldom refrains from "wholly/holy/hole-ly," "hack/hackneyed/hack-kneed," "knight/night," "Kathy/catheter" verbal snideness—is really a means of exchanging exploitation (in the form of terminations, abortions, and deaths) for exploits (cast as "stalemate[s] of erotic unattainability").[19]

A commitment to "possessionless love" (*Don Quixote* 24) is likewise intended to undo the corruptive model of the traditional male romance. The male-female polarities in *Don Quixote* tend to repeat those found in *Great Expectations:* while the male is associated with unification, order, unilateral statement, dualistic reductions, and terminals, the female is allied with magic, vision, collectivity (or anarchy), and open-endedness. We recall Virginia Woolf's depiction in *A Room of One's Own* of the obdurate "I" of a man's writing: "[T]his 'I' was a most respectable 'I'; honest and logical; as hard as a nut, and polished for centuries by good teaching and good feeding. . . . But—here I turned a page or two, looking for something or other—the worst of it is that in the shadow of the letter 'I' all is shapeless as mist. Is that a tree? No, it is a woman" (103–4). That "I," dispatched from the court of Rationality, is a general of a looming regiment of letters from which the woman writer must unsentence herself. Similarly for Acker, male reason

> is the court of judgement of calculation, the instrument of dom
> ination, and the means for the greatest exploitation of nature. As in
> De Sade's novels, the mode of reason adjusts the world for the ends
> of self-preservation and recognizes no function other than the

preparation of the object from mere sensory material in order to
make it that material of subjugation. Instrumental or ossified reason takes two forms: technological reason developed for purposes
of dominating nature and social reason directed at the means of
domination aimed at exercising social and political power. (*Don
Quixote* 72)

On the contrary, female "re-vision" renders life, literature, and human
interaction a ferment and a shambles. To make use of Barbara Claire
Freeman's categories, "Unlike the masculinist sublime that seeks to master, appropriate, or colonize the other, I propose that the politics of the
feminine sublime involves taking up a position of respect in response to
an incalculable otherness. A politics of the feminine sublime would ally
receptivity and constant attention to that which makes meaning infinitely
open and ungovernable" (11). Just as Acker's dismantled "I" (or "dis-men-
taled," if one will allow, in light of the priorities she rejects) demands
uneclipsed, proliferating agency, "[a]ll being is timelessly wild and path-
less, its own knight, free" (28).

As I have argued, we are faced with the paradox of a polemically
charged novel whose knight-errant, instead of being Cervantes's unwitting
victim of misprision, confesses her benightedness all of the time, in the
service of "romanticism of no possible belief" (42). Consider the following
syllogistic impasse: "Inasmuch as nothing human is eternal but death, and
death is the one thing about which human beings can't know anything,
humans know nothing. They have to fail. To do and be the one thing they
don't know" (35). The quester is a refugee from totalitarian understandings, a vagrant among vague surmises. While it may seem perverse to refer
to modesty during an examination of Acker's fiction, in regard to achieved
certitude, as squired by immaculate imagery (the coin of the patriarchal
realm), Acker turns out to be modest indeed. Among detractors, Acker's
fiction seeks a cheap pose of difference because conventional dimension-
ality eludes her. Exposing scavenged texts to shock treatment, so this argument runs, is the practice of a technician who cannot adequately handle
her tools. In fact, for all her rancor, her obsessive detailing of topical inde-
cencies, and her recruitment of other literature to her personal and political preoccupations, she is not so much polemical as "expressive" (Walsh
153–54). "I have no ideas," we are told in *Don Quixote*, by way of transition between two representative, lengthy broadsides (105).

In place of an art predicated on ideas, Acker pans excellence and opts instead for the art of the "cry." Ironically, perhaps, in view of so sordid a set of motifs as those ulcerating in novels like *Great Expectations* and *Don Quixote,* excess, escapade, and abundance express optimistic potential at optimum frequency, at which extreme the cry shrills and nothing comes to order. Primary, inarticulate, "stupid," yet poignantly alive, Acker's cry exposes "this want, this existence" that exceeds the deftness of craft and decorous figurative cunning (Acker, "Models of Our Present" 64). Forays of love and libel persist beyond the usual fusions of precedent and successor texts, self and community, male and female, quester and objective, and tenor and vehicle.

Chapter 8

DOWN THE RABBIT WHOLE
John Updike's Rabbit Novels

There is a tendency to think of metaphor in fiction in terms of the vertical axis of narrative instead of as a mode of development. Even an extended metaphor may appear to be more of a layered hiatus than the propulsive mechanism that "extension" suggests: a reinforcement of position, ornamentation, or ripening, rather than a progression. Certainly the overtly poetic quality of metaphor slows our passage, inviting us to linger at a scenic port.

However, in part because metaphor respects the contingency of conceptual housings, it can also operate as a linear connective and impetus for the story in which it flourishes. Therefore, when it comes to the way metaphor functions over a stretch of text, the live synapse may be a more appropriate analogy than the swollen node. "It's good to know there are infinite / Exponents within the arrays we've made," writes Alice Fulton ("The Fractal Lanes," lines 8–9), and the effect in fiction is to discover the developmental potential among strategically deployed verbal fixtures.

In DeLillo's *White Noise,* samples taken from contemporary American culture act like anticoagulants; they intrude like a barrage of preemptive stimuli, and coherence is often lost in the irreducible fallout (or the chaotic crowd). In John Updike's Rabbit novels—*Rabbit, Run* (1960),

Rabbit Redux (1971), *Rabbit Is Rich* (1981), and *Rabbit at Rest* (1990)—
lyrical instances reverberate not only throughout the novel in which they
are introduced but actually throughout the entire novel sequence. Concepts are siphoned and symbols revived, resulting in a kind of capillary
action that unites a prose project over four books and better than thirty
years in the lives of their author and their protagonist alike.

This characteristic recalls E. K. Brown's discussion of so-called expanding symbols in fiction. After Brown contends that symbols are especially
relevant instruments "to a writer who is not so confident that life is
perfectly intelligible, and who is impelled to render the part of life that
eludes his clear and convinced undertaking," he notes that, for all their
elusiveness, expanding symbols enact a "rhythmic evolution" that provides
"a form of order" (56, 58). Countless critics have emphasized Updike's
richly metaphorical style as his signature achievement (or, among detractors, as his maddening self-indulgence). Certainly he joins writers like
Paul West and William Gass in demonstrating the sort of mandarin sensibilities that thrive within sentence interiors—these are writers so de-
lighted by the folds within their phrases that they are said to overwhelm
more pedestrian narrative components of plot, character, and theme. In
fact, the poetic density of Updike's fiction creates a surface tension and
"self-apparency" that justifies the inclusion in discussions of metafiction
of a writer ordinarily categorized as a social realist.[1]

What Updike himself admires in the poetry of Walt Whitman provides
a phrase—"strenuous empathy," which infinitely expands the ego's field
("Whitman's Egotheism" 111)—that also approximates a similar, figura-
tively induced quality in his own prose.[2] One aspect of that strenuousness
has to do with that quality of metaphor which tolerates oppositional concepts without subsuming them under a reductive or finally reconciled system. In the Rabbit novels, as metaphors are redeployed and modified in
the course of their association with our aging protagonist, they function
as a series of locks and channels, regulating the narrative flow as they
enforce the sense that Harry Angstrom is running on a treadmill: not only
is he repeating the same sins and failures, but he is also confronted in his
movements by the same verbal landmarks, the same stalled front of associations. Rabbit does not transcend or progress so much as reaffirm his
habitat.

Still, despite the persistence of specific figures in Updike's four
novels, there is also a declension of metaphor to be witnessed as the Rab-

bit sequence progresses. While the coalescent capacities of those metaphors are remembered from book to book, as if they were satellites spiral-
ing further away from their initial launch site, their orbits begin to
deteriorate. Just as Rabbit's energies scatter and dissipate, the treatment
of given metaphors grows increasingly ironic in direct proportion to their
distance from origin.

The paradoxical behavior of metaphor parallels Updike's own ambiva-
lence about novel sequences. Speaking in the fresh wake of the publication of *Rabbit at Rest,* Updike explained that "a motive of the artistic life,
after all, is the completion of sets. That childhood instinct we have to
make collections, to tidy up and round out, affects adult enterprises as
well." Yet after offering this by way of justification for the writing of this
third sequel to *Rabbit, Run,* the author goes on to admit that if four novels serve to "bring all the threads to a gathering," a fifth would overwhelm
that gathering's capacities for coherence: "And with sequels, there is an
accumulation of loose threads, of characters you invented and used, so
that the elements increase geometrically, and beyond four would become
very messy" ("Why Rabbit Had to Go" 24, 25). Even as destinies are distributed during the course of the tetralogy, other threads diverge and fray
and thresholds multiply before they can be conclusively tied off.

Updike has frequently couched such formal equivocations in terms of
aesthetic principles. In his acceptance speech for the 1963 National Book
Award (earned for *The Centaur*), Updike railed against "whatever is lazily
assumed, or hastily perceived, or piously hoped," whereas the sturdier,
more genuinely rendered reality he champions turns out to be plastic,
blurred, fluxional: "Fiction is a tissue of literal lies that refreshes and
informs our sense of actuality. Reality is—chemically, atomically, biologi-
cally—a fabric of microscopic accuracies. Language approximates phenomena through a series of hesitations and qualifications. I miss, in much
contemporary writing, this sense of self-qualification, the kind of timid
reverence toward what exists that Cézanne shows when he grapples for
the shape and shade of a fruit through a mist of delicate stabs" ("Accuracy" 17). Lies that restore our sense of actuality, language that proceeds
through hesitations and qualifications, a pregnant mist of delicate stabs—
Updike seems very much at home in approximation, which he sees as the
fundamental quality shared by fiction and the world, as well as the most
defensible means of bridging them. "Everything unambiguously expressed
seems somehow crass to me," he explains, and this taste for "middles"

leads him to place his esteem and his belief in elastic tropes to relate what are forever and at best intimations of sense (quoted in Hunt 18).

For critic John F. Fleischauer, Updike's penchant for startling metaphors and for adjective and adverb modifiers at the "expense" of the linear responsibilities of the sentences they complicate represents "the author's implied mistrust of motives or goals" (278), which is to recognize a kinship between theme and technique. In each instance, the effect is to reassert distracting elements—the peregrinations of Rabbit, the dilations of Updike—as their own justification. Accordingly, Rabbit can regard his movements as belonging to a quest or a romantic crusade instead of as a concatenation of aimless gestures; Updike can defend his stylistic exhibitionism as constituting a set of similarly hopeful motions—an athletic grace pitted against common plodding. As Updike himself defends his high-voltage prose, "Novel-readers must have a plot, no doubt, and a faithful rendering of the texture of the mundane; but a page of printed prose should bring to its mimesis something extra, a kind of supernatural as it were, to lend everything roundness—a fine excess that corresponds with the intricacy and opacity of the real world" ("Special Message" 869–70). Metaphor's loose, subtle custody is especially conducive to the priorities of performance within the context of narrative development. In virtuosity lies virtue that rises above narcissistic performance, and one needs an appropriate locus—basketball court, bedroom, or paragraph—to accommodate it. Angstrom and Updike share a faith in an intuition of some underlying rhythm, some stabilizing pitch, which will counteract frustration, fragmentation, and arbitrariness. In this sense, artist and hero alike are fortified through deference to mystery, but mystery praised through attentive rendering, and mystery answerable to discipline.

To demonstrate, we may examine a few of the central metaphorical complexes that are introduced in *Rabbit, Run* and then track their reconditioning in subsequent volumes. The first and most prevalent of these is the enclosure. *Rabbit, Run* is a veritable network of claustrophobic images that verify Rabbit Angstrom's predicament and ultimately thwart his escape plans. From the kids gathered for basketball as the novel opens, and who "keep crowding you up" (3), to the scabby clutter and depressing narrows of his home (14), to the inept and cumbersome domesticity of his wife, Janice, everything conspires to hem him in.[3] When Rabbit suddenly bolts, the road map itself verifies his confinement: "The names melt away and he sees the map whole, a net, all those red lines and blue lines and stars, a net he is somewhere caught in." And while he may recall Joyce's Stephen Dedalus as that would-be artist sought to fly through the nets of his own history, Harry effects no escape; rather, in tearing up the map and letting the "bent scraps like disembodied birds flicker back over the top of the car," he ceremonially destroys a conventional symbol of liberation (36).

Indeed, particular references to "nets" and other entrapments occur as often as a dozen times within the first fifty pages of the novel. (No wonder Rabbit continues to worship the sport whose nets were makeable goals!)[4] All the conventional stabilizing influences of middle-class America are perceived as blockages or "clots of concern" (50).[5] What is worse, even those images or environments that might ordinarily have served as authentications of rejuvenation or release turn out to be deceptions. For example, seeking "the small answer of a texture" in the trees that line his street, Rabbit finds himself stranded at the corner, where "a mailbox stands leaning in the twilight on its concrete post. Tall two-petaled street sign, the cleat-gouged trunk of the telephone pole holding its insulators against the sky, fire hydrant like a golden bush: a grove. He used to love to climb the poles" (15). The grove has metamorphosed into urban junk; false relics occasion regard but inspire no faith, only a feckless nostalgia for a time when Harry could surmount things. Unlike Frost's pliable birches, however, these posts and poles are inflexible stays. After he drives back in defeat toward home, a mock enclave welcomes him in the form of "the dark grove full of cars each containing a silent coupling" (39). By the end of the novel, of course, the pastoral dream has dissolved entirely:

> above them all there was the primitive ridge, the dark slum of the forest, separated from the decent part of town by a band of unpaved lanes, derelict farmhouses, a cemetery, and a few raw young developments. Wilbur Street was paved for a block past Rabbit's door, and then became a street of mud and gravel between two short rows of ranch houses of alternating color erected in 1953 on scraped red earth that even now is unsteadily pinned by the blades of grass that speckle it, so that after a good rain the gutter-water flows orange down Wilbur Street. The land grows steeper still, and the woods begin. (219–20)

Security among these "steep streets" is an illusion that the perspectives created by distance dispel. When Harry takes Ruth, his lover and random

resolve, for a walk to the top of Mt. Judge, they discover that they have
made an exhausting spiral and that, precisely as was the case when Harry
made his horizontal flight, there is nowhere left to go but back. If "only
immensity can give us a sensible taste" of the abiding infinite, if "the true
space in which we live is upward space" (112, 113), why is it so difficult
to hack out accesses? Hints of death swarm their promontory; a dreadful
rankle in the deep structure of the city rises to meet them and lets them
know that there is no composed vantage, no release. In such surroundings, Rabbit's safety is compromised beneath "an invisible net . . . in whose
center he lies secure in his locked windowed hutch" (40). The hutch as a
claustrophobic sanctuary, the safety net that strangles, is a paradox continually cited in *Rabbit, Run,* and it brings into focus Rabbit's alternating
desires to succeed (or barring that, to assimilate) and to escape, as well as
his often simultaneous sensations of ruttedness and rootlessness.

When it comes to offering evidence of Harry's predicament, geometry
seconds geography. As was noted above, the clutch of imperious verticals
that preside over Wilbur Street may masquerade as promises of communication (the mailbox and the telephone pole), alternative direction (the
street sign), or replenishment (the hydrant), but they prove to be impasses,
presentiments of the futility of his departure to come. At the end of *Rabbit, Run,* verticals continue to imply a stifling rectitude, now made all the
more compelling by the multiplication of claims upon Harry's fidelity by
Janice, his wife, in the wake of their baby's accidental drowning in the
bathtub; by Ruth, his lover, by virtue of her news that she is pregnant; and
by family and church counselors, who have undertaken, by the light of
their respective beliefs and motives, the renovation of Rabbit Angstrom.
Now the intoxication of the horizontal, through whose blue expanse he
had once felt himself coursing like a shark (100), returns as "the sense of
outside space" that "scoops at his chest," and he seeks some hole in the
opaque pack of options left to him:

> Ruth has parents, and she will let his baby live; two thoughts
> that are perhaps the same thought, the vertical order of parent-
> hood, a kind of thin tube upright in time in which our solitude is
> somewhat diluted. Ruth and Janice both have parents: with this
> thought he dissolves both of them. Nelson remains: here is a hard-
> ness he must carry with him. On this small fulcrum he tries to bal-
> ance the rest, weighing opposites against each other: Janice and

> Ruth, Eccles and his mother, the right way and the good way, the
> way to the delicatessen—gaudy with stacked fruit lit by a naked
> bulb—and the other way, down Sumner Street to where the city
> ends. (305)

"The vertical order of parenthood"—stolid, upright—is a stick in the mud;
when he tries to oppose this contaminated image with a horizontal resolve (a breakaway to the delicatessen), he confronts "stacked fruit lit by
a naked bulb," another vertical sentry. The other way leads not to an
advent but to the end of the city and thoughts of "an empty baseball field,
a dark factory, and then over a brook into a dirt road, he doesn't know."
The outside air that had scooped invitingly at his chest has actually sub-
tracted from him: "He pictures a huge open field of cinders and his heart
goes hollow" (306). In short, the opposites he tries to balance in his mind
are not alternatives at all; rather, they are fuses gone dead at both ends.
The "blue beyond blue under blue" he imagines, awaiting him like some
cosmic gratification (100), becomes an impenetrable expanse, like Wallace Stevens's "dividing and indifferent blue" in *Sunday Morning* (3.15) or
Richard Wilbur's "still and woven blue" in "Merlin Enthralled" (line 36),
a universal carapace invulnerable to magic.[6]

It is instructive to contrast Rabbit's entrapment with a more optimistic
conclusion to the protagonist's feeling of confinement in Updike's story "A
Sense of Shelter." In that story, the bookish, stammering William, rumi-
nating on the impending completion of his high school career and upon
the start of college and a more conducive set of circumstances for the sort
of distinction he is suited for, suddenly feels the sheltering warmth of the
high school building growing heavy: "He was seized by the irrational fear
that they were going to lock him in. The cloistered odors of paper, sweat,
and, from the woodshop at the far end of the basement hall, sawdust no
longer flattered him" (100). Here, too, are those glowering verticals manifested as lockers, and "his self seemed to crawl into the long dark space
thus made vacant" by his removal of his coat, "the humiliated ugly, edu-
cable self." But this time the fated prey escapes: "In answer to a flick of
his great hand the steel door weightlessly floated shut and through the
length of his body he felt so clean and free he smiled." His having been
spurned by the tempting Mary Landis dissolves in favor of her prediction
that great things lie before him, until which inevitable time "he had nothing, almost literally nothing, to do" (101).

What machinations Rabbit goes through to achieve even momentarily the sensation of release that greets William like a benediction! Upon his return, he is taken in by his old basketball coach, Marty Tothero, whose restorative promises—clean clothes, a place to stay, an impending double date—awaken Rabbit's optimistic instincts like a clear lane to the hoop: "He feels freedom like oxygen everywhere around him; Tothero is an eddy of air, and the building he is in, the streets of the town, are mere stairways and alleyways in space" (49–50). The "crowding presence" of his pregnant wife and son has lifted like bad weather. Lines that earlier would have constituted a net are reimagined as enabling radials, outward vectors: "He adjusts his necktie with infinite attention, as if the little lines of this juncture of the Windsor knot, the collar of Tothero's shirt, and the base of his own throat were the arms of a star that will, when he is finished, extend outward to the rim of the universe" (50). But it is mood alone that interprets the knot and the star as symbols of centrifugal energy—a fragile, transitory mood at that. For it is literally a matter of seconds before Rabbit comes to wonder if anyone has seen his abandoned car, and "in the vast blank of his freedom Rabbit has remembered a few imperfections: his home, his wife's, their apartment, clots of concern" (52). That last, already familiar phrase will return in the form of divine retribution, which Rabbit perceives with tragic prescience as the certainty that either Janice or his baby will die: "His sin a conglomerate of flight, cruelty, obscenity, and conceit: a black *clot* embodied in the entrails of the birth" (196; italics mine).

Typically, the smooth-flowing apparatus of flight is halted. At the moment that Rabbit is presumably dressing for successful trespasses, the lines and stars that had demarcated his contraction in the form of the road map and which were momentarily recast as evidence of his freedom now revert and go for his throat. Indeed, "the vast blank of his freedom," an ironic refutation of the desired effects of freedom, will be echoed late in the novel when Harry tries in vain to clear his head of tragedy and sin, when he will find that although "what makes you move is so simple," "the field you move in is so crowded"; worse, as he learned while playing basketball, deftly passing the ball, like passing the buck, may make your accosters look foolish, but only because "in effect there was nobody there" for them to reach for. Rabbit consistently recognizes himself in the form of an outlined negative: "He feels his inside as very real suddenly, a pure blank space in the middle of a dense net" (306). In each case, purity is not the promise of purgation but the threat of erasure.

As if to certify his captivity, here is how clemency is exhibited at Harry and Tothero's first stop, the Sunshine Athletic Association, where Harry is passed among his coach's beefy cronies:

> Their alert colorless eyes, little dark smears like their mouths, feed on the strange sight of him and send acid impressions down to be digested in their disgusting big beer-tough stomachs. Rabbit sees that Tothero is a fool to them, and is ashamed of his friend and of himself. He hides in the lavatory. The paint is worn off the toilet seat and the washbasin is stained by the hot-water faucet's rusty tears; the walls are oily and the towel-rack empty. There is something terrible in the height of the tiny ceiling: a square yard of a dainty metal pattern covered with cobwebs in which a few white husks of insects are suspended. (51–52)

There is no mistaking the return of paralytic images, whereby Rabbit's brief wriggle has primarily served to prove the resiliency of his bonds. There is no mistaking this latest bout of vagrancy as a more sustainable liberation.

Even when he tries to escape the growing number of "mute dense presences, pushing in the dark like crags under water" by going to sleep, "the thought of the far shore approaching makes a stubborn lump in his glide" (231). Masturbating to relieve his stress, he thinks of Reverend Eccles's winking wife in terms of invitations to departure: canals, open gates, unraveled string. But his drift is interrupted by the memory of his failure to carry out his original getaway plan. He remembers "one of the red-haired girls that sat inside with her hair hanging down like seaweed," and he chastises himself for not having responded to her silent siren call and followed it instead of slinking back home (232).[7] His realization that the enduring compulsion *does* represent his following them, only "like a musical note that all the while it is being held seems to travel though it stays in the same place" (232), defeats even this modest effort to elude his life and troubles his sleep.

Two other metaphor complexes dominate the novel: athleticism and spirituality. Few contemporary authors are as attentive as Updike to the astonishing molecular dispensation that allows for human existence, an awareness that presides not only thematically but also stylistically throughout Updike's fiction in the sense that such lavish sentence making exemplifies and celebrates it. Whereas we might ordinarily expect the body's and the soul's respective prowesses to be in conflict with one another, in *Rabbit, Run* they tend to be equated because both are seen, at least initially, as reservoirs of hope and proofs of personal election. Were we to adopt Pascal's trinity of influence as it is offered in the novel's epigraph—"The motions of Grace, the hardness of the heart; external circumstances"—athleticism and spirituality, both forms of kinetic energy, seem to stand for the first of these, a rugged holiness which Updike refers to in a short story as "unceasing and effortless blessing" and which a few special writers and a few special players occasionally attain ("The Blessed Man of Boston" 228).[8]

We see them explicitly conspire from the opening scene of the novel, where basketball continues to provide Harry with an avenue of transcendence of sullen adulthood. The exploits of the best of the boys whose game he has crashed remind him of the "blessing" of physical aptitude, as well as of its deceptions:

> You climb up through the little grades and then get to the top and everybody cheers; with the sweat in your eyebrows you can't see very well and the noise swirls around you and lifts you up, and then you're out, not forgotten at first, just out, and it feels good and cool and free. You're out, and sort of melt, and keep lifting, until you become like to these kids just one more piece of the sky of adults that hangs over them in the town, a piece that for some queer reason has clouded and visited them. They've not forgotten him: worse, they never heard of him. (5)

Ascension precedes evaporation and disappearance into the "vast blank" lying behind the alluring sensation of freedom. It is true that for a moment the chance to play ball again grants him focus—Angstrom is temporarily less the embodiment of angst than the measurement of radiant energy—and Rabbit's skittishness is redeemed through the logic of feints and dodges on the court. Nevertheless, that his "touch still lives in his hands" (5) is little else than an engaging anomaly for the boys to kid about. (Despite his paunch and puffing, the old guy's still got it.) In an early story, Updike implies this fortunate "touch" in terms of the wordless desire of children for "the quality of glide. To slip along, always cool, the little wheels humming under you, going nowhere special. If Heaven existed, that's the way it would be there" ("Tomorrow and Tomorrow and So Forth" 36).⁹

We witness the clearest relationship between sports and religion when Reverend Eccles takes Harry golfing. However, we must be cautious about viewing their coincidence as a sign of unadulterated providence for Harry, notwithstanding his need to be validated both spiritually and athletically. After all, as he confesses to Eccles, his disappointment in Janice comes from his having had to settle for the second-rate after excelling in basketball (105), which had reliably keyed his intuition of "a realm / above this plane of silent compromise" (Updike, "The Angels," lines 5–6). Unfortunately, golf is not his game, and playing with Eccles will be a struggle at best rather than an opportunity to demonstrate anything first-rate about himself.¹⁰ In fact, the draw of competition is related to the "dangerous tug drawing him toward this man in black" (105) and to their initial greeting when Eccles caught up to his quarry at curbside: "Eccles' handshake, eager and practiced and hard, seems to symbolize for him an embrace. For an instant Rabbit fears he will never let go. He feels caught, foresees explanations, embarrassments, prayers, reconciliations rising up like dank walls; his skin prickles in desperation. He feels tenacity in his captor" (101). Familiar images of enclosure block out possibilities of the soul's revival, much less release, in his mind. If Rabbit believes for the time being that he can slip through the questionable welds of family, he is not so confident when it comes to "the fair young man with his throat manacled in white" (100)—an unsettling characterization of the holy fold, not to mention an unsavory allusion to the previously described knot at Harry's throat.

While Rabbit tries to protect his privacy against the genial prying of the minister, "Down in the pagan groves and green alleys of the course Eccles is transformed" (129). Here in this strenuous Eden appears to be Rabbit's long-sought haven, his serenely appointed hutch.¹¹ Unfortunately, Harry is flummoxed by the delicate art of golf; and as his vexation grows, the clubs and course hazards become human antagonists in his mind—Janice, Ruth, his mother. Meanwhile, "now at the corners, now at the center of this striving dream, Eccles flits in his grubby shirt like a white flag of forgiveness, crying encouragement, fluttering from the green to guide him home" (131). The conventional religious message seems clear enough: the self is truly freed through its surrender. The irony for Rabbit is that, despite his repudiation of middle-class trappings of marriage, fatherhood, job, and so on, he retains an urge to participate and locate himself within sacraments, no matter how secularized or diffracted they may be in this instance (Trachtenberg 10). As Marty Tothero boasts, the most telling goal of a good coach is to build a boy's heart by making him feel "the *sacredness* of achievement" (61), and whether one scores on the court or in bed, the feeling is the thing, the crucial source of separation from one's own skein of explicit griefs and the confounding drudgery of the everyday.[12]

It is only after Rabbit has endured Eccles's chastisements, delivered with the matter-of-factness of stroke instruction, that he has his vision:

> In avoiding looking at Eccles he looks at the ball, which sits high on the tee and already seems free of the ground. Very simply he brings the clubhead around his shoulder into it. The sound has a hollowness, a singleness he hasn't heard before. His arms force his head up and his ball is hung way out, lunarly pale against the beautiful black blue of storm clouds, his grandfather's color stretched dense across the east. It recedes along a line straight as a ruler-edge. Stricken; sphere, star, speck. It hesitates, and Rabbit thinks it will die, but he's fooled, for the ball makes this hesitation the ground of a final leap: with a kind of visible sob takes a last bite of space before vanishing in falling. "That's *it!*" he cries and, turning to Eccles with a smile of aggrandizement, repeats, "That's it." (133–34)

"That's it"—is this gut reaction to the first satisfying, solid drive he has had to be taken as dismissal and vanquishment of an adversary or as validation of Eccles' argument prior to the shot that Rabbit is a coward who worships nothing except his own worst instincts? "Let us not mock God with metaphor, / analogy, sidestepping, transcendence," Updike writes in "Seven Stanzas at Easter" (lines 13–14), a grouping that appears to accuse of apostasy not only verbal approximation (metaphor and analogy) and evasion (sidestepping) but any departure (even transcendence) from literal miracle. Is the consolidation and redemption of several of the novel's images in this paragraph, including the blue sky, a presentiment of death, and the finicky star ("stricken" by its having been struck), to be taken as a verification of the collusion of athletic and spiritual aspirations, with the levitation of the golf ball rainbowing over a suddenly inviting sky like the arc of the covenant?[13]

Rabbit is typical of Updike's heroes in that he is eager to be guided by vivid presentiment. One welcomes news of the scrutable wherever it arises: if for Emerson the world's fat stash was stored in a forest of symbols, like an ideal poem awaiting our devices, then Rabbit's vision of a pastoral arena suited to his own peculiar capacities seems credible. To be sure, for all his ready palaver and legislative bromides about the Deity, Eccles does not have the sense of "It," of some authentic, authenticating presence, that Rabbit achieves, however temporarily, through furtive instinct. (When Rabbit maintains, "There's something that wants me to find it," Eccles can only read "it" as an excuse for selfishness and vaga-bonding.) As Reverend Kruppenbach angrily points out to Eccles, belief must burn hot and absolute at the center of solicitude. The rest is clubby irrelevance.[14] In this sense, Jack Eccles, who does not have that to offer, joins the forces of the inauthentic that Rabbit associates with Janice and Ruth, those "mute dense presences" who obstruct his vision.

On the other hand, golf is only a game, and a day's ventures along a golf course, like Rabbit's interstate breakaway in the night, leads him back where he began. Or, to borrow the words of J. D. Salinger's Teddy, another mystic of the quotidian, "Life is a gift horse in my opinion" (181).[15]

In short, the entropic figures of *Rabbit, Run* shadow the declining prospects of its protagonist. Not even the concluding passage of the novel, which many readers have interpreted as a kind of rejuvenation of options, is excepted from the influence of phrases alluding to corrupt contexts elsewhere in the novel: "He wants to travel to the next patch of snow. Although this block of brick three-stories is just like the one he left, something in it makes him happy; the steps and window sills seem to twitch and shift in the corner of his eye, alive. This illusion trips him. His hands lift of their own and he feels the wind on his ears even before, his heels hitting heavily on the pavement at first but with an effortless gathering out of a kind of sweet panic growing lighter and quicker and quieter, he runs. Ah: runs. Runs" (306–7).

Acceleration is an unburdening, yes, but one whose logical extremity is disappearance, as we recall his sense, introduced only a paragraph before, that he has become a "pure blank space." We recall Rabbit's reply to Eccles's question about what was inside him: "Hell, it's nothing much . . . It's just that, well, it's all there is" (124). While this is a preview of the galvanizing "it" Rabbit encounters during golf, it is also serves (when the comments are held accountable to their antecedents and "well" is recognized as a potential noun) as a sobering equation of hell and the absolute zero toward which Rabbit's sundry runs have tended: hell is "nothing much," a dismissal that is also a definition, and hell is "just that well," an eternal hole. Moreover, the next block, like the next patch of snow, is not a new arrival but more of the same restrictive scenery, as yet another avenue collapses like a bad vein before him. The respite is deceptive, and evanescent at that. That the buildings seem to imitate, and thereby validate, his own rabbity manner, all twitches and shifts, is the illusion that "trips" him—triggers his sprint, but also, like the internal fibrillations that rule his personality, causes him to stumble. For the "sweet panic" recalls an earlier passage whose darker import—the key parallel to "sweet panic" is "indefinite urgency"—casts a pall upon the close of the novel, as we come to appreciate the historical regularity of the trammeling of Rabbit's evasions: "Rabbit pauses at the end of the alley, where he has an open view. He used to caddy over there. Pricked by an indefinite urgency, he turns away, going left on Jackson Road, where he lived for twenty years. His parents' home is in a two-family brick house on the corner; but it is their neighbors, the Bolgers, who have the corner half, with a narrow side yard Mrs. Angstrom has always envied. *The Bolgers' windows getting all that light and here we sit wedged in*" (18). Updike's italics (in the revised Fawcett paperback edition of *Rabbit, Run*) are not all that rat him out. Urgency is an exacting ethic but a vague one as well. The open view is not only refuted by the golf course, where Rabbit was just a caddy ("second-rate," if you will) and where, as noted in the discussion of his golf outing with Eccles, all pasturing proves futile; it, too, like the block Rabbit comes upon at the end of the novel, is "bricked" in. Indeed, the Bolgers ruled the corner, obstructing the Angstroms, hoarding the light. We need only contrast the opaque prospect afforded by the view from his childhood home with, say, the forgiving sight awaiting Joey from the window of *his* childhood home in *Of the Farm* to appreciate the possibility, denied Rabbit, of a resolving membrane between soul and world: "It was a window enchanted by the rarity with which I looked from it. Its panes were strewn with drops that as if by amoebic decision would abruptly merge and break and jerkily run downward, and the window screen, like a sampler half-stitched, or a crossword puzzle invisibly solved, was inlaid erratically with minute, translucent tessarae of rain. A physical sense of ulterior mercy overswept me" (*Of the Farm* 107).

It is true that, thanks in part to the squinting modifier, Rabbit grows "lighter and quicker and quieter" along with his panic, and that the unaccountable "lift" he senses in his hands brings back the ballplayer's electric "can't miss" sensation (which, significantly, onlookers will disdainfully refer to as being "unconscious"); it is true, in other words, that *Rabbit, Run* appears to end by overcoming phrases that had marked Rabbit's confinement. But Rabbit's muscle memory of values whose frame of reference once stretched baseline to baseline seems somehow absurd at this point, as he oscillates among ruinous truths (Janice's accidental drowning of their baby, Ruth's pregnancy, and his respective desertions). The old motility is still there, but like the shooter's touch he retains, it exists outside of any legitimating context.[16] We remember the description of Mrs. Smith's garden, in which "invisible rivulets running brokenly make the low land of the estate sing" (135). If only Rabbit's broken-field running could transform the streets of Brewer in this way instead of making him feel like a trespasser wherever he goes. From another viewpoint, even Mrs. Smith's garden is not the privileged landscape it seems: its flower beds are "bordered with bricks buried diagonally, are pierced with dull red spikes that will be peonies," with "the earth itself, scumbled, stone-flecked, horny, raggedly patched with damp and dry" (135). The garden hoe, like the golf club, had the reassuring heft of connection to the abiding, restorative earth, but it is the same deceptive landscape of denial everywhere.

Running is not running *toward*. Rabbit is still a would-be pilgrim without a course, still surrounded by the same residual strictures of family, religion, and moral convention, the same opaque suburban structures drawn tightly together against alternative. The planet remains shut tight as an apple against him. The heart's probation continues.

The title of the sequel, *Rabbit Redux*, forecasts the centripetal fate of Updike's hero, but for our purposes here it also implies the recursion of the metaphors that dominated *Rabbit, Run*. However, just as the implication of a return to health is handled ironically in terms of Rabbit's family circumstances in *Rabbit Redux*, so too do the metaphors themselves resist restoration, as the "sweet panic" of the first novel shifts into the "stale peace" of the second (*Rabbit Redux* 6). On a personal level, evidence of Rabbit's recuperation appears limited to the mere fact of his having stayed home for the past ten years. Otherwise, he has become all the more sexist and disdainful. Rabbit now blindly flies with the Right Wing of America First. He spares no minority from his bigotry, a fact which makes his harboring two standard countercultural representatives—Jill, a young hippie runaway grown lean with reckless disregard, and Skeeter, a manipulative vocalist for Black Power—all the more remarkable. Actually, Rabbit tends to be identified with staples of fixity in *Rabbit Redux*—the majority of the novel's scenes show him at home or on the job—and he serves as a point of intersection for the travels of other characters. That most American of mottoes, "Let Freedom Ring," implies the undermining of faith in motion, for freedom does finally appear to be more like a series of concentric, confining rings (as foreseen in the collection of net and circle images texturing *Rabbit, Run*) than unhedged vectors. Put another way, Rabbit's return confirms that his outward ripples were really bounded, and in *Rabbit Redux* they, like the hero's effronteries, double back upon themselves. Rabbit's flight reflex has generally inverted into a tendency to cringe beneath the collisions.

Stewing in resentment, dissipation, and the *Brewer Vat*, where his job as typesetter is at the brink of obsolescence, Rabbit looks to the same stolid verticals that had so consternated him in the previous novel as reassurances. His politics tenuous, his erections frail, Rabbit clings to the props of the propertied despite his inability to behave as his fellow Penn Villagers would expect. He "sleeps best when others are up, upright like nails holding down the world, like lamp-posts, street-signs, dandelion stems, cobwebs" (26), notwithstanding the fact that he seldom sleeps with his own wife. A hollow shaped by the departures of *others* now, most notably the haunting death of his infant daughter, and most recently the frank adultery of Janice with Charlie Stavros, a liberal coworker at her father's Toyota dealership, Rabbit determines that "the world is quicksand" and conventional rectitude is the only outpost that can last it out (32). This is the rootedness of solid citizenship, as vested in the crisp intolerance of neighbors defending their subdivision against the wrong sorts of inhabitants while they champion complacencies of the boudoir and *davven* over the Sunday barbecue.[17]

No matter how his transgressions escalate during the destructive course of *Rabbit Redux*, Harry Angstrom has discovered that he craves regulation and its trappings. An expedient seduction of Peggy Fosnacht, who like Rabbit means to counteract her spouse's abandonment with diligent promiscuity, rewards him with the following realization: "that even while he and Peggy were heating their little mutual darkness a cold fluorescent world surrounded them in hallways and down stairwells and amid unsleeping pillars upholding their vast building" (317). Late in the novel, wandering in the wake of his most recent loss (the death of Jill in a fire at his home), he watches the machinery of civic maintenance, thinking, "These appliances of a town's housekeeping seemed to Harry part of a lost world of blameless activity; he felt that he would never be allowed to crawl back into that world" (345).[18] In other words, the mute sentries of the quotidian may continue to go about their business, but they remain blunt and unsympathetic toward this inveterately prodigal son.

Hence the bankruptcy of Harry's tactics is evident in the insurrection of the imagery they inspire. For example, although Harry seeks fortification in straight lines and sharp angles, Charlie Stavros, his ideological antagonist and sexual rival, is rendered as a barrage of aggressive geometry: "a squarely marked-off man" endowed with "potent gravity," with eyebrows that run "straight across" "rectangular" horn-rims, "deep squared sideburns" (40–41). As opposed to Rabbit, who is consistently rendered as a vacancy or blur, Stavros is all directed fervor; and his skewering of Rabbit's rabid political agenda, just like his sexual impact upon Janice, is associated with mutinous planes. Rabbit sizes him up as a playmaker, meaning to reduce him in basketball terms to a subordinate to the prolific scorer Rabbit had been, but the joke is on him: Stavros is making a successful play for Janice.[19]

Skeeter similarly betrays Harry's expectations. His jumping bail— indeed, the radical politics and religious zeal behind his repudiation of the status quo—recommends him to his host as a higher order of runaway than the currently moored Rabbit had been before. Loitering with intensity as a member of the perversely ecumenical household of Harry, Jill (who acts by turns as Harry's lover, daughter, and mother), and Nelson, Skeeter defies containment in a way that Harry had only nebulously, temporarily approximated a decade ago. Skeeter remains an unknowable quantity: not only does Rabbit not know his real name or ulterior motives (apart from his Svengali-like control of Jill through sexual humiliation and drug addiction) for certain, but Skeeter never fully resolves out of the smudges and shadows that swaddle him (205). Actually, it is this characteristic, which Rabbit identifies as the liquid sheen and "curious greased grace" of blacks (138, 251), that tantalizes him, for it appears to combine the qualities of athleticism and escape artistry that Rabbit had once enjoyed and still cherishes. Yet the insubstantiality that is a constitutional insufficiency in Rabbit's case is a calculated evasiveness in Skeeter's.

Surely the sports analogy betrays Rabbit on this occasion. He senses how "this black man opens up *under him* " like a basketball hoop, but by no means to reward Harry's prowess: Skeeter is "a pit of scummed stench impossible to see to the bottom of" (208; italics mine). When Rabbit does draw close to Skeeter, he is met by the same aggressive imagery: "when Rabbit pries at him he has no opening, just abrasive angles shaking like a sandpaper machine" (211).

Sexual encounters are more plentiful and explicit in *Rabbit Redux* than they were in *Rabbit, Run,* but it is even more apparent here that for Rabbit intimacy is an invitation to annihilation. His obscene references to female anatomy mask his horror of the tear that precedes a plummet into the void. Whereas Janice is positively exuberated by the way her proficient lover encourages her to let go, Rabbit has long refused her, ostensibly because he has not wanted her to get pregnant again after the tragedy of the drowning of their baby, but more precisely because he equates sex with darkness and death (36).[20] When he does make love to his wife, Rabbit imagines her body to be "a stretch of powdery sand, her mouth a loose black hole, her eyes holes with sparks in them," and "her appetite frightens him, knowing he cannot fill it, any more than Earth's appetite for death can be satisfied" (70). Not even his masturbatory fantasies can be practiced apart from thoughts of the gallows (378–79). The snares of *Rabbit, Run* have returned as lethal envelopments in *Rabbit Redux.*

Given this neurotic condition, it may be fitting that Rabbit rather blithely accommodates Janice's own extramarital adventures, but it is ironic, to say the least, that he continues to rely on sex for his own security when it consistently exposes his inadequacy, his desolation, or his mortality. When Jill offers her body absently, as compensation for Harry's dubious nurturing attentions, he is initially struck by its barren landscape, a stark contrast to the "boneless" nestle afforded by Janice (27): "The horns of her pelvis like starved cheekbones. Her belly a child's, childless. Her breasts in some lights as she turns scarcely exist" (142–43). Jill challenges Harry to "fuck all the shit out" of her (201), but he compounds it instead. Whereas Janice had accused Harry of lacking presence and definition and of meaning to avoid contracting that condition, Harry senses in women a call to oblivion. They are alternately perceived by him as parched domains, looming pits, or squalid viscera. His wife in bed "is all confused mocking darkness where he dare not insert himself" (378). Comparable hazards lurk inside Jill's body. At times he is Prufrock repelled by the dank: "[H]e is holding wind in his arms. He feels she wants to be fucked, any way, without pleasure, but to pin her down. He would like to do this for her but he cannot pierce the fright, the disgust between them. She is a mermaid gesturing beneath the skin of the water. He is floating rigid to keep himself from sinking in terror" (284). "He cannot overcome his fear of using her body as a woman's—her cunt *stings*, is part of it; he never forces his way into her without remembering those razor blades" (157). Intercourse is a matter of complicit lacerations, mutual corrosions. Even sex with Peggy Fosnacht, which has far less threatening implications for Harry (he considers her in terms of bland candy that he can take or leave), is inflammatory and jacketed in wicked adjectives; the "dim charged space" it establishes offers little in the way of revelation or refuge (313).

Briefly, human interactions in this novel may be classified in one of two ways: they are ravenous and scalding, like the sexual combustions that suggest that fire (passion, anguish, rage, or the communal vengeance by arson against the accursed House of Angstrom) is our essential fact, and so "we shimmer at all moments on the verge of conflagration" (346); or they are sparse and fuddled, as represented by the impaired speech of Harry's mother, stricken with Parkinson's, whose telegrammatic fragments tragically imitate the cumbrous communications transmitted by astronauts. Apparently the atmosphere in *Rabbit Redux* is too thin to support anything other than stammered sentiments.

Sex with Jill triggers more traumatic images. Jill's childlike proposal that people substitute love for fear and fury is pitifully insufficient, in part because the universe of *Rabbit Redux* lurches back and forth between fire and ice (170), and in part because love is no balm anyway. Not that this hapless girl can recruit anyone to so naive a conception of love anyway. Introduced as a refutation of her own pretension to innocence—"standing there *prim*, in a *white* dress *casual* and *dirty* as smoke" (125; italics mine)—she is quite willing to accept her lover's patently false expressions of love; moreover, when she later maintains that sex "just happens on the surface, a million miles away" as a means of consoling Harry about her having had relations with Skeeter (213), she is inadvertently discrediting the sole evidence of their own intimacy.[21] Regardless of her dismissal, Harry imagines her being "defiled by Skeeter's kiss," which injects her with "his luminous poison" (254). And to be sure, the thought of Jill reminds Harry of nothing so much as one of Prufrock's mermaids tempting him to drown—we remember with him, too, the tragic death of his baby girl—or worse, of "sour gas bottled in churches, nothing to rise by" (284). Embraces multiply absences, tighten the hollows.

Meanwhile, as he tries to fend off images of his own immolation during sex, Harry imagines his ejaculant as acid, which brings the war home by transforming Jill into a napalm victim. When anonymous neighbors, determined to cauterize the wounds against neighborhood propriety, burn the Angstrom house, Jill's death by fire seems an inevitable extension of the very fate she had bargained for by taking up with Harry in the first place. Survival requires a refuge. Skeeter is impenetrable; Mim, Harry's sister, is a Hollywood prostitute whose talent for becoming "hard clean through" sustains her in predatory company (361); Babe, the Negress who entices Harry at the bar, shows no "soft hole in her, she is all shell" (379). But while Jill affects hardheartedness, the drugs she uses to ensure it actually leave her "peeled" and vulnerable (264).

At the conclusion of *Rabbit Redux*, Harry and Janice try to soothe their respective bruises in bed together, and the scene is not so much one of requital as of cooperative recoil reminiscent of the close of John Osborne's *Look Back in Anger*, in which the Porters agree to the painless remove of a game of bears and squirrels. (Harry and Janice's drey is, appropriately, the Safe Haven Motel.) Husband and wife meet up in a motel bed like moonwalkers; hoping to gauge one another again, they rely upon exaggerated gestures and unnatural adjustments in the course of trying to establish a reasonable docking procedure after long neglect (405). The novel has effected its own metaphorical return. Janice's presence in bed had originally qualified its contours, making it "a laden hollow, itself curved" (27), seemingly suited to the unredeemed "blank" Janice lies with, rounding his little life with a sleep. At the end of the book, Rabbit "ducks into the bed as if into a burrow, being chased," and he takes solace for a change in his wife's mossy privates—a consoling "patch there, something to hide in" (404).[22]

Nevertheless, in spite of the relative optimism represented by his being able to locate an "inward curve and slip along it" (407), although Janice's curves had previously seemed so forbidding and unavailing, the sensation that he is being "bombarded" continues inside this shelter. They do not make love; "coupling" has not yet been completed. The Angstroms are back in bed together, but as restless ions floating in "a dim charged space." "O.K.?" the novel concludes, in the last of some twenty uses of that surprisingly flexible word in the book. It implies solicitation, validation, petulance, and concession; however, it never really approximates the assured quality of an astronaut's "A-OK."[23] The Angstroms' Tranquillity Base is at best an uneasy sleep.

The sight of his scorched house makes it clear to Harry that "death is in heat": it is death's fertile period, and death prospers in the tropics of passion, be it born of desire or hate (324). No wonder Harry rejects Skeeter's vitriolic prophecy of the new order to come, for it is characterized by these same assailing images of erasure, chaos, and flame. Skeeter waxes optimistic when he extends his politics to the physical universe: "[T]hough it is true everything is expanding outwards, it does not thin out to next to nothingness on account of the reason that through strange holes in this nothingness new somethingness comes pouring in from exactly nowhere" (261). The future of the race, like the women he has slept with, is thereby characterized for Harry as an ambiguous combination of advents and abysses, and like these women, it terrorizes and seduces him at the same time.[24]

Macrocosmic parallels to the diminishment of human relationships in *Rabbit Redux* form a consistent background throughout the narrative. Despite the recuperative promise of the title and the general impression that the novel is set during a particularly vital period of American evolution, Harry inhabits a landscape of arrested motion—a lunar surface. The opening pages of the novel are wreathed in a pallor whose choking, inconsolable atmosphere conditions every personality, motive, and event:

> In winter, Pine Street at this hour is dark, darkness presses down early from the mountain that hangs above the stagnant city of Brewer; but now in summer the granite curbs starred with mica and the row houses differentiated by speckled bastard sidings and the hopeful small porches with their jigsaw brackets and gray milk-bottle boxes and the sooty ginkgo trees and the baking curbside cars wince beneath a brilliance like a frozen explosion. The city, attempting to revive its dying downtown, has torn away blocks of buildings to create parking lots, so that a desolate openness, weedy and rubbled, spills through the once-packed streets, exposing church facades never seen from a distance and generating new perspectives of rear entryways and half-alleys and intensifying the cruel breadth of the light. The sky is cloudless yet colorless, hovering blanched humidity, in the way of these Pennsylvania summers,

> good for nothing but to make green things grow. Men don't even
> tan; filmed by sweat, they turn yellow. (3–4)

A dismal lyricism prevails over the city and the people who "have dried
up with it" (5). Light does not reveal opportunity or portal; it lays a
"cruel breadth" upon the population. The stars are just mica bits stuck
in granite curbs; glinting ridiculously beneath the feet of men who
trudge home with "the look of constant indoor light clinging to them,"
they suggest no frontier. Not even an "explosion" rouses, for it too is
"frozen" in place. Instead of the wishful expanse encouraged by running,
a "desolate openness" implies that there is no escape from the habits of
languor and contempt. Things seep instead of progress. Everywhere is
found the same swamped surrender: "The day whines at the windows, a
September brightness empty of a future: the lawns smitten flat, the
black river listless and stinking" (199).

   The novel is replete with pessimistic references: traps and trenches,
wretched huddles and vacant lots. Harry may live on Vista Crescent, but
there is only more of the same narrowing fate to see at the precipice of
the decade. His cares have made him feel more claustrophobic than ever
(19, 240), and he often feels his heart tremble in its hollow, another desolate openness, rattling like the last stale candy in the box. Time has
been ruthless to both his parents, while signs of decrepitude are already
upon the ex-athlete, for whom a "quick one" at the beginning of *Rabbit
Redux* refers not to joining in a game of basketball as it did in *Rabbit,
Run* but to a stop at the local bar. Rabbit's slackened dash, the fact that
his primary run has been a run to fat, suggests that death is stalking
him still. It accosts him everywhere, as though it were a personal
vendetta spawned from environmental decay. Here it is nature that is
"running out" (12). Civic flourishes are the masquerade of the nation's
death throes; a walk through West Brewer realizes the enervated vision
described in Eliot's "Preludes":

> But beneath these awesome insignia of vastness and motion fat
> men in undershirts loiter, old ladies move between patches of gos-
> sip with the rural waddle of egg-gatherers, dogs sleep curled beside
> the cooling curb, and children with hockey sticks and tape-handled
> bats diffidently chip at whiffle balls and wads of leather, whittling
> themselves into the next generation of athletes and astronauts.

Rabbit's eyes sting in the dusk, in this smoke of his essence, these
harmless neighborhoods that have gone to seed. (113)

The country seems plunged in relentless twilight, its doom mapped out in
bleak faces and strangled avenues, "streets that end with, as a wrung neck,
a sharp turn over abandoned railroad tracks into a sunless gorge where a
stream the color of tarnished silver is now and then crossed by a damp
covered bridge that rattles as it swallows you" (267). Future athletes and
astronauts, America's most promising and as of yet its least cynical dream-
ers, unwittingly operate within the same entropic context as the next generation of "penumbral ghosts, suppliants ignored" (184).

For it is 1969, and the disqualification of space exploration mirrors the
disqualification of athleticism as a transcendent ploy. By turning to outer
space, America sought to revive the frontier of splendid possibility that
had served as its mythic validation. However, from Harry's perspective,
instead of renovating a context for the American Dream, the Apollo program simply translates our inner emptiness to the heavens, the "big round
nothing" they waste their aim at (22). The "pure blank space" of *Rabbit,
Run,* with its implosive threat, becomes the "dim, charged space" of *Rabbit Redux,* which further decertifies the symbol. If the local landscape
seems barren and unavailing, if Harry's "slowly turning cold house" is a
dead planet and his own pain a crater no attentions can fill (133, 90),
where can anyone muster enough thrust to break out of earth's atmosphere? In *Midpoint,* Updike defines an aesthetic principle that is not
inspired by but must be achieved in contrast to the example of Space:

> Sickened by Space's waste, I tried to cling
>
> to the thought of the indissoluble:
> a point infinitely hard
> was luminous in me, and cried *I will.*
>
> I sought in middling textures part-
> icles of iridescence, scintillae
> in dullish surfaces; and pictured art
>
> as my descending, via pencil, into dry
> exactitude. (1.39–47)

Here again is Updike's "small answer of a texture," recognized as "middling" as much for its dialectical positioning as for any hint of secondariness or thinning compensation.

The point is that the defamiliarization of the local landscape in *Rabbit Redux* does not represent a reversal of earth and moon, whereby the latter would have been a hospitable alternative; on the contrary, it represents the poisoning of earthly habitation by the moon's airless, uninspiring example, as though the satellite were encroaching on an inward spiral. Beds that retain their coldness no matter how often or how furiously they are shared; the dry skin and chapped lips of Jill, a flower child turned Harry's "moon child," who, like other drug users and denizens of the blues lounge, abjures the sun; the hard blanks of the Las Vegas faces Mim admiringly describes as desert adaptations—"Look out for it, Harry. It's coming East" (359); and a host of images of stasis, numbness, and vacancy continually reassert the fact that contact with the moon is no antidote. To indict that favored phrase from *Rabbit, Run,* how much faith is to be found in "the small answer of a texture" when every texture is compromised, or worse, contaminated? And what difference would a responsive texture make anyway to a player who dolefully admits that his "touch" is gone?

Harry can no longer sustain his youthful faith in the renewing power of space. "Space kills," he thinks. Departure, be it directed toward another woman or toward an unspoiled world, lengthens our shadows, extends our fatal attachments (92). The curvature of space recalls for him the treacherous curves of Janice. Space "frightens Rabbit with a sense of ultimate blindness, of a blackboard from which they will all be wiped clean" (93). All of that vague commotion on the moon just colonizes additional dust.

Yet perversely, despite the evidence, Rabbit is as stubborn as the country in his commitment to a philosophy of acquisition and subjugation. Just as America would reconstitute Vietnam in its own image and swallow the moon, Rabbit would "cash in" proximate women. "Everything is blank until you fuck it," he concludes; but fucking erases him, a phenomenon that Peggy Fosnacht, that most readily cashable of checks, recognizes as the next logical step in the collapse of his athletic career: "She has seen him coming to nothing" (310).[25] The skies may captivate us and allow us temporarily to borrow greater dimension from their example, but in the end we remain the same dull, sublunary lovers. Sex, according to Mim's expert testimony, is not a matter of filling a hole or a need but a task of scouring, draining (360).

In the end, Rabbit feels antagonized rather than vindicated by Skeeter's argument that it is not only possible but inevitable for something—truth, political solution, or cosmic omega—to come out of nothing. All fervor and self-approval, this militant messiah promotes a God of/as Chaos, who in turn supervises a lurid birth: "The moon is a baby's head bright red between his momma's legs" (262). Part of what makes Skeeter so mesmerizing an adversary for Rabbit is his talent for appropriating so many of the issues that preoccupy his host—on this particular occasion, they include the abyssal hole, the moon as locus of renewal, and the equation of love, authority, and violence—and, by mangling the symbols Rabbit customarily associates with them, unleashing their terrorist potential.

Transcendent principles are the chief casualty of the deflation of metaphor in *Rabbit Redux*. Rocketry is the way technology prays; nonetheless, while preoccupation with the moonshot invites numerous references to the rousing spirit and vocabulary of transcendence—ignitions, launches, liftoffs, and starry destinations—they are immediately exposed as poetic deceptions. There is nothing to rise by. If the moon proves to be just another lonely outpost, "a cold stone above Mt. Judge" (384), the firmament is a reflection of static captivity here on earth, its lights nothing other than confusions of distance. Stars are either mocked by local replicas, such as after-images from a television screen that sustain no faith (7), or they dwindle into the very images of entrapment introduced in *Rabbit, Run* but which the space race had been counted on to contradict. Indeed, over his burnt house, "a half-moon rests cockeyed in the blanched sky like a toy forgotten on a floor," and the view above, an inexorable darkening perforated by stars, recalls one more massive net: "The soot is settling on Harry's bones. . . . The freshening sky above Mt. Judge is Becky, the child that died, and the sullen sky to the west, the color of a storm sky but flawed by stars, is Nelson, the child that lives. And he, he is the man in the middle" (329–30).[26] It is a rule of physics: "all things must fall" (376). The only thing that ascends from the ruins is smoke.

Rabbit retreats to his childhood home after this latest tragedy, but transcendence fares little better there. He finds things relentlessly unmagical: "These mundane surfaces had given witness to his life; this chalice had held his blood; here the universe had centered, each downtwirling maple seed of more account than galaxies. No more. Jackson Road seems an ordinary street anywhere" (373). A chasm has opened up between his childhood vision that equated the rich, expectant radiance of churchly col-

ors fanning out of the beveled glass over the front door with a kind of spiritual sanction (91) and the stifling sensations that dominate the place
now: "When he was a child this chair was downstairs and he would sock
it to release torrents of swirling motes into the shaft of afternoon sun;
these whirling motes seemed to him worlds, each an earth, with him on
one of them, unthinkably small, unbearably. Some light used to get into
the house in late afternoon, between the maples. Now the same maples
have thronged that light solid, made the room cellar-dim" (95). The grace
that had seemed an ever-basting divinity over the Angstroms has shown
itself to be, as their respective declines have demonstrated, a trick of the
light that Harry and the old neighborhood have both outgrown.

In Updike's contemporary America, Burger Bliss and Pizza Paradise
make cheap novelties out of nirvana; the Pinnacle is a hotel, and what daz-
zles is a "lake of parking space" (113).[27] Meanwhile, Harry drives a Falcon,
but he is clearly grounded, as Janice has long recognized (34). (On the
other hand, she sells Toyotas at her father's lot, yet again "betraying" her
husband as she associates him with outmodedness.) His publishing company, a sinkhole whose torpor no real light can escape (28), is home to
transient flyers, too. The dull fluorescence clings to him like the summer
humidity.

In *Rabbit, Run* God alternately haunted and intoxicated Harry Angstrom. The Lord's habitats ranged from the contested pulpit of Kruppenbach and Eccles to the jump shooter's best moves and the sweet descent
of a golf ball to the center of the green. He was in evidence. In *Rabbit
Redux* God is the nullity that indicts us; He is that "immensely missing"
something in Updike's "Short Easter," an absence ever impinging (102). If
He exists, it is in some impenetrable blackness, which in this novel is
less likely to stand for a pure refuge than for the unplumbable pit of
scummy stench Harry connects with Skeeter, or for something hopelessly
marooned in deep space. "I think God is everything that isn't people,"
Harry tells Peggy, who has bothered to vex him with the question
(110).[28]

According to critic Frederick Crews, this logic parallels the influence of
the religious philosophy of Karl Barth seen throughout Updike's writings.
In Barth's economy, human failings enable us to distinguish Creator and
Creation from one another, consequently inspiring us to embrace the Savior. God is "Wholly Other" from us, and by extension, from our musings,
deeds, and petitions (Crews 8). Seen one way, as divinity school professor

Roger Lambert argues in *Roger's Version,* the universe without God is "crushing to contemplate"; but contemplating God through "those grandiose and prayerful efforts to flay, cleave, and anatomize the divine substance" is crushing, too (17, 22). God's fundamental and irreparable otherness may be a ground rule of our salvation. If we accept Harry Angstrom's theology, it is definitely necessary to His salvation from *our* pale imperfections.[29] "Only by placing God totally on the other side of the humanly understandable can any final safety for Him be secured" (*Roger's Version* 32).

It is a sobering concept, but God fares better here than elsewhere in Rabbit's ruminations over the degraded forms He takes when He slums among us. At best, Rabbit's God is an attendant in a nightgown waiting for us "at the end of a glossy chute" like a slick death canal; at worst, He is a drug hallucination, a disappearance down a whirlpool, or an adversary in some cosmic game of one-on-one looking to exploit His opponent's weaknesses (146, 349). We may compare Jerry's vulgarized equivalences in Edward Albee's *Zoo Story:* "WITH GOD WHO IS A COLORED QUEEN WHO WEARS A KIMONO AND PLUCKS HIS EYEBROWS, WHO IS A WOMAN WHO CRIES WITH DETERMINATION BEHIND HER CLOSED DOOR" (496). In *Rabbit Redux,* worship warps in the direction of the characters' doubts and recriminations. Harry masturbates into the sheets so as not to come toward Him, while Nelson panics at the notion of His coming and prays not to see Him. Faith in the arrival of a supply of mescaline or in sustaining an erection supersedes more sublime considerations. A voyage to the moon may be a more glamorous exploit, but it brings God's loving visage no closer.

In sum, futility has tightened its grasp on the metaphorical preoccupations of *Rabbit, Run.* In a way, all of American society in the 1960s is rabbity, restive—"Everybody now is like the way I used to be," Harry confides to Stavros (182)—and inspired to movements more anxious than an athlete's exhilarant break to daylight. The conviction that "Nothing stands still" (340) is not a testimony to American progress but a capitulation to manifold misfortune. (The line is uttered by Rabbit's superior at Verity, who has informed Rabbit that Linotypers are being phased out.) Nets and webs continue to exact their confinements in *Rabbit Redux,* ranging in subtlety from barricaded streets (91), to the wrinkles around the eyes of Peggy Fosnacht like "a net flung at his head" (108), to the suffocative L-dopa dreams of Harry's mother (194).[30] At the Linotype machine, as in the skies stung by spaceships, "the matrices rattle on high" and operate all the more fiercely as we challenge them (339).

But with the fading of Harry's physical prowess has come a loss of confidence in his capacity to give the world the slip with a quick first step or a good "head fake" to open up some space to make his move (357). He no longer feels the touch that used to live in his hands (255), and being "out of touch," having spent his election, Harry cannot summon the same conviction from his own motion anymore.[31] Conformity and conventional contentments are still stagnant traps, but running now is a joke, or more comparable to the anxiety of running late to school, instead of a sign of liberating verve. As Rabbit corrects Jill, it is not love but fear that "makes us poor bastards run" (170). Even Peggy, who still harbors the fantasy of the flat-bellied athlete who took the court before his inheritance of loose flesh and tragedy, ridicules Harry's decision to run the mile and a half from her bed to his house when he gets the call from Skeeter, and she makes him take her car instead (316). A subsequent joint autopsy with Janice of his affair with Peggy, as we witness in the dimming of antecedents in the following exchange, leads to the conclusion that running neither exalts nor gratifies:

> "But all this fucking, everybody fucking, I don't know, it just makes
> me too sad. It's what makes everything so hard to run."
> "You don't think it's what *makes* things run? Human things."
> "There must be something else."
> She doesn't answer.
> "No? Nothing else?" (397–98)

Mim's summary of her brother's philosophy—"Be crazy to keep free" (358)—could be read as a paraphrase of his strategy or as a remonstrance from the voice of experience.

Early in the novel we learn that Janice now understands something of the relief that running could afford. As opposed to Harry's interstate adventure at the beginning of *Rabbit, Run,* it is she who gives directions as they drive early in the sequel. The Falcon feels like her car now (35).[32] In another reversal of the conditions of the first book, in which Janice presided over the death of an innocent, she "resuscitates" Stavros, thereby demonstrating a kind of compensatory nurture (Updike, interview with Reilly 132). For his part, Rabbit, who is an uninspiring harborer of another girl whose death he cannot prevent, has not as yet shown a similar positive capacity. Nonetheless, Janice's newfound sexual glibness and fluency land her back with her husband.[33]

As for Rabbit himself, bereft of the justifying instincts and the nutritional supplement of likability that buoyed him through *Rabbit, Run,* he dismisses the dropping out he tried to engineer ten years ago now that it has become a commonplace of the counterculture. There are rules of conduct he cannot outrun now. (Interestingly, Harry complains to his mother that in "any decent kind of world" there would be no need for those rules [373], but it is not certain whether that is because everyone would be spontaneously good or because his utopia would be absolutely permissive.) "I once took that inner light trip and all I did was bruise my surroundings," he tells Jill, derogating commitments both to the open road and to spiritual awakening. "Revolution, or whatever, is just a way of saying a mess is fun. Well, it *is* fun, for a while, as long as somebody else has laid in the supplies. A mess is a luxury, is all I mean" (172). America First and Me First are revealed to be equally irresponsible, equally unsustainable. Jingoism is egoism writ large.

The incursion of outer darkness, then, aborts the "inner light trip" and forecloses larger motions. "Sunshine, the old clown, rims the room"—it is a fragile benediction at best, and it is repeated verbatim from *Rabbit, Run* in *Rabbit Redux* (*Rabbit, Run* 206; *Rabbit Redux* 301). The perspectives launched toward and from outer space, adulterous departures, and social revolution, much less the middle-class aspect of Vista Crescent, show no redemption of that light either: "Rabbit finds there is nothing to say, just mute love spinning down, love for this extension of himself down into time when he will be in the grave, love cool as the flame of sunlight burning level among the stick-thin maples and fallen leaves, themselves flames curling. And from Peggy's window Brewer glows and dwindles like ashes in a gigantic hearth" (309). Another blasted vantage, another window giving onto holocaust. Love meekly competes with incineration, makes its silent way down the grave site. In the second novel in the sequence, Rabbit is led back on a tether, as another run winds down. He burrows into mute compromise.

Sitting with Mim in their parents' house near the end of *Rabbit Redux,* Rabbit remembers a childhood dream that the hassock beneath her feet was "full of dollar bills to solve all their problems" (307). That condition seems to have ripened over the next ten years, after which we rejoin the

Angstroms in *Rabbit Is Rich*. If there is any truth in Hazel Motes's conviction in *Wise Blood* that a man does not need to be justified if he has a good car, a man with a profitable car lot—Rabbit is now co-proprietor of Springer Motors—must be one of the Chosen People, especially in view of the fact that Japanese cars (Springer Motors is a Toyota dealership) appear to be the best bet to ride out the economic stupor of the Carter years. In 1979, Rabbit's speculations are as likely to be financial as sexual or philosophical, and an "ample square peace" (*Rabbit Is Rich* 5) sustained by the profit margin is the perceptible, unexpected reward for all the running he has done over the past two novels and twenty years. Prosperous and swollen as a pasha, Rabbit endures "the gut pull of steep maturity" with unprecedented ease (Updike, "Upon the Last Day of His Forty-ninth Year," line 14), thanks to his newfound ability to participate in the enduring structure of American materialism. In place of the hectic atmosphere of its predecessors, there is in *Rabbit Is Rich* a feeling of cozy amplitude and muted repercussions; the caress of wealth provides an agreeably numbing nexus. The "push" of venture capital has supplanted spiritual and athletic adventures (406), and Rabbit has managed to situate himself rather cozily within a class upholstered by country clubs, Caribbean vacations, and *Consumer Reports*. A studied "muchness" reigns (368).

Updike has said that he intends his books to be moral debates examining the question of what goodness is ("One Big Interview" 502). In *Rabbit Is Rich*, as Rabbit confides to a potential customer, virtue is in goods (16). If serenity is a delusion, it is a delusion one can purchase. If one is fortunate enough, if he can marshal enough extravagance, he can hover indefinitely above death: "Lately he no longer ever feels he is late for somewhere, a strange sort of peace at his time of life like a thrown ball at the top of its arc is for a second still" (227). As Big Daddy declares in *Cat on a Hot Tin Roof*, "The human animal is a beast that dies and if he's got money he buys and buys and buys" (403). Amplitude affords everything, it seems, and Rabbit converts his self-approval into swags of gold, silver, and fat. The center of the novel finds him having sex with Janice on a bed strewn with Krugerrands—a harmonic convergence of his desires, favorable balance sheets drawn back over a fresh erogenous zone.[34] Love is love of the fungible. "Nothing like the thought of fucking money," he considers over the sleeping form of his cash cow of a wife (188), much as he cashed in Peggy Fosnacht in *Rabbit Redux*. Rabbit, if one will pardon the expression, has come into his fortune.

But if *Rabbit Is Rich* is a comparatively "happy book," as Updike has maintained, it attests to pleasures stolen from a "flimsy" national context (Updike, interview with Bragg 226). And like the American "sickness" to which President Carter notoriously referred, Rabbit's own middle age is at best an ambivalent arrival, a soulless peace: "When he was fifteen, forty-six would have seemed the end of the rainbow, he'd never get there, if a meaning of life was to show up you'd think it would have by now" (231). Grace as eternal postponement, as a ball in perfect loft, has succumbed to the natural fact that "A certain Sinkingness resides in things" (Updike, *Midpoint* 5.147). This listless sedimentation pervades even the previously protected precinct of the golf course, where "he can't stop seeing the fairways as chutes to nowhere," and "[t]ime seeps up through the blades of grass like a colorless poison" (178). Certainly, his general improvement as a player comes at the expense of those exquisite, miraculous shots that had first inspired him to pursue the game. His handicap shrinks, but the presiding "angel" has departed from the scenes of privileged intervals; and the scuffs, tails, and fades that qualify the flights of his drives make the game seem like work, "a matter of approximations in the world of the imperfect" (179). The hustling supplicant of *Rabbit, Run,* who placed his trust in solid shots and open fairways to the green, feels in *Rabbit Is Rich* the weight of contrivance, which brings back his awareness of "the Sinkingness in things." That verdant elsewhere is the painted veil: "The fairway springy beneath his feet blankets the dead . . . . The earth is hollow, the dead roam through caverns beneath its green skin" (177).

Clearly, his relative prosperity provides precious little insulation from the old fears. Dollars make a sterile heap. As Rabbit tours his new house, plumbing the expensive rummage of successful days at the lot, he confirms that what is bought will also decline: "He roams through his house warily exulting in the cast-iron radiators, the brass window catches, the classy little octagonal bathroom tiles, and the doors with key-lock knobs; these details of what he has bought shine out in the absence of furniture and will soon sink from view as the days here clutter them over. Now they are naked and pristine" (457).[35] One who had placed his faith in unabridged motion through clean, pure space has settled for, and into, a plush crypt, and even that will foreclose.

Ironically, Rabbit's current interest in upgrading rather than escaping his hutch has done nothing to quell his suffocative episodes. For twenty years now his family has been warehousing blame and disappointment in him. The predicament is that he feels, while clamped between his wife and his mother-in-law, at once throttled and exposed: "[T]here isn't a corner of the Springer house where Harry feels able to breathe absolutely his own air, feels the light can get to him easily," yet at the same time he craves a private den, "a room where people would have trouble getting at him" (38, 453). Rabbit still exhibits the casual bigotry refined to habit over the past twenty years, as well as the same misogynist scorn of the women he is drawn to. A familiar circle revealed to be a voracious drain for his seed to drown in—that is how he sees Janice, whose drunken scrabbling below his waist strikes him as vexatious, part of a complicated task in the "fumbly worried dark," which recalls the awkward body docking and dull adhesive impulses at the conclusion of *Rabbit Redux* (52–53). Both are marooned in parallel confusions, isolated needs. (He reads while she engages him; she sleeps when he finally enters her, an unresisting cleft at best.) Nelson takes on this attitude indiscriminately, despite himself, toward his own "dumb slot": "Women. They are holes, you put one thing in after another and it's never enough, you stuff your entire life in there and they smile that crooked little sad smile and are sorry you couldn't have done better, when all is said and done. He's gotten in plenty deep already and she's not getting him in any deeper" (360).[36]

Thus the paradoxical complex of Rabbit's dream house: "Stone outside, exposed beams inside, and a sunken living room" (45). The angst-stream of *Rabbit, Run* is redefined in retrospect: "In a way, he sees now, he grew up in a safe pocket of the world . . . like one of those places you see in a stream where the twigs float backward and accumulate along the mud" (162–63). Thanks to the passage of years, the bolstering of a financial portfolio, and the amassment of family disasters, Rabbit has altered his point of view sufficiently to deem the stagnant secure and inertia safe entrenchment. No wonder Rabbit prefers Pru Lubell, Nelson's pregnant fiancée, to Melanie, the more spontaneous girl with whom Nelson originally returned to Brewer. Whereas Melanie recalls Rabbit's commitment to freedom, Pru and he share the solidarity of recoil: "They agreed about things, basic things. They knew that at bottom the world was brutal" (316).[37]

And this is fundamentally what he and Janice have effected together— a muddled repose, a conspiracy of settling for less. Possessed by the same griefs and disappointments, beset by the same consortium of ghosts (Becky, Jill, Skeeter, and their own youthful expectations), they can even experiment with spouse swapping during a Caribbean vacation because they are confident of one another's station: "He likes it now when she gets all flustered and frowny, her breath hot and somehow narrow with grief; she seems most his then, the keystone of his wealth. Once when she got like this, her fear contaminated him and he ran; but in these middle years it is so clear to him that he will never run that he can laugh at her, his stubborn prize" (455). Faithful in his fashion to Janice, he has reached with her, if not bliss, armistice. From the reflexive swervings of *Rabbit, Run,* to the cautious docking of *Rabbit Redux,* we come to the wriggling adjustments and consensual lethargy of *Rabbit Is Rich.* Nowhere does this progression come through more clearly than in the concluding structural refrain of this third novel in the series, in which Nelson and Pru's baby is deposited in the new grandfather's lap. Nelson has at least temporarily run from responsibility—belatedly, too, in view of Rabbit's silent urging during the wedding ceremony that he take off before the vows, as well as in keeping with his father's private conviction that "Like water blood must run or grow a scum" (46)—while Rabbit considers this "oblong cocooned little visitor" with the "tiny stitchless seam of the closed eyelid" as almost smug in her posture of self-containment. In brief, the baby enjoys the indulgence of others, a condition Rabbit boasted about in *Rabbit, Run* as the reward for having the intrepidness to make people defer to your superior sense of self. At the same time, however, she is "a real presence hardly weighing anything but alive. Fortune's hostage, heart's desire, a granddaughter." Compelling and closed in at once, she is the possession that, like all possessions, enslaves: "His. Another nail in his coffin. His" (467). He, too, is Fortune's hostage, his affluence sometimes a guarantee of contented laze, sometimes the basic component of his feeling "too fuddled to move" (157). The coffin-under-construction is the logical extreme of Rabbit's battened-down hutch.

This image is the last of several reminders of death that punctuate the novel. For all of his material gains, Rabbit's "ample square peace" delivers onto a wasteland, its occasional open spaces seen as the blighted wake of extravagant bad news both home and abroad. While Rabbit appreciates the dead for their commodiousness and generosity in terms of moving aside, the room they lease is one they continue to pry into like juridical gods (5, 462). In *Rabbit, Run,* running was running out on others; now, things—dreams, gas, America—are running out. While Rabbit has not yet been "caught" because of his fortuitous connection to Toyotas, their better mileage is just a momentary stay against entropy.[38] What is more, Rabbit's position at Springer Motors came to him as a result of the death of Janice's father, who managed to rally sufficiently only to have a coronary! In other words, Rabbit's opening—his lot, as it were—is cast by death: "The great thing about the dead, they make space" (5).[39] Basically, Rabbit's ennui parallels the world's wearing down, the discontented residue of reckless getting and spending. Mortality presses in, decertifies the depleted spirit. The whole country suffers from burnout that grounds all flights: "The Chuck Wagon too seems quiet today. Beyond its lot littered with flattened take-out cartons a lone tree, a dusty maple, drinks from a stream that has become a mere ditch. Beneath its branches a picnic table rots unused, too close to the overflowing dumpster the restaurant keeps by its kitchen door. The ditch marks the bound of a piece of farmland sold off but still awaiting its development. This shapely old maple from its distance seems always to be making to Harry an appeal he must ignore" (7). Ecstatic flashes dim to artifice. The times call for the awful daring of a Fisher King, perhaps, but the pastoral is "touched by wilt" (243), and "the ditch marks the bound" of the contemporary pioneer. Rabbit's yellowing credentials, the old newspaper clippings about his high school basketball exploits, like bank accounts that cannot keep up with inflation or the waning of longings and capacities, confirm the deathward stretch of everything. "Everywhere in this city . . . structures speak of expended energy. . . . These acres of dead railroad track and car shops and stockpiled wheels and empty boxcars stick in the heart of the city like a great rusting dagger" (32–33).

Twenty years ago, Rabbit had taken Ruth into the sparkling heart of the city, whose massive neon advertisements for Sunflower Beer provided a bit of gaudy bounce to his "bounder's" progress, until they were stopped by the sound of a monotone bell, railroad crossing gates like a guillotine, and the sludge of traffic (*Rabbit, Run* 71). The same scene today contains none of those comical signs: "[N]ow only the Brewer Trust's beacons trained on its own granite facade mark the center of the downtown, four great pillars like four white fingers stuck in a rich black pie, the dark patch made by the planted trees of the so-called shopping mall." A web of lamplight, trawling in the shallows for the few errant pedestrians who might be haunting the "deadened heart of the city," reaches until its "glow flattens to a horizon swallowed by hills that merge with the clouds of night" (*Rabbit Is Rich* 321). The noumenal is further skewed, more deeply secluded, in *Rabbit Is Rich*.

Rabbit looks at his distracted son, and his disdain is tempered by pity because the boy faces "a worn-out world to find his way in" (227). Why does this obstinate boy refuse America's license and Nature's imperative to keep moving? It turns out that a dying system, as well as the faith that had fostered it, has long been cannibalizing itself. Oil, electricity, industry, ingenuity—everyday use uses things up. America, flagship of the century, is "going down with all her lights blazing" (302). Furthermore, the national energy crisis also appears in the home as a heritage of squandering like some genetic disorder. In human nature, too, as witnessed through its standard sacraments of marriage and family, life wakens to smother, and every flower contains its fading (28, 47). For Rabbit, each frisk—sexual fillip or fairway shot—is tinged with irrelevance, and so despair.

"Carter is smart as a whip and prays a great deal but his gift seems to be the old Eisenhower one of keeping much from happening, just a little daily seepage" (127). If Rabbit runs in this novel, he hurries over a delicate, precious "membrane removed from the hosts below" (141–42) to keep from falling through, to resist a little longer the ceaseless pull of the grave. *Rabbit Is Rich* features no spectacular fatalities on the order of those seen in *Rabbit, Run* and *Rabbit Redux*; instead, there is this slow but persistent leak, "a little daily seepage," the undertow of quiet desperation.[40]

Death beckons—"The land under Rabbit seems to move, with the addition of yet another citizen to the subterrain of the dead" (111); "the dead reach up, they catch at his heels" (225)—but death is leavened by glimpses of connection and legacy. Nelson's coiled moodiness, his hapless cruising for damage (he smashes up no fewer than three Springer cars during the course of the novel), his free-floating viciousness and vulgarity, and his inclination toward recoil constitute one persistently accusing aspect of that continuity—the vengeful satisfaction of failing right in his father's face, the sapped features of "a big dead man on Nelson's chest" (314). Meanwhile, Rabbit's obsessional pursuit of the girl he suspects may be his daughter with Ruth is another take on continuity, which, although Ruth confirms that she did indeed have the abortion, still revives the prospect that family may be a source of transcendence rather than an obstacle to it.[41] So while the Angstroms are captive to one another's witnessing of the calamitous family record, at least they possess the occasional sense of "the camaraderie of survivors" to cling to: "The voices come from the sunporch. These voices lessen Harry's gravity, seem to refute the world's rumors of universal death" (73).

The way that death trumps our evasions, of course, is by contaminating the very biological strategies we employ against it: having children, we propagate futures only to give our ghosts extended tenancy. Buried intimates join the primordial elements but never forsake our consciousness for long. Hence the swallows that skirt the television aerials scraping their middle range above Brewer are more imperiled than Wallace Stevens's swallows at the close of *Sunday Morning* (*Rabbit Is Rich* 46), and they have not as yet found a glide path to inspire a similarly benedictory descent.[42]

It is at once a miracle and a curse "how things grow, always remembering to be themselves" (86), in that resilience and disorder alike evolve into fixed appointments, providing a fold yet anticipating transgressive tendencies. The metaphorical project of the Rabbit books persists as well, but in the manner of a deceleration, as down the decades their hero careens further and further from the twin sanctifications of freedom and physical prowess. For example, Rabbit still resists being "crowded up," a reflex he now realizes to be a family trait variously practiced by Mim and Nelson—the latter, like his father, being "too twitchy" to stick to selling cars (129).[43] Rabbit still runs, but he seldom enjoys the euphoric release of motion anymore; instead, because he jogs to improve his health, running is now fraught with consciousness. His father's having been "taken off by his heart" (144) refers to a health risk, not to a romantic departure. A further mortification, given his priorities, is that Janice has become a rather graceful tennis player at the country club, while the one-time jock lumbers through the game.

Supplanting the image of the ecstatic athlete is that of the tardy child hurrying home to get his punishment over with, or, as Updike puts it in one of the short stories, of "an animal caught in a gunsight" ("A Sandstone Farmhouse" 129). The radius of his escape, too, has shrunk to a couple of blocks at most. As Rabbit extends his jogging, he reaches "the waist of the hourglass" of his private course, symbolically giving out where the terrain is most constricted by time's passage and characterized by "dwindled descendants, the swimming pool drained, the tennis courts overgrown, energy gone" (140). In a summer of "captive moths beating their wings to a frazzle on the screens," the furious buzz of an unseen car escaping into the distance is a vicarious pleasure and a representative scourge (80, 318).

Rabbit surveys the rutted countenance of Brewer, as well as the chafed complaints of his son, the woeful geography major who cannot stand how he has grown to fit his father's tragic mold, and prays for both of them against being boxed in. But as for that, of course, Rabbit's adventures have stopped at jobs his father-in-law has gotten him. He understands that running confirms rather than attenuates his indenture. "The world seems indestructible and won't let you out"; and these days, when running out is running down, there seems to be "less reason than ever to move" (35, 38): "He sees his life as just beginning, on clear ground at last, now that he has a margin of resources, and the stifled terror that always made him restless has dulled down. He wants less. Freedom, that he always thought was outward motion, turns out to be this inner dwindling" (97).

"This inner dwindling" is clearly proportional to the "stony truce" that currently prevails between Rabbit and God (140). Shards of faith still present themselves to him, usually as memories of buoyant episodes on the court, whose showboating lifted no one but himself and only temporarily (255), or in occasionally revived commitments to the natural purity "woven into him at birth" (138). Regardless, his suspicion of the "invisible" has generally increased. "Every time in his life he has made a move toward it somebody has gotten killed" (162), and the conviction that everyone needs a little religion to keep from "sinking" makes for an unreliable counterweight to the heft of bullion or the novel's frank sexual presences (198), not to mention the "gut pull" of time and the inherent "sinkingness" in things. When he thinks of "those pieces of bread in the miracle," it is in association with sensations of fragmentation, chaos, and the irrecoverable; they have little to do with the satisfactions of largesse or humble plenitude (189). And if Jack Eccles was at worst an earnest but unprepossessing wasp, their current clergyman is, well, "Soupy."

In other words, Rabbit still has a talent for, or suffers the stigma of, detachment, for not being answerable to the conventional. More to the point, instead of recognizing the ways in which deflective strategies reduce spirituality to ceremony, he actually equates them with religious practice (202). It is a position encapsulated in the story "Trust Me": "[T]he space of indifference is where we breathe" (7). Cynicism fortifies the shield that had once been constituted by beatific shimmer alone, as seen in the Angstrom bedroom, where angels now grapple obscurely in the flawed glass: "Ten years of habitancy, in the minutes or hours between when the bedside lamps are extinguished and sleep is achieved, have borne these luminous rectangles into Harry brain as precious entities, diffuse jewels pressed from the air, presences whose company he will miss if he leaves this room. He must leave it. Intermixed with the abstract patterns the imperfect panes project are the unquiet shadows of the beech branches as they shudder and sway in the cold outside" (352). Would that these gem-like presences were unalloyed by woeful shadows; would that they were so "dense" as those family presences he daily endures! Here the sun discovers the lair of forbidding shadows. Later, in the Springer Motors showroom, the sun slants along the plate glass and turns the dust to gold, an optical illusion because "the arc of each day is so low" (378).

The word "obey" is left out of Nelson and Pru's vows because it is out of fashion. Faith is a fool's game, and, by Rabbit's reckoning, the world has even the Pope on the run like the wayward rest of us (293). God is in sporadic evidence, but He rises and falls in Rabbit's imagination with the salesman's level of inebriation or the vicissitudes of the market. (Rabbit prefers the purr of his Toyota to "Savior, Keep a Watch Over Me" playing on the car radio, finding greater redemptive authority in his Supra than in the rumored Supreme Being [436].) Perhaps God is only the most eminent of the dead, alternately crowding him up with conscience or generously making way for his aspirations; perhaps "God is in the universe the way salt is in the ocean, giving it a taste," yet quenching no thirst (462–63). When Rabbit was young, God was a ball at the top of an unbroken parabola, a weightless curtain hovering like some cosmic athlete over our harried mundanities, until "He entered into the blood and muscle and nerve as an odd command and now He had withdrawn, giving Harry the respect due from one well-off gentleman to another, but for a calling card left in the pit of the stomach, a bit of lead true as a plumb bob pulling Harry down toward all those leaden dead in the hollow earth below" (231). The description of God as a compatible business associate darkens, indicts. "We're not God," Janice says to Rabbit, encouraging his aid in shaping some sort of forgiveness for the two of them. "Nobody is," he replies, scaring himself with the height of the bar he believes not even God can clear anymore (312).

With God banished alternately to flippancy or to negligence, His prior manifestations in the novel sequence summon less and less inspiration. Space, for example, is not a precipitous expanse but rather the vacancy the dead leave upon departure. Rabbit longs for the "good solid space they were lost in" in the 1960s, as opposed to the "soupy psychedelic space they have on TV now" (181), as though being lost amidst the vaulted, vaunted dark were preferable to being rooted to shabby suburban certainties.[44] (Now people get "spaced" on alcohol and marijuana.) Absent God, the heavens reflect the black "vacuum of the heart," where "love falls forever" (271), and whose defining extremity Rabbit enters during anal sex: a sensationless "casket of perfect nothingness" (417). Since the time of *Rabbit Redux*, the dusty moon barely looms at all, while the stars, so central to Rabbit's sense of efficacy in *Rabbit, Run,* provide no place to get a grip on (226).[44] At least occasionally while surveying Springer Motors, Rabbit can picture himself as "the star and spearpoint of all these two dozen employees and hundred thousand square feet of working space" (4), and thereby view that star's center as the center of what matters instead of the cipher at the core . . . that is, until he considers how Charlie Stavros is really the better salesman, or how he himself is ascendant thanks only to nepotism. Even during his Caribbean vacation, Rabbit is spooked by the stern firmament, with its stars "that hang in the sky with a certain menace, fragments of a frozen explosion," or that "hang unbudging in their sockets" (395, 409).

The grave gapes; the indifferent sky pushes down. To Ruth, to whom Rabbit comes for the consolation of regenerative possibility, he was "Mr. Death"; to Nelson, to whom he would give counsel about treading lightly over a world determined to take you down with it, he is a shameful sellout and accomplice to the deaths of Jill and Skeeter. In *Rabbit Is Rich*, he contends for Stevens's title of "King of the Ghosts." With each ten-year reunion, Rabbit's ruinous descent into middle age picks up speed.

"There is no reconciliation between the inner, intimate appetites and the external consolations of life," Updike explains. *Rabbit, Run* "is a novel about the bouncing, the oscillating back and forth between these two kinds of urgencies until, eventually, one just gets tired and wears out and dies, and that's the end of the problem" (quoted in "John Updike" 92). Pascal's tripartite involvements—"the motions of Grace, the hardness of the heart; external circumstances"—threaten to overwhelm their single housing with their competing stresses. By the time of the fourth and final entry in the sequence, Rabbit is pushing sixty and soured on the whole edgy business of whittling desire down to the size of diminishing options. As Updike puts it, fiction is designed to provide characters a space "where they can find the freedom to fulfill their tendencies," a formula which has as much to do with determinism and inexorability as with freedom. Regarding *Rabbit at*

Rest, the author explains, "I wanted . . . while plausibly portraying a spec-
imen American male's evolution into grandpaternity, frailty, lassitude,
sensations of dispensability, and even inklings of selflessness, to allow the
thematic tendencies, conscious or unconscious, of the three other novels
to run to their destination, to wind up" ("Special Message" 872). For thirty
years Rabbit's thoughts have been snagging on the same salvage. There is
a wound-down quality to *Rabbit at Rest,* a sense of the nets being drawn
in at the end of the venture, and, as Updike's assessment implies, a final
accounting for the constitutive images of Rabbit Angstrom.

In *Rabbit Redux,* Janice followed Rabbit's adulterous example from
Rabbit, Run; in *Rabbit at Rest,* by virtue of her sole inheritance of Springer
Motors, she has assumed the mantle of financial status her husband had
pretended to in *Rabbit Is Rich.* While Rabbit is bloated on junk food and
wide-ranging reproaches, Janice "has been building up an irritating confidence"; while her husband has become increasingly aimless and indolent,
she is working toward the successful completion of her real estate license
in *Rabbit at Rest,* and her "body's elastic health" contrasts with his jammed
arteries and bunched, bundled heart (113, 156). The routine integrations
of their marriage, the repellent shells they have grown and which have
enabled them to accommodate their mutual abuses, create a tie that Rabbit suspects may be religious, for "it made so little other sense" (204). She
is still his dope of a wife, that dumb slot down which his options dropped
so many years ago, yet "he admires her as you admire children you've
raised, whose very success pulls them away, into the world's workings, into
distance and estrangement" (280). For her part, Janice unaccountably
finds corners where traces of the old intangibles she loved reside, yet she
realizes that she has been preparing for widowhood with unaccustomed
equanimity in face of Rabbit's deteriorating health (309). In a sense,
Rabbit's frailty is both a hold on her and another profanation of the gifts
he had risen with as a teenager. "We are each of us like our little blue
planet, hung in black space, upheld by nothing but our mutual reassurances, our loving lies," Rabbit thinks (264); and the sporadic lusts and lacerations they trade are in the end equivalent efforts to bridge the essential
distances between them. We may remember in this regard Updike's beleaguered Maples, whose "conversations, increasingly ambivalent and ruthless as accusation, retraction, blow, and caress alternated and cancelled,
had the final effect of knitting them together in a painful, helpless,
degrading intimacy" ("Twin Beds in Rome" 76).

We could argue that Rabbit's heart is itself a principal character in *Rabbit at Rest*. A longtime adversary that refuses to fall for his feints and crossover dribbles, his heart is now the internalized version of his having felt "crowded up" all his life. We may ruefully recall William Butler Yeats's conception of "All that man is, / All mere complexities, / The fury and the mire of human veins" ("Byzantium," lines 6–8) as a fitting diagnosis of our hero's predicament. Rabbit suffers two heart attacks during the novel—the first while trying to rescue his granddaughter when their boat capsizes, the second while gasping his way through an ill-advised game of one-on-one that completes the frame begun in the opening pages of *Rabbit, Run* when he joins a group of kids on the court to prove that his touch had never really left him. That heart that used to "float" now just seems part of the weight he lugs about. All motion is exertion now, everything an ordeal marbled by fat and exasperation. The cruel medical procedures he suffers, obscenely splayed on overhead monitors as though laying bare not just his heart's clogs but the crabbed and spiteful contents themselves, berate him with the fact of mortality. He flinches from "a twitching pale-gray ghost dimly webbed by its chambered structure and darkened in snaky streaks and bulbous oblongs by injections of the opacifying dye" (273), amazed somehow that a regimen of self-approval, sexual reverie, and viciousness have done nothing to stave off its ossification.

"Get interested in something outside yourself," his cardiologist advises, "and your heart will stop talking to you" (476). But it is late in the game for him to cultivate anything of the sort. Staggered by each new jab of recognition of himself in his son, Rabbit cannot speak to Nelson except to upbraid him for his studied bitterness, drug addiction, and fantastic debts. He abominates Nelson for his relentless reflection of him, so that the kid is another weight on his chest (178). (In *Rabbit Is Rich*, we recall, Nelson felt that those positions were reversed, with his father "a big dead man" on *his* chest [314].) His grandchildren show flashes of the energetic quality of Angstrom, but they challenge Rabbit's patience and, in the spectacular case of the near-drowning of his granddaughter (with its horrifying reminder of the death of baby Rebecca), inspire further withdrawal.[45] He actually has a one-time liaison with his daughter-in-law, Pru, when Nelson's vileness and negligence have left her heedless and hating herself; but her owning up to it reveals that episode to have been another trap, and Rabbit is still not mature enough to act responsibly. (He takes off from Pennsylvania for the Florida condominium he and Janice winter in and, in doing so, completes the blown getaway from *Rabbit, Run.*) As for past companions and forsaken lovers, they have one by one been forgotten or, dying, submitted to minerals, reminding Rabbit, as surely as the televised evidence in the hospital did, of "Mr. Death's" own appointment. "The deaths of others carry us off bit by bit," we read in "Deaths of Distant Friends," but strangely there is a mercy in this, in that "Witnesses to my disgrace are being removed" (89).

The meditative and physical preoccupations of the first three Rabbit novels, in addition to the verbal structures on which they depended, are also rather fruitless pursuits these days. To take a line out of another of Updike's stories, "Actuality is a running impoverishment of possibility" as the series winds down ("Bulgarian Poetess" 230). For instance, Rabbit still has that ubiquitous sexual itch, but Janice is stingy about "rewarding" him (typically reserving it for his demonstrating docile conduct in face of bad news), while his single transgression with Pru leads to an operatic confession that spooks him so that he gets all the way down to Florida this time before looking back to see if anyone is following. "How disgusting we are—disposable meat," he thinks as he considers a display of explicit magazines (18)—this from a man who once suspected that godhead and maidenhead might be duplicate aspirations!

When Rabbit golfs these days, it is at Valhalla Village, whose very name, unlike the rousing promise of Flying Eagle, suggests a home for dead gods. Here he struggles to revive the magic of "perfect weightlessness and consummate ease," which he has always associated with athletic success but which a combination of self-consciousness about his play, chest pains, and the joking remonstrances of his playing partners, whom he believes he should be beating regularly, has confiscated. The holy satisfaction of "That's it!" from his initial round with Eccles in *Rabbit, Run* has been diluted into the defeated nostalgia of "That would be *it*," as he sullies one shot after another (56–7). In fact, even his good holes are cheapened for him, a man who could once count on the world's melting before his capricious whistle, by the awareness that the Florida courses have been tailored "for the elderly and lame. They baby you down here" (59). He remembers having told Eccles ("a prying clergyman," as he currently recalls him) that somewhere there was something that wants him to find it. "Whatever it is, *it* has found *him*, and is working him over" (136). That treacherous pronoun surfaces once again during a discussion with Judy, his granddaughter. "Don't force it. Let nature do its work," Rabbit advises her in the matter of her frustration with adolescence (496). This reads like solid advice for a golfer as well, but Rabbit, for all of his efforts to prolong his adolescence indefinitely, realizes that he is at an impasse: his game will never get any better, and "Let nature do its work" has less to do with how to recapture an unerring touch than with surrender to mortality, the last, smooth, natural uncoiling.

The study of history, or at least musing about history, is a relatively recent hobby for Rabbit, but that procession of the dead hardly compensates for the "vast colorful jostling bristling parade" of life in which he feels himself falling further and further behind (115). Not surprisingly, it offers little psychological gratification: "It has always vaguely interested him, that sinister mulch of facts our little lives grow out of before joining the mulch themselves, the fragile brown rotting layers of previous deaths, layers that if deep enough and squeezed hard enough make coal as in Pennsylvania" (44). AIDS, economic woes, congestive foreign entanglements—history has a wicked memory, holding the race accountable for its profligate conduct just as Rabbit is made to answer now for actions whose consequences he was at one time able to ignore. History is not just the record of Rabbit's scandalous behavior and faded promise, it is Time's growing equity against us, the spreading slag heap that America has to drag toward the next millennium. "Though the stars recycle themselves and remake all the heavy atoms creation needs, Harry will never be that person again, that boy with that girl" (437). What could be more ironic than Harry Angstrom marching in an Independence Day parade as an Uncle Sam patched together with adhesive tape, stubborn bunting, Nitrostat, and hedged resolve? Indeed, he cannot shake his sense of humiliation or obsolescence, or figure out where he is going, or put aside the feeling that history is a chronicle of losing propositions for the country just as it has been for him. In the estimation of one critic, "Harry is contesting versions of history and Emersonian individualism, one which asserts, with Pink Floyd, that he is just another brick in the wall, whereas the other tries to hold onto a sense of the centrality and 'infinitude' of the individual, a position which reduces history to a parable of the ever 'becoming' infinitude" (Wilson 22). History fails him on two counts: as a legitimating arena for self-reliant action and as a fortifying communal identity.

A woman's arms, a richly appointed den, a jingoistic reverie—how long before the world's inimical forces root him out of those burrows? "Hey

man, you're history!" a boy taunts him when Rabbit tries to compete in a
shoot-around he happens upon near the end of the novel (491). Like his
antiquated set shot, Rabbit has lived long enough to witness his irrelevance (the newspaper accounts of his basketball exploits, which used to
adorn Springer Motors openly, are now curling in his private office), and
there is little left for him to do but go under, join the mulch.

As for God, whose ambiguous stirring slurs the stars but leaves no legible sign in the sky, He seems to have diminished in Rabbit's imagination
into one more sort of occupational therapy. "When God hadn't a friend in
the world, back there in the Sixties," Rabbit thinks during his drive to
Florida, "he couldn't let go of Him, and now when the preachers are all
praying through bullhorns he can't get it up for Him" (450). On the radio
the evangelists mingle with the oldies music as slight, compatible claims
on his attention. At the beginning of *Rabbit at Rest*, Rabbit overhears
someone shouting to his sluggish wife at the airport, "Come *on*, Grace!"
(6), and the pun is telling: Rabbit has developed a real petulance about the
recalcitrance of Grace; especially in his later life, it keeps getting lost in
the crowd. Worse, the elusive "it" that used to propel him to athletic transcendence typically alludes in *Rabbit at Rest* to death alone. The "pressing
essence" he senses inside his chest is no longer something blessed working its way in but something pushing out, threatening to burst the heart
that essence should strengthen (7).

God's stubborn otherness plagues him. Instead of the cosmic caddy
who watches over his handicap, He is that which did not pull the bathtub
plug to save Rabbit's baby nor "delete from the universe whatever it was
that exploded that Pan Am 747 over Scotland" (10). The visionary gleam
has fled, "and the things he looks at all seem tired; he's seen them too
many times before. A kind of drought has settled over the world, a bleach-
ing such as overtakes old color prints, even the ones kept in a drawer"
(56). It appears that neither God's creation nor Rabbit's scoring records
resist eclipse, as "even the sky, where your eyes can usually find relief, is
dirtied by jet trails that spread and wander until they are indistinguishable
from God's pure clouds" (66–67). Rabbit's golden vistas lie behind him. A
fruitless beauty estranges, reducing Rabbit to a Prufrockian murk and the
status of those meddling Brewer ghosts:

> And up top where there is most light the leaves are beginning
> to unfold, shiny and small and heart-shaped, as he knows because

he is moved enough to pull the Celica to the curb and park and get out and pull off a single leaf to study, as if it will be a clue to all this glory. Along the sidewalk in this radiant long grove shadowy people push baby carriages and stand conversing by their steps as if oblivious of the beauty suspended above them, enclosing them, already shedding a confetti of petals: they are in Heaven. He wants to ask one of them the name of these trees, and how they came to be planted here in these hard brick blocks of Brewer, luxuriant as the ficus trees that line the avenues of Naples down in Florida, but feels shy in their gaze toward him, himself a shadow in this filtered tunnel light of blossoms, a visitor, an intruder from the past, and figures they would not know anyway, or if they did know would think him too strange for asking. (187–88)

It is hell to be a creature under these circumstances, betrayed by genetic instructions and atomic decay. That "sinkingness" in things infiltrates us and adds to the "great heaviness of being" (76). No wonder Rabbit has affection for President Reagan, who seemed to float above the facts that drive Rabbit and the rest of us earthward. Like God Himself, Reagan displayed that "dream distance," which demonstrated the outward look, if not the genuine substance, of transcendence (62, 295).[46]

Having pretended for so long that his dissatisfactions denote a personal discipline, Rabbit has tried to encourage God to descend favorably as though urging an errant ball to curve back toward the fairway. Gently mocked by his doctor because he shudders at the notion of having his blood run through a machine, Rabbit silently responds to his remonstrance—"What else do you think you are, champ?"—that he is a warranted essence exceeding the images of worn valves and blockages: "A God-made one-of-a-kind with an immortal soul breathed in. A vehicle of grace. A battlefield of good and evil. An apprentice angel" (237). How can bulbous ruins and sluices account for all he is in his own estimation, not to mention God's observance? But such assertions pale before the stark on-screen evidence. "How could the flame of him ever have ignited out of such wet straw?" (270). So when Rabbit looks skyward, it is to confront, in a phrase from "A Sandstone Farmhouse," a "heavy heedless dynamism" (118)—not a sheltering certainty but an indifferent seal.[47]

Nor can the steadfast devotion of Thelma Harrison inspire piety in her agnostic lover, for her faith is primarily a desire for faith, one that she contrives to ease, if not fully justify, the lethal grip of her lupus: "She has kept her strongest feelings contained, and the affair has enriched her transactions with God, giving her something to feel sinful about, to discuss with Him. It seems to explain her lupus, if she's an adulteress. It makes it easier on Him, if she deserves to be punished" (195).[48] The spiritual dilemma Rabbit confronts is that without God's insinuation we are nothing but garbage, but "no old wispy Biblical God would dare interfere" with the sad trash of the human body, much less the redoubtable heap of the material world (344, 272).[49]

As we would expect, celestial images in the closing novel of the Rabbit series parallel the steady erosion of the hero's spiritual confidence. The news event that precipitates this tragic connection is the bombing of Pan Am Flight 103 over Lockerbie, Scotland. Rabbit comes to imagine the scene frequently and in ghastly detail: "a roar and giant ripping noise and scattered screams this whole crazy world dropping away and nothing under you but black space and your chest squeezed by the terrible unbreathable cold, that cold you can scarcely believe is there but that you sometimes actually feel still packed into the suitcases, stored in the unpressurized hold, when you unpack your clothes, the dirty underwear and beach towels with the merciless chill of death from outer space still in them" (9). The unpressurized hold of the doomed plane serves as a kind of mirror image of the excessively pressurized hold of Rabbit's own chest— an outer representation and validation of inner anxieties.

As Rabbit awaits the landing of the plane that carries Nelson and his family, it closes in like a star stripped of beneficence; rather, its bright flash suggests the verge of an explosion. As we can see, not only has space lost whatever frontier charisma it may have gathered in *Rabbit Redux*, the stars likewise have lost any optimistic symbolism. They are ridiculed by mundane allusions, like the maroon Ford Galaxy he tries to avoid rubbing fenders with in the airport parking lot, in which a good space is not a locus of freedom but a snug port for his car (22); or they represent an invidious assault or mad spatter, the galactic void pressing down upon the presumptive bastion of Florida retirees the Angstroms annually seek out: "In this gap of unillumination, the stars leap down at them out of the black warm sky. . . . Harry, Roy's breath moist on his neck and the child's head heavy as a stone on his shoulder, looks up at the teeming sky and thinks, *There is no mercy*" (84–85). Stars apathetically verify our evanescence; the passengers on Flight 103 must have gone down with that last awareness.

As his heart labors to regain composure, Rabbit understands that we are all of us planes ready to detonate at any time (493). Whenever he considers how his light is spent, Rabbit quickly considers how *all* light is spent, and the interplanetary scope of indifference and disposability is devastating.

Physical infirmity, coupled with habitual discouragement, makes Rabbit wary of former intensities. Apart from his fatal last dash south, Rabbit is by and large content to let his mind wander and to relegate himself to "internal roaming" (356). Certainly the "inner light trip" that he came to denounce in *Rabbit Redux* provokes even more cynicism in middle age: "'Driving is boring,' Rabbit pontificates, 'but it's what we do. Most of American life is driving somewhere and then driving back wondering why the hell you went'" (29). Shaking the organizational structure strikes him as intolerable. Freedom induces motion sickness. Accordingly, the image of the road map as the constricting net that so defeated him in his original escape attempt early in *Rabbit, Run* is significantly reinterpreted when the frame is completed in *Rabbit at Rest*: "Lost in the net of thread-lines on the map, he sleeps as in his mother's womb, another temporary haven" (457). And yet, the completion of his trip to Florida does not stave off the threat of so many immensities. Like the Toyota customers he seduces into the dream of the open road, Rabbit learns there is still no way to get out, nowhere really to get to.

In view of this revision, space is space between. It does not encourage our growth but instead coaxes us toward a plummeting fall. Our blind intersections are all collision sites, and we are the "little blue planets" that clack and break apart into separate densities. And again, if outer space offers the purity of infinite emptiness, inner space defines purity as infinite contraction, as Rabbit so often feels that "the space inside him has compressed, so that as he hangs there he must force down thin wedges of breath into a painful congestion" (133). Rather than cancel one another out, claustrophobia and agoraphobia actually increase one another's terrifying impact.

It is useful to test the ultimate treatment of the firmament in the Rabbit tetralogy against alternative appraisals of the idea in three of Updike's stories. In "Harv Is Plowing Now," we read the following striking confession: "Something distant is attracting me. I look up, and the stars in their near clarity press upon my face, bear in upon my guilt and shame with the strange, liquidly strong certainty that, humanly considered, the universe is

perfectly transparent: we exist as flaws in ancient glass. And in appre-
hending this transparence my mind enters a sudden freedom, like insanity; the stars seem to me a roof, the roof of days from which we fall each
night and survive, a miracle. I await resurrection" (182). The passage is
rife with contradictory notions: the stars attract, yet they expose guilt
and shame; their effect is first termed "near clarity," then is upgraded to
"certainty"—a certainty somehow "liquidly strong," tough yet flexible (as
opposed to the seeming implacability of the stars that force themselves
down upon Rabbit in *Rabbit at Rest*). We are flaws that disrupt the perfect transparency of the universe, yet we help to establish that perfection
by virtue of our perceptions, which are somehow, magically, endowed with
that same transparency—a liberating sophistry that may be due to insanity instead of strong certainty. Most important, the protective canopy may
not forestall our fall, but the fortunate fall it occasions is always miraculously cushioned. What excites faith in resurrection—it suggests an elas-
ticity that Rabbit's disease has robbed him of—may be this very capacity
to accommodate opposites like certainty and uncertainty, control and
surrender, "sudden freedom" and God's sheltering presence—His unpredictable, predicating "touch."

"Geoffrey Parrish, approaching sixty, had long enjoyed an uneasy relationship with the stars," begins the short story "Conjunction" (46). Parrish
apparently shares a form of Rabbit's cosmic discomfort when he views
their "seethe of activity that went on without him, all night" and whose
dimensions, "senselessly large and distant and numerous," reduce him to
stupor (47). But here, too, as a man approaches a speculative brink in his
life *about* his life, he locates (with the aid of a telescope) "a small comfortable space in the spangled void where his gaze could rest" (52). As in
"Harv Is Plowing Now," there may not be a harmonious resolution between massive constellations and mired consciousness, but a compensatory suspension is reached.

Such a progressive resacralization of the heavens also characterizes
Updike's "The Astronomer." The story opens with an image of impending
destruction comparable to those that burden the opening of *Rabbit Is
Rich*, as our narrator peers over the Hudson: "The river would become
black before the sky, and the little Jersey towns on the far bank would be
pinched between two massive tongs of darkness until only a row of sparks
remained. These embers were reflected in black water, and when a boat
went dragging its wake up the river the reflections would tremble, double,

fragment, and not until long after the shadow of the boat passed reconstruct themselves" ("The Astronomer" 180). Soon afterward, he and his wife host a dinner for the visiting astronomer. They are seated near the window, "from which the Hudson appeared a massive rent opened in a tenuous web of light" (182). By the end of the story, however, simple human communion helps to create a dissenting, albeit modest, image, as "the ashtrays and the ashes were hastily swept together into a little heap of warm dark tones distinct from the universal debris" (186). "Universal debris" is not refuted, but a more charitable conception of the human condition and of our galactic station concludes the story: "In memory, perhaps because we lived on the sixth floor, this scene—this invisible scene— seems to take place at a great height, as if we were the residents of a star suspended against the darkness of the city and the river. What is the past, after all, but a vast sheet of darkness in which a few moments, pricked apparently at random, shine?" (186) We may recall Saul Bellow's Herzog, who, flying to Chicago to see his daughter, thought our local star to be "the spot that inoculated us against the whole of disintegrating space" (*Herzog* 241). Imagination can effect a more hopeful focus, a momentary metaphorical release.

Returning to *Rabbit at Rest*, we are regularly met with less forgiving phrases. Rabbit keeps running hard up against a terminus; his horizon haunts through the gloom, boxed and confounding. In contrast to the stories just examined, *Rabbit at Rest* serves more as a consolidation of the crises, personalities, and thematic obsessions of the three previous novels, not as a breaking out of the captivity they suggest. Meanwhile, almost all of the characters to whom we had been introduced in the series either make cameo appearances in *Rabbit at Rest*, even including a brief, serendipitous walk-on by Ruth's (and, it remains undetermined, Rabbit's) daughter, who is a nurse who attends to Rabbit at the hospital after his first attack; or they are recollected with their destinies extrapolated on by the principals. This is in keeping with the recursion of specific figures and symbolic predilections throughout the tetralogy, the point being that if no one is ever really lost to consciousness, no significant verbal rendering proves echoless either.

Preeminent are eloquent presentiments of death, which eloquence does nothing to mitigate. These begin on the opening page of *Rabbit at Rest*, when Rabbit realizes that it is not so much his son's family he is waiting to land but "something more ominously and intimately his: his own

death, shaped vaguely like an airplane" (3). We track it through literally
scores of references to the absurd expenditure of our meager ration of
zestfulness and the world's limited resources; through the unredemptive
materiality of the body and its fetid betrayal of our impulses, as impres-
sively portrayed not only in the descriptions of Rabbit's fishy viscera but
also in the extended comparison of their bedeviled fleshes by Rabbit and
Thelma during their last lovers' "rendezvous"; and through the "chutes to
nowhere" variously exposed as hopeless roads, fairways hiding rough,
blocked arteries, grave sites. Deleon, Florida, promises rejuvenation in its
name, but it is really the contemporary end of the line for the process of
human wreckage. The whole state strikes Rabbit as cautious and brittle
(70), its landscape featuring a sort of institutionalized condescension toward the crippled, the elderly, and the otherwise forgettable. Deleon is a
way station where ghosts-in-waiting are temporarily humored by those
impatient for the room (353). "There is nothing beneath these rocks,
these steep lawns and proud row houses, but atoms and nothingness,
waiting for him to take his tight-fitting place among them" (267).

As Rabbit and Janice shuttle between Brewer and Deleon, they tighten
the weave of their checkered, inevitable interdependence. They scan the
obituaries, gossip over the rise and fall of friends' health as though dis-
cussing the stock market, and reminisce about their respective heresies
when at least they felt they had the space to stray in. Now, especially for
Rabbit, life seems a series of goings under: the toppling of the Sunfish,
his son's succumbing to cocaine, mounting debts and misgivings. The old
buoyancy is a lasting joke he tells on himself. By the end of the novel, he
feels himself undone by encroachments—shocking news stories, Hurri-
cane Hugo, his bedside history of the Revolutionary War, familial quick
fixes, and fast food—until all animation drains away and he is ready to go
under for the last time with the rest of the ghosts. Momentarily, "It" is the
return of Rabbit's shooting touch or the designated catcher of fleeing children in playground games, but these incarnations pale before so many
portents of a clawing, vortical, rapacious Death—the unremitting "It" that
brooks no elevation of the spirit, that "wants it all" (218). As Rabbit takes
on "Tiger" in the game of one-on-one that causes his fatal infarction, "The
nature of this exertion is to mix him with earth and sky" (504), but he is
not accorded anything like the sober consolation of Wordsworth's Lucy,
who in death is "Rolled round in earth's diurnal course, / With rocks, and
stones, and trees" ("A Slumber Did My Spirit Seal," lines 7–8). On the

contrary, Rabbit's adversary calls his final basket "Pure horseshit," and it
is into nothing nobler than this epithet that Rabbit irretrievably falls.

As we witness the declension of metaphor in Updike's Rabbit tetralogy,
therefore, we must locate saving possibilities in the luxuriant quality of
attention instead of in the inherent value of the demolition attended to.
Novels of manners enriched by mannered prose style: this is the consen-
sus regarding Updike's fiction, and it is often commented upon in the
course of deeming it superficial—ornaments strewn through suburban
alleys, filigrees squandered on middle-class row houses.[50] I would contend,
however, that social, political, moral, and aesthetic interests validate and
mutually reinforce one another. To use a phrase from *Rabbit at Rest* in
this context, they "all make together a little enclosed climate, a burrow of
precise circumstance" (128). If "the straight path is made smooth" (*Rabbit, Run* 202), it is not because of the strident enforcement of ethics but
because of its having been "smoothed and packed firm by the passage of
human feet . . . . Such unconsciously humanized intervals of clay"
("Packed Dirt" 246–47), along with the verbal passages that particularize
and commemorate them.

Updike's deft, richly outfitted catalogs of the ordinary, his minutely
rendered fascinations, "give a ripple of balladlike vividness to the stream
of consciousness" (Pritchett 202). The poetry of the material world vital-
izes the brute materiality of the world. Updike pits the poetry of mortality
against mortal circumstances. (Updike has noted his humble appreciation
of Renaissance artisans who decorated the undersides of chairs, subtly un-
dergirding their creations with "needless" beauty.) In a tribute to Proust,
Updike indirectly provides an insight into his own brand of worshipful
impressionism: "The remorseless pessimism of Proust's disquisitions on
the heart, the abyss he makes of human motives, the finality of all our little deaths, did not appall me . . . . In the interminable rain of his prose, I
felt goodness" (quoted Cooper 321). Through style, Updike, too, adopts a
posture of reverence apart from the pieties we would usually expect to
occasion it. The writing he champions displays "that elusive but essential
something, that sense of music, of voice, of phrase-by-phrase unexpect-
edness, of constantly retuned attentiveness, which makes some texts wine
and whose absence leaves others watery" ("Virtues of Playing Cricket"
298).

Updike tracks "that elusive but essential something" through *Rabbit,
Run, Rabbit Redux, Rabbit Is Rich,* and *Rabbit at Rest,* detecting its scent

in bedrooms and locker rooms, lifting prints from local streets and tender fleshes; but, in deference to the metaphorical nature of his approach, he contents himself with approximation and conjecture. Like an ellipsis that trickles past the perimeters of what can be securely stated or comprehended, metaphor is a "rabbity" construction—skittish, vagrant, tentative, pasturing. In the end, "the irrepressible combinations of the real" (*Roger's Version* 56) will not be contained by any orthodoxy, be it religious or stylistic. Instead of "the resolution or final 'conversion' that a Bunyan pilgrim might seek and find, Updike's pilgrimages will be dialectical in character and ambiguous concerning any 'resolution'" (Hunt 38).

Hence, we return to Updike's avowed bias in favor of "middles . . . where ambiguity restlessly rules" and, compatibly, his appreciation of fictions conducive to their maintenance (quoted in Hunt 18). In the meantime, even though the fundamental speculations of the Rabbit novels never infuse their hero or his community with anything so unassailable as belief, their descriptions radiate grace. Happily, we find that over the course of Harry Angstrom's thirty-year run, even the smallest textures remember a uniquely redemptive touch.

Conclusion

ON THE ETHICAL BEHAVIOR OF METAPHOR

So often it is the image that sticks, the tailored saying that becomes the enduring distillate of all that's said. In the course of wiring for demolition the latest Judith Krantz novel, critic Anthony Lane contrasts her glutted, gulping style with that of Anita Brookner, whose prose, he notes, is "as sad and tidy as a suitcase on a single bed" (83). Long after the self-satisfied skewering of Krantz has dissolved for me—indeed, long after I forget the subject in whose service the line was delivered—I am sure that I will remember having halted at that line. Can there be any denying that figure, any recovery from it? For there is not only the sublime rightness of the metaphor itself, which one could readily imagine captioning a painting by Edward Hopper, but also the adhesive quality of alliteration that packs the "s" and "t" of "sad" and "tidy" into the modest first syllable of that equally modest "suitcase," then primly, chastely ties up the aural package by overlapping the "s" of "single"—"sad" and "single" hasped over the unexceptional contents and, undoubtedly, sealing the character and reception of its sad, tidy, single possessor.[1] There she perches, a bleared pastel, keeping vigil over some vain, unspoken hope. She will dine alone again tonight. Again she will hear the fork scrape the plate . . .

To linger over a passage is not to loiter but to tease out as much treasure as possible. In fact, there is more than madness to the diagnosis of a writer's compulsive "instead." I believe it to be true to the very nature of language, not to mention the literature it constitutes, that we break off our assigned routes as we progress through a text, which is the way, often as not, that the larger yardage is made. "The heart has need of some deceit / To make its pistons rise and fall" (Cullen, "Only the Polished Skeleton," lines 1–2). At the expense of rigorous definition, the pinched legalism of denotation, figuration wakes slumbering assumptions and widens the field of inquiry.

A good metaphor is not only a novel, dilatory means of delivering ulterior meaning like the day's mail. When my students accuse me (with their silence) of exaggerating the importance, much less the intention, of wordy sleights up authorial sleeves; when they cry "Relevant!" and "Practical!" as though those precious dactyls were airborne and escaping to the far horizon of the class while I dream over verbal cud; when they plead for me to cut to the chase when it comes to interpretation (more than willing to receive textual bodies already embalmed) and in doing so disclose their doubts about there even being a chase to cut to, I remind them of the slanted approaches and departures of Emily Dickinson's truth, its irredeemably lowercase appearance. Try squinting to see through all that clamorous sun, I suggest. Or I exercise a favorite escape clause of Thoreau's: "The world is more wonderful than convenient."[2] But I am talking to people who pay tuition, and their impatience grows. There is a Jack Ziegler cartoon from the *New Yorker* (February 12, 1996) in which a grumpy man complains to his dog: "Can we forget about our dainty little tracks in the snow for five seconds and try to concentrate on what we're out here for?" (5). The implication is that art is apparently a luxury better suited to a warmer climate than to the coldly deductive classroom and only to be indulged after the real business of self-help has been conducted.

As representative fictions by Paul West, Don DeLillo, Steven Millhauser, Paul Auster, William Gass, Richard Powers, Kathy Acker, and John Updike have indicated in this study, metaphors are unstable compounds, which is a source of their wonder and of their inconvenience. Conclusions taper; metaphors embark. This realization, of course, will do little to warm the core of the humanities curriculum or the hearts of those who campaign to require the installation of literature into it. Their presumption is that literature shows us what it is to be good; more optimistically, it makes us better people. One imagines a would-be perpetrator entering a local 7–Eleven store, then suddenly remembering a piece from his sophomore survey anthology, dropping his weapon, and dramatically swearing from this day forward to support the new hospital wing, children's library, or telethon. If only Oswald had read "Ozymandias," say, or Dillinger dipped further into the Dickens on reserve, they might have been transformed into infinitely gentle, infinitely suffering things, and America might have been spared countless traumas.

As it happens, literature is an unreliable pharmaceutical at best. A good deal of unsavoriness appears in it, survives exposure to it, and truthfully, if we are to believe the capsule biographies of some of the misanthropes, brutes, and suicides who inhabit the typical anthology, has been exhibited by several who have produced it. Art seems rather incompatible with ethical programs and ideological lobbies. As W. K. Wimsatt Jr. observes, "[A] moral code must be by its nature too rigid to accommodate, or at least too rigid to account for or specifically sanction, the widely heterogeneous concreteness of the world's recognized poetry" (89). The chief obligation of literary creation, argues Seamus Heaney, is pleasure, whose foundation is neither moral improvement nor political edification but a studied brilliance. What it affirms is "the mind's capacity to conceive a new plane of regard for itself, a new scope for its own activity" (Heaney 159–60). We are going to be disappointed when we try to use subtle texts as blunt objects, regardless of the righteousness of the cause in whose name we flail. As for the time-honored search for a capitalized Truth, Philip Wheelwright reflects in *Metaphor & Reality* on the need for even the most "enterprising explorer" to retreat from the vision of a star, luminous and alone, heralding an absolutely paraphrasable firmament: "[T]he best we can hope to do is catch partisan glimpses, reasonably diversified, all of them imperfect, but some more suited to one occasion and need, others to another. If we cannot hope ever to be perfectly right, we can perhaps find both enlightenment and refreshment by changing, from time to time, our ways of being wrong" (172–73). Figuration invests in gems embedded in impurities, but the consolation may be that "truth, like certain precious metals, is presented best in alloys. In that case the way toward it will be through a guided succession of tentative errors" (Wheelwright 173). That last phrase in particular—"a guided succession of tentative errors"—seems especially congenial to such flexible concepts noted in my introductory chapter as Frost's planned obsolescence of metaphor or Dickinson's strategy of slant. There is at least as much raucous complication as algebraic proof in the metaphors we strive by.

Yet for all of this rhetoric of disclaimer, literature does retain an intimate connection to ethics. Its narrators exhibit and provoke ethical reflection; its characters exemplify and enact ethical options; its enduring
evaluative standards—veracity, beauty, depth of feeling, philosophical
viability—are ethical precepts. Nevertheless, the fundamental ethical
dimension of literature has relatively little to do with our approving or dis-
approving of saintly performances by the author or his fictional proxies, or
with the level of life affirmation after a story's events shake out. What literature *can* do is introduce us to the concepts and conditions under which
moral agency is initiated and, at its best, simultaneously show moral stre-
nousness through deft, sinuous, considered use of words.

Integrity is basically an aesthetic matter. As Susan Sontag declares,
literature's moral pleasure and its moral service derive from the same quality: "the intelligent gratification of consciousness" ("On Style" 24).[3] A startling metaphor, a sentence that ripples after the turning of the page
enough to turn us back, a paragraph whose acoustics occasion as much
wonderment as the argument it bears—these are ethical demonstrations,
ethical accomplishments, as sure as any sermon might be. The good word
is the right word; the writer's virtuosity is his virtue, not mere bunting
about a thesis. The will to truth in literature is inseparable from its verbal
conveyance. We cannot for the sake of expediency extract the point from
the embroidery and, having liberated it from all that language, bear it
effortlessly and unencumbered away.

The complaint "If that's what the writer meant to say, why didn't he
simply *say* so?" confuses disparate realms of behavior, the literary with the
literal, and disrespects distinctive methodologies of justice. Successful
literary works, Harold Bloom reminds us, "are achieved anxieties, not
releases from anxieties." And for all of his renowned conservationism
regarding the Western Canon, Bloom does not exempt that bastion from
that same rule: "Canons, too, are achieved anxieties, not unified props of
morality" (38).[4]

It would be pretty to think that we could apply Ethics like any cologne
at the cosmetic counter, for surely its name pretends to no greater magnitude than Infinity, Desire, or the rest of that aromatic fellowship. If only
people who recalled the pulse of a motif in Fitzgerald made better parents,
sophomores soothed by consonance in Stevens kissed with more articulate passion, and the literate never littered. On the contrary, even if we
could install moral character like air bags in late-model graduates and

inspire them to civic disciplines—recycling without complaint, adhering to curfews, smiling at crossing guards—metaphor, with its inexact tolerances and slippery penchants, is not the dependable instrument for accomplishing these things.

Janet Burroway writes on behalf of the moral employment of words as a stand against tyrannies of all sorts—in human institutions and in human communications. "Literature is my credo because it is capacious, tentative, and empathetic; because it acknowledges irony and anomaly, because it poses dilemmas, for which it declines to offer a way out, in small acts of perpetual reconciliation" (14). Burroway's steady preference for the open over the constrained is apparent in her cautious, undogmatic diction. Along with Wimsatt, Heaney, Wheelwright, Sontag, and Bloom, Burroway holds to a creed which, while it may consternate doctrine, is exceptionally responsive to metaphor. "Splendid also to feel the curious and potent, inexplicable and irrefutably magical life language leads within itself," exclaims Updike's narrator in "Wife-Wooing" (110). If moral development is to be found in literature, it most likely lives there, too, among the orchestral ambitions and trembling latencies of wordplay.

As we have seen throughout *This Mad Instead*, figuration has not been abandoned in this skeptical and decadent age. From the harrowed confinements of West's Walter Sickert or Gass's William Kohler, from the staticky academic climes of DeLillo's Jack Gladney or Powers's faltered ego, from the obsessively coiled voices of Paul Auster or Kathy Acker, and from the lapidary addictions of Steven Millhauser and John Updike, metaphor breeds and seduces, plumping even neuroses and poverties to sumptuousness. At the same time, intricate textures and compositional beauty do not in the end represent composed contracts between authors and their fictionalized arguments or their linguistic materials. Doubt, misgiving, serendipity, desire, and the seeming obstreperousness of the alphabet they employ variously combine, along with other troublesome components, to prevent the deification of literature into a kind of "cultural superego."[5]

A metaphor is a beachhead that crumbles under the straining stakes. As we have seen, for many writers the pleasures of connection are fleeting. We think of West's insidious motion pictures, decadent and treacherous as the crimes they portray; of DeLillo's aural blurs, hinting at codes that fret and subside into a sea of white; of Millhauser's harried curatorships and paragraphs like reticule bags; of Auster's dark alleys and dead ends of detection, where definitions go out like bad fuses; of Gass's private and professional documents covered with rubble, recrimination, and blood; of Powers's leading-edge Gnostics and the technology of unmappable minds and motives; of Acker's toxic wastrels and the violences done to and in the name of voice control; of Updike's long-distance runner forever chasing down his generation's trends of worry and worship. All of the fictions featured in this study present characters who seem uncomfortably situated outside both of the Edenic options with which I introduced *This Mad Instead.* Surely, they despair of finalizing some concordance of the world's surge. Very often the data they gather (statistical, experiential, testimonial, or otherwise) leaves them, instead of completing a draft of reality's essential patterns, riding out "a storm of single instances" (Graham, "Who Watches from the Dark Porch" 5.77).[6] Furthermore, when a memorable metaphor is struck, its initial satisfaction impacting like a hard-won vantage or privileged fix on things, its conjunctive essence does not dissipate in the wake of the new coinage. A polished poem or finished fiction does not operate with impunity. It connects and meshes, sometimes rigorously, sometimes recklessly, credited by cleverness instead of accuracy, in a dizzying context of alternatives that might as well have served.

"If there is too much uncontested meaning on earth (the reign of the angels)," writes Milan Kundera in *The Book of Laughter and Forgetting,* "man collapses under the burden; if the world loses all its meaning (the reign of the demons), life is every bit as impossible" (61). In the case of metaphor, ethical governance yields to this paradox and prospers in the margin between mythic absolutes: dreams of finalized meaning and their inexorable dimmings. And if "vehemence and ecstasy" are intrinsic to metaphor, it is perilous to harness metaphor to partisan drives (Ricouer 249). The man of metaphor, a self-effacing prophet, is an unpractical politician and worse warden. He turns ethical imperatives into literature.

We watch the soft Brownian motion of boats roped loosely together, knocking indolent hulls in the harbor; we watch ants deploy and scrabble over the odd granular tract; we watch the stars suggest and betray configurations, whose illuminations imply a blueprint of some indiscernible master project or caution us like signal flares flanking massive absences we would be wise to travel around. Our hunger for formal empathy in the environment is unceasing. When we think that we have hit upon something hospitable—a reward for concerted alertness, for alertness to concert—we make a show of poetry to recruit admiration, not to proselytize or to proclaim the reign of Truth, which, benevolent despot though it may be, is still a despot. Or it may be that the eloquent way the writer paves to the treasure *is* the treasure after all. A compensatory ethics of lucid communion may be the best that metaphor can accomplish. "Metaphoric juxtaposition can arouse us to tensive new awareness, but it cannot repay us for what that new awareness costs" (Cable 31). Furthermore, "the fresh kind of knowing that is provided by the metaphor may offer pleasure, or shock, or thrill of discovery. But what it cannot offer (and has no intention of offering) is assured *gratification* of the kind it had disrupted in the first place for the sake of its own assertion" (Cable 33).

Metaphor's bonding and breaking are perpetual conditions that manifest perpetual traits of the imagination. Like human perception, metaphor appreciates and supplants. Respectful of the novelty of "isolate flecks," it is nevertheless geared toward the seduction of comparability.

> What binds
> one shape to another
>
> also sets them apart
> —but what's lovelier
> than the shapeshifting
>
> transparence of *like* and *as:*
> clear, undulant words? (Doty, "Difference," lines 44–50)

Figures make their quizzical assent. They proceed while conceding to their flaws. And yet, the manufactured instance of a mad instead is not principally a grim petition against a world that will not clarify. It is principled wit: a festive shape, a resonant occasion, a conceit as sweet on itself as it is dedicated to ulterior linkages. In the end, if we try to measure them by morals, "fictive things / Wink as they will," as Wallace Stevens confides. "Wink most when widows wince" ("A High-Toned Old Christian Woman," lines 21–22).

Notes

INTRODUCTION

1. Among countless poetic treatments of this same theme, see Elizabeth Bishop's "The Fish" (48–50). Not only does Bishop's speaker have to resort to repeating one adjective ("wallpaper") to describe first the fish's strips of brown skin and, two lines later, its pattern of darker brown, as though anxious to confirm that single small speculation (lines 10–14), she also ends up retracting the reference to the fish's lip with "if you could call it a lip" (line 49), admitting the impudence of human imposition. Like the shallow eyes of her uncapturable captive, her subject "shifted a little, but not / to return my stare" (lines 41–42). The humblest objects—Williams's bush, Bishop's battered catch—repel poetic intentions.

2. The same irony opens Stevens's "Study of Two Pears," whose announcement that "The pears are not viols / Nudes or bottles" actually belies the claim that "They resemble nothing else" by virtue of that "anti-association" (1.2–4). In fact, Williams himself creates a comparable method of ironic constraint and self-betrayal at the start of "Queen-Ann's-Lace": "Her body is not so white as / anemone petals nor so smooth— nor / so remote a thing" (lines 1–3).

3. See David Lehman's discussion of Stevens's use of "negative simile," whereby the poet "frequently uses *not* as a more accurate way of saying *like*," as Lehman puts it in the second of his "Three Meditations on Wallace Stevens" (37).

4. In this light, Karl Shapiro's determination that Williams "sheds figurative language as a snake sheds its skin; . . . he is naked, a poet without decoration, without metaphor" (quoted in Wagner 43), however commonplace, proves insupportable, as Linda Wagner confirms in "Metaphor and William Carlos Williams."

5. Similarly, in a letter to Williams, Stevens reminds him that "the *process* of adjustment is a world of *flux*" (quoted in Sheehan 66; italics mine), reinforcing the unsettledness of the imagination and its products.

6. "Inside the Onion" Nemerov discovers "the beautiful inexact" (line 4), an especially terse, telling comment on how qualified his findings are. The title of Nemerov's first published volume of poetry, *The Image and the Law* (1947), also appears to focus upon how fact and artistic configuration are mutually conditioned.

7. Coinciding is the finical yet forever vigilant interest of Bishop's "Sandpiper," obsessively on the alert "for something, something, something" amidst the "dragging grains" of the beach (lines 17, 12).

8. "The common object is known in its immanence, but not until it is touched by the hand of poetic metaphor is it informed and made vivid with the rich garments of thought and feeling," says semantic philosopher Weller Embler (130), who clearly delights in both the redemptive capacity of poetic metaphor and the way it lays a supportive hand upon him and vests his interests in this very sentence.

9. Given this logic, it is not surprising that Black champions what he calls "strong metaphors," which he defines as those that demonstrate "resonance and emphasis" ("More about Metaphor" 27). Evidently, the goal is not to erase the tracks of figuration but to exploit the inevitability of figuration as provocatively as possible. See further Wallace Stevens's "Metaphor as Degeneration," whose point is to deny its title by arguing that being mandates imagination and is not deprived but made vital and "undulant" through contact with its imagery (lines 19–21).

10. In this regard I would return to Williams's "A Sort of a Song" to fault the suggestion that Williams abjures metaphor because it somehow robs things of their precious individuality. A word should be used "in such a way that it will remain scrupulously itself, clean perfect, unnicked beside other words in parade," the poet contends (quoted in Miller 297). But as I have argued, sterilizing the horizontal plane, as it were, proves impossible. Whereas J. Hillis Miller celebrates Williams's devotion to the incomparable object and the chaste word (306–7), in a poem like "A Sort of a Song" such resonances seem to me to be precisely the poem's directive. In fact, rocks that obstruct proliferation are left fractured in its wake. Absent symbolic depths, Williams's urgent flower could neither take root nor muster the momentum to burst complacent surfaces and join (or "compose," organically or lexically) the things of this world whose latencies it awakens.

11. I note here in passing that Kuhns appears to assume a rather more distinctive status for philosophy than Harries would allow. "The descriptions provided by science and philosophy are not based on some aperspectival mode of vision but conjectures responsive to the ineradicably perspectival evidence furnished by the body, expressed in language that has to bend ordinary language to its demands" (Harries 85).

12. Alan Singer subtly connects this characteristic of metaphor to "the 'identity principle' of *denouement* whereby apparent differences miraculously integrate new criteria of relatedness; conflict is appeased by revised parameters of inclusiveness" (157). In other words, the essential components of narrative can be said to display the same tendencies as the language that constitutes it, a thesis fortified by Singer's belief that language and its products are inherently metaphorical (176).

13. Not every writer is so sanguine about this superinteraction. Thomas Pynchon, for instance, fears that the meaning program that language effects or unlocks could be repressive and exclusionary, depending on who makes the metaphors: "The act of

metaphor then was a thrust at truth and a lie," he writes in *The Crying of Lot 49,* "depending where you were: inside, safe, or outside, lost" (95).

CHAPTER I

1. It is significant that Ruskin uses this phrase in the course of describing members of "the first order of poets," whose ability to "feel strongly, think strongly, and see truly" is not affected by "whatever and how many soever the associations and passions may be that crowd around" the object of perception (168).

2. James A. W. Heffernan's definition of *ekphrasis*—"the verbal representation of graphic representation" (299)—is more exclusive than Krieger's, and it effectively summarizes the double distancing of verbal depiction.

3. "After the first enthusiasm," West continues, "I get quite deliberate about things, making charts and curves, of themes and colors and motifs, also of word-numbers per chapter, and then the less-than-aleatory side of my head takes over, making patterns and schemes" (interview with Morrow 157). The anchoring of organic creation in definitive structure is also evident in West's reference to some enabling "architectonic of rhythm" (interview with Morrow 168). And as he avers in *A Stroke of Genius,* "I have a fidgety, though lyrical mind, trying always to smooth heterogenous or discordant experience into a big, holistic swoosh" (103).

4. Alexander Theroux, a fellow inebriate of dictions richly devised, echoes West in his call for *amplification* in "Theroux Metaphrastes," which, like West's "In Defense of Purple Prose," gushes with and for surplus value. And in his prefatory note to *The Women of Whitechapel* West prepares us for a reading that is "more operatic than informational. Where nobody knows, we must invent . . . giving the mind a ride, leading it a chase."

5. Compare *U and I: A True Story,* in which Nicholson Baker praises narrative "cloggers." Instead of interruptions of the "it" we are presumably supposed to get on with, these instances of stuck vertical hold are chiefly what he reads for and tries to emulate in his own writing: "I wanted my first novel to be a veritable infarct of narrative cloggers; the trick being to feel your way through each clog by blowing it up until its obstructiveness finally revealed not blank mass but unlooked-for seepage-points of passage" (73).

6. Wilbur specifically juxtaposed these lines in the course of a reading he gave at the 1992 Modern Language Association convention in New York on December 29.

7. Playing upon John Updike's title for his collection of essays on art, *Just Looking,* leads to a similar complication: there is "just looking" in the sense of a casual bit of innocent observation, and there is "just looking" in the sense of engaged ethical examination.

8. For West's formal retort to the "flatulent pietism" that characterized many of these initial responses to the novel, see "Deep-Sixed into the Atlantic."

9. In *The Horse's Mouth* a blonde model named Lolie abruptly dismisses the value of the abstract, to which Abel, a sculptor, had unfortunately turned: "What is there to bite on in the abstract? You might as well eat triangles and go to bed with a sewing machine" (239).

10. Compare Gull's vision to the sadomasochistic will of Seigneur in John Hawkes's *Virginie: Her Two Lives.* Seigneur is another "artist" who ruthlessly and lovingly conducts his experiments over women.

11. When Sickert considers the failure of life to express itself as something decipherable, as more than "a cacophony of cancelled afterthoughts, a maelstrom of botched quotations," he thinks of God as being an artist altogether too receptive to accident. "Why was God not like Brahms?" he complains to himself (288).

12. "He knew now that to get rid of something you did not externalize it in a work of art, for that work of art hung around your neck" (379). Furthermore, Sickert admits to himself that the memories are not entirely unwelcome: "He half-liked having been henchman to a Ripper, and he realized he enjoyed the Netleys, the Gulls, as creatures who dared to make love to their own depravity, spending their seed in empty and rotten eye sockets because it was the spirited thing to do" (387). In contrast to Philip Roth's contention that the artist "needs his poisons: to motivate works of art that will serve as their antidote" (quoted in Plimpton 43), Sickert's productions rather increase the toxic concentration and effect of the experiences that compel them.

CHAPTER 2

1. By contrast, the same novel relates through James Axton the risk analyst's lament: "We have our self-importance. We also have our inadequacy. The former is a desperate invention of the latter" (5). The liberated artist may be the marooned artist.

2. In the following exchange, the possibility is advanced that this subterranean buzz is not just death's harbinger but the thing itself:
"What if death is nothing but sound?"
"Electrical noise."
"You hear it forever. Sound all around. How awful."
"Uniform, white." (*White Noise* 198)

3. "At the edge of every disaster," we learn in *Great Jones Street*, "people collect in affable groups to whisper away the newsless moment and wait for a messenger from the front" (254). In this novel as well, people come to rely on tranquilizers to short-circuit input and to help "run the lucky hum through our blood" (138).

4. In an example of a simulacrum readily relatable to *White Noise* and meriting the attention of Jean Baudrillard, these were also the days of "ghost game" broadcasts, in which nimble announcers had to re-create on radio the illusion of games wholly on the basis of inning-by-inning statistics received over the wire. "In this half-hell of desperate invention he did four years of Senators' baseball without ever seeing them play" (*Pafko* 45).

5. Consider in this regard the paradoxical tourist trap of the most photographed barn in the world. The collective perception confers an aura of importance upon its object, but because its uniqueness is based on extraordinary familiarity, uniqueness is actually overwhelmed by the cumulative effect of a "maintained" image. We no longer see the barn so many see the same way (*White Noise* 12–13).

6. Mr. Gray serves as a nominal and psychological precursor to Bill Gray, the shadow-dwelling author who is rudely thrust into the spotlight of world events in *Mao II.*

7. Compare the novel-in-progress being authored by Tap in *The Names,* whose dynamic, untotalizable progress of "White words . . . Pure as the drivelin' snow" (336)

offers an optimistic spin to DeLillo's consistent sense that language proliferates enig-mas it cannot dissolve. Art is not the antidote to the environment it derives from.

8. Arguably, he does not have the *ability* to mind. In "The Ecstasy of Communi-cation," Baudrillard describes his pathology as "this state of terror proper to the schizo-phrenic: too great a proximity of everything, the unclean promiscuity of everything which touches, invests and penetrates without resistance, with no halo of private pro-tection" (132).

9. A related malady afflicts James, the mathematician's assistant in DeLillo's play *The Engineer of Moonlight:* instead of grunting, he says "grunt," or, panicked, says "Loud and prolonged cries for help" (44).

10. Similarly, DeLillo's refusal to tie up the numerous loose ends of his narrative (the result of Jack's diagnosis, whether Murray gets approval for his Elvis Studies cen-ter, and so on) actually helps keep *White Noise* from the inevitable deathward progress toward which, so it is rumored in the novel, all plots tend (Zinman 77).

11. John Frow suggests that we might speak of an "airborne *aesthetic* event" in the wake of the toxic scare. He quickly notes, however, that this does not replace the poi-sonous cloud but joins with it (176). In other words, the beautiful, protracted sunsets that conclude *White Noise* are, like good metaphors, mysterious incorporations, open-ended messages.

12. "I do sort of emit a certain feudal menace," concedes a character in *Players* (171), and this is the manner of expression Bawer indicts. In fact, this quality goes beyond the conversational arcane. At the end of that novel, for example, the sight of a naked woman asleep in bed prompts the following considerations: how women "seem at such times to embody a mode of wholeness, an immanence and unit truth"; how motels tend "to turn things inward" and serve as repositories of private fears; how bucolic street names constitute "a liturgical prayer, a set of moral consolations"; and how sunlight through the window reveals "the animal glue of physical properties and functions," thereby "absolving us of our secret knowledge" (209–12). Apparently, nothing is offhand in DeLillo. Every moment is richly textured and tilled, charged with scholarship and suspicion.

13. The trick, of course, is to distinguish this presumably enabling "hovering sum" from the tactical deceptions of the power elite, as David Ferrie puts it in *Libra:* "There's something they aren't telling us. Something we don't know about. There's more to it. There's always more to it. This is what history consists of. It's the sum total of all the things they aren't telling us" (321).

14. Capitulation to the void takes several forms in the novel, including Steffie's eager acceptance of the role of disaster victim during simulation exercises and compe-titions among Jack's colleagues as to who can drive longest on the highway with his eyes shut. This is the Zen of self-erasure without transcendent end.

CHAPTER 3

1. "For is there any end to true textures, to true / Integuments," Wilbur wonders, in a "maculate, cracked, askew, / Gay-pocked and potsherd world" ("Objects," lines 26–27, 28–29).

2. Whenever one of Millhauser's characters happens upon the border between realms, the precariousness is described as palpable and exhilarating. See for instance those moments in *The Barnum Museum* in "A Game of Clue" (32), "Behind the Blue Curtain" (65), and "The Sepia Postcard" (96).

3. A similar occurrence may be found in "The Invention of Robert Herendeen," Millhauser's update of Borges's "The Circular Ruins." As Herendeen more and more exclusively devotes himself to scrupulously imagining "Olivia" into existence, his aging, Polonius-like father begins to fade from lack of attention. At one point, his "sudden appearance struck me with all the force of a haunting"; later, "he reminded me of a soft white tuber growing secretly in moist soil" (196, 198).

4. "Boredom is dissatisfaction with things as they are—it is an extreme form of refusal," Millhauser says (interview with Ross 326). But his protagonists tend not to shed "things as they are." Sensory overload keeps them grounded in the world they abjure. And in stories like "The Dream of the Consortium" and "The Eighth Voyage of Sinbad," particularizing wholly imaginary and "ratifiable" items in the same list has the effect of equating them—in "The Dream of the Consortium," making the fantastic more mall ballast. For additional commentary on the imperial nature of boredom, see Millhauser's "Cathay" (*In the Penny Arcade* 151).

5. Thus John Barth's comment that a pork chop turns into garbage when it is dropped into the trash can but turns into art when it is dropped into Proust reflects a different emphasis than do Millhauser's invisible boundaries. On the other hand, it is true that Millhauser's museum compares with Barth's opposed contexts in that it is as likely to confer as to confirm the value of its contents.

6. Mary Kinzie points out a similar condition in "The Eighth Voyage of Sinbad": "When Baghdad is a place of respite, creaturely self-absorption, and thrilling clarity in the present moment, the adventures appear remote, cerebral, and grotesque. When Baghdad is repetitious and overly familiar . . . then his adventures seem to Sinbad utterly clear and real" (Kinzie 126).

7. In *Portrait of a Romantic*, Arthur Grumm encounters a mechanical clown whose very lifelikeness reveals instead of obscures its artful contrivance, "so that it was difficult to say whether the pleasure of the observer lay more in the lifelike illusion of the performance or in the perception of the deceiving artifice itself" (208–9).

8. Cornell said that a "world of complete happiness" is one in which "every triviality becomes imbued with a significance" (quoted in Simic 18). Evidently it is a significance based on the sorts of juxtapositions that lists approximate in verbal form. Charles Simic states: "Every art is about the longing of One for the Other. Orphans that we are, we make our sibling kin out of anything we can find. The labor of art is the slow and painful metamorphosis of the One into the Other" (62).

9. Compare Ronald E. Martin's analysis of Whitman's passion for catalogs: "He is attempting a kind of object-evocation, in which the independent *otherness* of the object is his main concern—and additionally, perhaps, some more deeply interfused quality" (20).

10. See also in this regard the tantalizing premise of Millhauser's novella *Catalogue of the Exhibition*, which tests an artist's life story against the life work that presumably

reveals it—a dream of correspondence that might eliminate otherness, but which Mill-hauser consistently interrogates.

11. In spite of his title's implications, A. R. Ammons apparently calls for a comparable form of tolerance at the beginning of "The Unifying Principle":

> Ramshackles, archipelagoes, loose constellations
> are less fierce, subsidiary centers, with the
> attenuations of interstices, roughing the salience
>
> jarring the outbreak of too insistent commonality. (lines 1–4)

Ammons, too, does not want to eradicate "the forms / things want to come as" when he includes them in his poetry ("Poetics," lines 11–12).

CHAPTER 4

1. As Blue realizes in *Ghosts,* his proclamation of the "snugness" of words does not hold up when he tries to view Black through a dark window: "He's there, but it's impossible to see him. And even when I do see him it's as though the lights are out" (26).

2. We could also refer to Vladimir Nabokov's connection between fiction and chess, both of which display how "value is due to the number of 'tries'—delusive opening moves, false scents, specious lines of play, astutely and lovingly prepared to lead the would-be solver astray" (quoted in Kuehl 84).

3. The narrator of *The Locked Room,* like Aaron entrusted with the manuscript of a shadowy, absent friend, like Aaron exploits that absence by advancing his designs upon the deserted wife, proving that some collisions are not merely coincidental but rich with solicitude.

4. Lest we forget A. R. Ammons's instruction in his poem "The Unifying Principle" (remarked upon in the preceding chapter on Millhauser), *the* principle is really *a* principle, and it is necessarily one that defers to the "preconceived" forms of things upon their arrival, usurping, or at the very least tutoring, our conceptions of them.

5. This represents an advance on Quinn's irrepressible bias in *City of Glass* for "reading" Stillman's erratic walks through the streets of New York as a letter-by-letter deployment of clues to a design (TOWER OF BABEL) that, whether utopian or murderous, is definitely spellable.

6. Not that Fanshawe's shadow would be any less consoled than Quinn by this assertion, as he seconds Quinn's frustration: "In the end, each life is no more than the sum of contingent facts, a chronicle of chance intersections, of flukes, of random events that divulge nothing but their own lack of purpose" (*Locked Room* 35).

CHAPTER 5

1. Defying such structures is not simply a stylistic challenge: "The first sort of mistake we might make would be to attribute to nature properties which properly belong

only to the medium of its description; hence the error of imputing necessary connection to causality on the grounds that the hypothetical syllogism seems a perfect model for it, so that affirming the antecedent is like producing a cause" (Gass, "Representation and the War for Reality" 90).

2. Implied disqualification of this reasoning can be found not only in Planmantee's declaration that "heady self-awareness" is "historical superfluity—the randy dance of light in a cake of melting ice" (142) but also in Kohler's disparagement of Herschel's scholarly efficacy and of his impactlessness, historically speaking.

3. History has to make room for Lou, who easily trumps the other contents of that slice of time (109).

4. "Waste not even waste," writes Gass in praising the "blessed method" of collage: "never cut when you can paste. . . . It works wonders, because in collage logical levels rise and fall like waves" ("Carrots, Noses, Snow, Rose, Roses" 282).

5. In Gass's universe, using the terms provided in "Representation and the War for Reality" (94–97), Kohler is an untidy Thick, whereas his "anal retentive" colleague Planmantee, who champions compartments and legislative rigor when it comes to the writing of history, is an inveterate Thin (390–96), and hence, intolerant of the vagaries of metaphor.

6. We may consider in this regard Kenneth Burke's proposal at the conclusion of his essay on the ambiguous division between "Semantic and Poetic Meaning": "The ideal word is itself an act, its value contained in its use at the moment of utterance. Its worth does not reside in its 'usefulness' and promise (though that is certainly a part of it) but in its *style* as morals, as petition, in the *quality* of the petition, not in the *success* of the petition" (167). Similarly, in "The High Brutality of Good Intentions," Gass explains that Henry James merges moral problems and moral passions with aesthetic ones (183, 190).

7. Another relevant version of this justification appears in Gass's essay "The Artist and Society": "A work of art may not utter the truth, but it must be honest. It may champion a cause we deplore, but like Milton's Satan, it must in itself be noble; it must be *all there*" (282).

8. Kohler describes "The Barricade" (243–44) as an abstraction weighted by mundane components. In other words, barriers are composed of worldly materials, instead of being stainlessly steeled against them.

9. Gass expands on the word as a "silted-up symbol" in "Representation and the War for Reality" (96). In "Groping for Trouts," he asks us to appreciate how every word "is, like a piece in chess, the center of a network of astonishing relations" (274). And in "Culture, Self, and Style," Gass reacts to an excerpt from *A Farewell to Arms*: "'River' does not mean 'river' in this passage; it means all the things that rivers mean" (199).

10. Of particular interest in this regard are the four essays on the nature of literary language that constitute part 1 of *Fiction and the Figures of Life*; "Carrots, Noses, Snow, Rose, Roses" and "The Ontology of the Sentence, or How to Make a World of Words" in *The World within the Word*; and "Representation and the War for Reality," "The Soul Inside the Sentence," and "Tropes of the Text" in *Habitations of the Word*.

11. It bears noting that, like *Omensetter's Luck* and "The Order of Insects," this novel makes use of the spider as an image of the secluded artificer. Kohler sees the

historian as a stationary spider waiting "until that little shiver in the web signals the enmeshment of our prey" (71). We might think specifically of the spider called the tunnel weaver (or tube spinner), which connects a flat web to the tubular nest it hides in.

12. He consistently describes cyclones experienced during his boyhood as vertical tunnels, majestically apart, whatever damage they may do.

13. *In the Heart of the Heart of the Country* offers a considerable ancestry for the tunnel-obsessed Kohler, from Jorge, who dreams of burrowing into a warm, wonderful sleep under the snow in "The Pedersen Kid" (*In the Heart* 57) and settles for the Pedersen basement; to the narrator of "Mrs. Mean," who lingers on lascivious dreams of squeezing his way inside her dark house (*In the Heart* 118–19); to Fender, the feckless protagonist of "Icicles," who stalks his life from another iced-in cave; to the narrator of the title story, who lives behind jaundiced eyes the way Israbestis Tott lives in his wall in *Omensetter's Luck*.

14. Also compare Kohler's panic in the wake of the grasshopper episode as he plucks bits of insect from his body or finds a live one holed up in his hair (104), with the quiet, meditative enchantment of the narrator of "The Order of Insects" caused by these manifestations of "the dark soul of the world" (*In the Heart* 168).

CHAPTER 6

1. A celebrated nature writer whose subjects extend from the human senses to physiological peculiarities of the animal kingdom, Ackerman often packs her poems with biological phenomena. See for instance the give-and-take of marvels constituting "A. R. Ammons amid the Fungi" (171–72).

2. For more on the odds-defying fact of us, the numbing, embarrassing All, see young Heinrich Gladney's argument on the human eye (*White Noise* 158).

3. Prior to the publication of this novel, Richard Powers had been a notoriously reclusive author, stingy with interviews and maintaining a nearly Pynchonesque silence and distance from the public scene. (See Baker's characterization of Powers's anonymity in his *Publishers Weekly* interview.) But especially in *Galatea 2.2,* whose setting is clearly based on the University of Illinois (the U being Urbana), autobiographical nuggets are ripe for the panning; in addition, the fictional Powers reveals much about the circumstances and intentions behind the previous novels, even going so far as to comment upon verbatim phrases from salient reviews. It also bears noting that this novel's dust jacket is the first to provide a photograph of its author.

4. There is always the danger that for an especially word-drunk person like Powers, life may tend to become "an interruption of my description of it" (215), and held-off friends abandon him while he busies himself with their portrayals. But if "the point of stories was what you did with them" (108), in the case of the Powers hero, the point is to repeat them in the service of correction and cure. Whether it is to redeem a father and a family history in *Prisoner's Dilemma* or to soften the dying of children in *Operation Wandering Soul,* a Hebbian rule applies to narrative, in that repetition makes reality into a more tractable, durable plot and fosters our sense of living "in advance retrospective" (268, 98). Helen herself picks up on this appeal when she relates Pow-

ers's motivation for rehashing the loss of C. to the compensation of books: "Something that seems always, *because* it will be over?" (310).

5. Powers identifies this paradoxical opener as a tradition of Persian fables (319). Roman Jakobson notes a parallel formula among the Majorca storytellers who begin, "It was and was not," which similarly achieves the poetic prerogative of affirming and undermining what follows (cited in Cable 20).

6. Witness the illustration by a colleague of his young daughter trying to deliver her sense of the word and concept *goose*. He misinterprets her intentions by assuming she means birds or things that fly, until she finally manages to make clear to her father that by *goose* she means an action: "To move fast. To be free. To escape" (224–25). The episode compares with Powers's reading of his correspondence with C. to the indefatigably alert Helen. They show love to be waxy, overwrought, excessive, and words, words, words . . . and like all stories, as well as like Helen herself, "not a thing but a distributed process" (270).

7. Powers says much the same thing in *Gold Bug Variations*, when it is suggested that the genetic code is subject to Gödel's Incompleteness Theorem: "*We* are the by-product of the mechanism *in there*. So it must be more ingenious than us. Anything complex enough to create consciousness may be too complex for consciousness to understand" (102).

8. "'Mother goes to fetch the doctor,'" C. reads from her family's English primer. "Imagine my brother trying to explain to his parents, at age ten, why mothers do to doctors what dogs do to sticks" (63). And when it is compared to the job of unknotting a line of Keats, leaping between those concepts would be only the smallest victory for intelligence, artificial or otherwise.

9. Once again, Powers duplicates in Helen's instruction the answer to his own needs. He realizes, for instance, that for his infatuation with A. to gather momentum, he needs pictures of her to substantiate experience of her. Like Helen, he wishes for reifying images to facilitate deep storage of abstractions.

10. A frail child lies "narrow in his bed. He seemed so slight, such a vulnerable line. A lima bean germinated on damp paper towel for the science fair" (136). Later on, "Outside, a gang of grackles combed the landscaped lawn like a homicide squad dragging a field for evidence" (150). Critical appraisal of Powers's prose tends to focus on two interdependent qualities—scientific ideas and literary wordplay—so as to make one skeptical of C. P. Snow's lament over the separation of the "two cultures," given their consistent negotiation in the Powers canon.

11. Admittedly, Percy is somewhat more guarded than Barthelme about depending too greatly on shuffling words from diverse contexts. However splendid the effects, the pastime of "rolling out the pretty marbles of word-things to see one catch and reflect the fire of another" is bound to "go stale" in the absence of "the meaning situation" (76–77). Nevertheless, Percy holds with the findings that dominate the introductory chapter of this study when he concludes, "This 'wrongness' of metaphor is seen to be not a vagary of poets but a special case of that mysterious 'error' which is the very condition of our knowing anything at all" (81).

12. Seeming to corroborate this is the prank played upon Powers by Lentz's colleagues: by infiltrating its readouts and thus masquerading as the computer to dupe the

humanist, they perform a sort of reverse Turing Test, causing human intelligence to be mistaken for artificial intelligence (121–24).

13. This is reader-response theory with a vengeance. Intriguingly, Helen craves Powers's voice for its own sake, contextlessness notwithstanding. She fastens on songs and jabber with at least as much fascination as she accords Keats.

14. For more on these complements, see John Updike's *New Yorker* review of the novel (113–14).

15. In this context, Powers states that the "common denominators" uniting scientific and literary disciplines (a division he believes masks complex internal divisions on both sides) are reliance upon "symbolic manipulation" and "awe at our ability to say anything at all about where we find ourselves" (quoted in "Bordercrossings" 108).

CHAPTER 7

1. In "The Geography of Enunciation," Karen Brennan expands on parallels and deceptive divisions between the "new homoerotic orders" devised by Acker (specifically in *Blood and Guts in High School*) and Genet (244–52).

2. The protagonist of Gail Godwin's *Odd Woman* also reads compulsively to find answers and, like Acker, learns that she must avoid absorption by "already-written stories" if she is to locate an identity undefiled by preconception (quoted in Greene 8). She fits the mold of Blanche H. Gelfant's "hungry women," defiantly avid for books, voracious "for knowledge, for power, for possession of her self" (223).

3. See in this regard Rosa's metafictional epistolary complaints in *Great Expectations* (25–30).

4. Friedman's straw man critic is F. R. Leavis, whose "Great Tradition" only allows access to women's fiction when it can be perceived as conforming to its strictures.

In this context, the "moral seriousness" demanded by Leavis is "revealed as a code, rationalizing patriarchal dominance. The operation of this code is evident in the particular vocabulary of his judgments, including key terms such as 'morality,' 'reverence,' 'civilization,' terms driven by imperatives defined and maintained by a strict system of patriarchal constraints" ("'Utterly Other Discourse'" 354). While Acker is not specifically covered in this essay by Friedman, her unruliness would clearly exempt her from consideration by an F. R. Leavis; as she puts it in *Empire of the Senseless*, "Literature is that which denounces and slashes apart the repressing machine at the level of the signified" (12). Friedman might say that Acker's experimental integrity is a justification for her unmanageability.

5. Cixous is interested, in "The Character of 'Character,'" in bringing the subject "back to its divisibility," as befits the Ego outside of its usual compression into "character." The following comment is inspired by Hoffman's tales, but it suits Acker's novel admirably: "No preperson is ever held back in his precipitation into the other who speaks to him in his name or who makes him reverberate with the convulsive airs of his libido" (390). Or as Luce Irigaray puts it, "'She' is indefinitely other in herself" (28).

6. See for example the passage in *Don Quixote* in which the androgynous hero imagines a closed, forbidding circuit among "the image," "a man's suit," untouchability,

imperviousness, and being "totally elegant" (56). Cixous's concept of "vatic bisexuality" also seems relevant to Acker's gender editing (quoted in Moi 108–9).

7. Another Acker title, *Empire of the Senseless,* neatly expresses this coup.

8. It is useful in this instance to bring in someone like Sven Birkerts for counter-point. Birkerts celebrates our experience of "deep durational time" as it is traditionally guaranteed by the novel, which "through language, through the complex decelerating system of syntax, pushes us against the momentum of distraction" (10). By contrast, Acker's novels are positively permeable affairs, keen for sensation. They do not combat "the momentum of distraction"; they welcome it.

9. Douglas Shields Dix prefaces this comment by depicting the paradox of a col-lective radical movement, in that collectivity makes the rebel force ripe for co-optation by the existing order (56–57). (If Love is Don Quixote's goal, it must be a sleepless, unconsolidated love.) Thus the female must resist her tendency toward collectivization in order to sustain her polymorphic power and her threat of uncompromising emotion.

10. As Walsh goes on to explain the deliberate failure of progress in the novel, "The combination of the argument's thematic stasis with its dynamic linear structure results in the incorporation of this dynamism *within* stasis, producing an argument in dynamic equilibrium. The cyclical form that constrains the narrative is therefore not viewed from outside, as repetitious and fruitless, but from within, as a potent condition of frustra-tion" (140).

11. As "dehumanized victims" of the ideology of "a crude self-interested material-ism," it is to be expected that the dogs would prove to be less than attentive to poetry (Walsh 136).

12. Arthur F. Redding wonders more or less the same thing, as he maintains that any emancipation effected by Acker's outrageous poetics is "illusory and provisional at best" (283–84). See also the discussion in Toril Moi's *Sexual / Textual Politics* of how deconstructive texts confess their parasitism, whereby subversion retains the taint of the assaulted "host" (139–43).

13. Luce Irigaray's commentary on woman's "consignment to passivity" further glosses this "O": "While her body finds itself thus eroticized, and called to a double movement of exhibition and of chaste retreat in order to stimulate the drives of the 'sub-ject,' her sexual organ represents *the horror of nothing to see.* A defect in the systemat-ics of representation and desire. A 'hole' in its scoptophilic lens" (26; author's italics).

14. There may be a critical price to pay for assigning the quality of "betweenness" to woman: the subordination of her presence to the status of "interval" or "copulative link." See Irigaray 108–9.

15. In his chapter "Theories of Desire," Jay Clayton pits Bersani against Peter Brooks, who underscores the social benefits of sublimation toward the creation of "an enduring civilization," the very defining constructions of which Bersani's version of desire may be directed to overturn (78). As for Bersani's reference to the possible involvement of "brutally dehumanizing activities," Clayton obligingly samples a number of contemporary novels in which sadistic sex is prominently considered (64)—a bang gang Acker's books could readily consort with.

16. The dubious values of the "phallocracy" are listed by Irigaray as "property, pro-duction, order, form, unity, visibility . . . and erection" (86). By refusing to subscribe to

these values, a writer like Acker presumes a female presence under another model of truth and/in discourse.

17. In his discussion of Peter Brooks's *Reading for the Plot: Design and Intention in Narrative* (1984), Clayton highlights Brooks's consideration of metonymy and metaphor, which are here, too, seen as an "organizing principle of narrative middles" and as "the figure that governs totalizing interpretations at the end of story," respectively (66). It should be noted that Brooks treats these as stages in the reading process, in which deferrals are necessary but temporary. Meanwhile, Acker's interest seems rather a matter of sustaining the dynamism of desire for its own liberating (and indefinite) sake.

18. Also relevant to Acker is the phrase "enunciation's motility," which Kristeva employs in "The Novel as Polylogue" (175). See also Fredric Jameson's contrast between Modernist parody and postmodern pastiche, the latter which does not restore the paradigm of "normal healthy discourse" (cited Brennan 247). By way of contrast to Kristeva's idea, see Arthur F. Redding's analysis of masochism in Acker's writings, in particular the contention that "Even a victim is entrenched within a discursive figuration that allows only limited semantic flexibility" (284).

19. Richard Walsh coins this last phrase and proceeds to list instances of these stalemates in the novel (146–51).

CHAPTER 8

1. We may note the surprising company Updike keeps in Jerome Klinkowitz's *Literary Subversions: New American Fiction and the Practice of Criticism* (1985), where he is united with "innovationists" Grace Paley and Robley Wilson, as well as with other more conventionally designated metafictionists like John Barth, Ishmael Reed, and Kurt Vonnegut, all of whom fit beneath the broad criteria of having revised the terms of criticism by virtue of their rebellion against mimetic constraints and their "self-apparent" techniques. (Klinkowitz coins the term in his 1984 study *The Self-Apparent Word: Fiction as Language / Language as Fiction*.)

2. In this respect, we could likewise turn to Updike's admiration of Virginia Woolf's writing—the way Woolf "give[s] us actuality in all its sliding, luminous increments" ("The Importance of Fiction" 86)—for another insight into the possible horizontal imperative of metaphor.

3. Janice bears comparison to the lumpish Molly Bingaman in "Flight," whose devotion to erudite young Allen Dow threatens to scuttle the aspirations his mother, friends, and teachers have for him. Like Janice, Molly is described as a negative space, a death's head (*Rabbit, Run* 7; "Flight" 63). As we might expect in a story entitled "Flight," Updike again uses images of enclosure prominently: Allen's own brain, shot through with conflict and especially with recriminations inherited from his mother, seemed to him "one dense organic dungeon, and I felt I had to get out; if I could just get out of this, into June, it would be blue sky, and I would be all right for life" (69).

4. See Burhans's extended attention to the contrasting line and circle image complexes in *Rabbit, Run*.

5. Paradoxically, for all her unbudging soddenness, Janice Springer Angstrom exhibits a reflex similar to Rabbit's instinct to flee: she is given to "kicking out in . . . her

panics" (8). Conversely, it is Rabbit, not his conventional drudge of a wife, who has the
obsession with neat rooms and folded clothing. Updike does not allow the reader to
become too complacent about the directions his satire of 1950s domesticity takes.
Indeed, Rabbit's flight from Janice lands him in another pregnant woman's arms. In
other words, Rabbit's run determines the regularity of his confinement better than it
locates openings in the seams.

   6. Yet another tension between arrest (vertical) and process (horizontal) resides in
the subtitle Updike had originally added to the novel: "A Motion Picture." Stanley Trachtenberg takes this as a cue to analyze the filmic nature of the narrative and the movie
version of *Rabbit, Run* (5–7), but we can also appreciate the oxymoronic quality of the
phrase, its relevance to Rabbit's desperate, thwarted course, and its neat approximation
of metaphor's dual capacity to retard and to project the reading experience.

   7. This evident reference to "The Love Song of J. Alfred Prufrock" (the self-
absorbed "sea-girls wreathed with seaweed red and brown") is joined by at least two others in the episode in which Harry and Tothero prepare for their night on the town.
Rabbit's Windsor-knotted tie recalls Prufrock's "necktie rich and modest, asserted by a
simple pin," both of which begin as marks of dignity and self-confidence and turn trea-
sonous. Next, Tothero's embarrassing relish over the way women are covered by hair—
"They are monkeys, Harry" (53)—recalls Prufrock's startling discovery of the brown,
downy arms of the women in Eliot's poem. (See also my discussion of how Harry finds
Jill's embrace a destructive threat in *Rabbit Redux*.) As for Lucy Eccles, the subject of
Harry's sexual reverie, her "compact arc of skull under her short-clipped fluffed hairdo"
which "suggests that she's been turned on an exceptionally precise lathe" (121) may
remind us of Madeleine, Herzog's tortured, vindictive wife in Saul Bellow's novel, who
cuts her bangs with shears as if with a vengeance.

   8. From Tothero's apartment, Rabbit hears the raucous sounds of the body shop
below, and he is comforted to think "that while he hides men are busy nailing the world
down, and toward the disembodied sounds his heart makes in darkness a motion of
love" (46). The same three components arise here, with love identified as companion to
other "motions of Grace," regardless of the libidinous musings (about decidedly *embodied* lovemaking, another combination of spiritual and athletic priorities) that immediately precede this thought.

   9. Contrast Ruth Leonard, who has been rendered rather earthbound and prosaic
by her sins. Not only is she scornful of Rabbit's wish to be Jesus Christ to her Mary
Magdalene (149) even as he encourages her to do to him what she has done to other
sex patrons; she is privately unappreciative of Rabbit's viewing sex as some transub-
stantiation of primal motives. Thinking of the male genitals, "That was the great thing
she discovered, that it was no mystery" (146–47). Furthermore, "when they're good
together she feels like next to nothing with him" (revised Fawcett paperback edition
138). Ruth takes comfort in the vanquishment of complexity, whereas Rabbit is cast in
the role of the nothing she lies next to. For his part, Rabbit emerges from this embodiment of oblivion with his nerves all combed (282)—until she levels her questions and
cares at him. "The way she is fighting for control of herself repels him; he doesn't like
people who manage things. He likes things to happen of themselves" (revised Fawcett
paperback edition 281).

10. Predictably, Rabbit remembers having enjoyed first-rate sex only back when he was a star high-school basketball player, with a girl named Mary Ann: "He came to her as a winner and that's the feeling he missed since" (198).

11. Golf has been a perpetual source of spiritual considerations and equivalences for Updike. In his essay "Tips on a Trip," Updike expands upon the mystical propensities of golf, marveling at how it "so transforms one's somatic sense, in short, that truth itself seems about to break through the exacerbated and as it were debunked fabric of mundane reality" (95). Beyond this, Updike concludes that his rare, luminous achievements on the golf course represent a reprieve from the limitations of philosophy, psychology, and physics: "These things happen in spite of me, and not because of me. On the golf course as nowhere else, the tyranny of causality is suspended, and men are free" (98). See also his review of Michael Murphy's *Golf in the Kingdom*, "Is There Life after Golf?," which undertakes by way of introduction this particular game's ability to inspire transcendental parallels (98–99). Then in the story "Intercession," soul and ball coalesce on the fairway: "If miracles, in this age of faint faith, could enter anywhere, it would be here, where the causal fabric was thinnest, in the quick collisions and abrupt deflections of a game. Paul drove high but crookedly over the treetops. It was dismaying for a creature of spirit to realize that the angle of a surface striking a sphere counted for more with God than the most ardent hope" (151). But for the last word on the subject, we may look to "The Pro," who tells his frustrated pupil in no uncertain terms that "there is no life, no world, beyond the golf course—just an infinite and terrible falling-off" (174).

12. A would-be bane of the domestic, Rabbit demonstrates a kitchen gadget, the MagiPeel Peeler, for a living. Coach Tothero, who takes special pride in his star player who never fouled (63), approves of this job as a "noble calling," cinching the joke even as he underscores the inviolable status of spiritual ecstasy.

13. Even Rabbit's symbolic dream of the struggle between life and death employs the context of athletics, as he witnesses this parabolic contest in the skies from below "on a large sporting field" (281).

14. A presentiment of Eccles's hollowness can be located in his name, with its echo of "ecclesiastic" (De Bellis 35–36). No wonder Rabbit prefers the proverb delivered by Jimmy, television's adult Mouseketeer—Know Thyself (which Rabbit conveniently paraphrases as an invitation to Be Yourself, a sentiment that sustains his putting instinct first)—to anything Eccles utters (Brenner 94–95).

15. Rabbit is anointed by the dying Mrs. Smith among her failing rhododendrons: "That's what you have, Harry: life. It's a strange gift and I don't know how we're supposed to use it but I know it's the only gift we get and it's a good one" (223). Her aphoristic firmness, however, is peculiar at best in the context of the fatal reversals to come, and will be replaced by Ruth's discovery that Rabbit is "Mr. Death himself," a contagious void (301).

16. We may recall Updike's poem "Ex-Basketball Player" in this context. Flick, whose "hands were like wild birds," has the same natural gift as Rabbit, but it now exists without relevance as he works at Berth's Garage, occasionally dribbling an inner tube or nodding "towards bright applauding tiers / Of Necco Wafers, Nibs, and Juju Beads" (lines 18, 29–30).

17. Penn Villas, an endowed bower of achieved affluence, does not escape the curse of the wasteland. It is a place of embedded blackness and drowsy decay (99). Whereas Harry remembers his childhood neighborhood as snug and secure, "Here, there is a prairie sadness, a barren sky raked by slender aerials. A sky poisoned by radio waves. A desolate smell from underground" (60).

18. Rabbit remains fundamentally a toy of primal sensations in *Rabbit Redux,* and while he does board Jill and Skeeter, he offers no real nourishment or protection but merely witnesses—at times promotes and participates in—their addictions and excesses.

19. Meanwhile, Janice herself, a creature of arcs and curvatures (43, 201), works with Charlie, shares his jargon, eats off his plate. And Charlie readily compensates and gratifies her. What troubled Harry about his wife—"he had fled her cunt as a tiger's mouth" (27)—evidently charms Charlie (who relishes the lover he refers to as "tiger").

20. In her lover's company, Janice senses "a falling, a falling away, a deep eye opening, a coming into the deep you, Harry wouldn't know about that" (57). Janice is not just noting her husband's relative ineffectiveness in bed but also coming to an understanding of how his long-standing irresponsibility was not a way of letting go of something but of holding on to something. In a reversal of the first novel's opening gambit, it is now Janice who tries to escape from the ballast of their domestic muddle.

21. And if nothing does count when it occurs a million miles away, here is yet another sobering comment upon the lessons America had banked on with the Apollo program.

22. Janice's return is also a retreat. In part it is due to the upheaval caused by Charlie's having had sex with Mim; in part it is due to Charlie's prohibitive heart condition; and in part it is due to the rediscovery of something that she had sensed during her first confession of the affair: "A gate she had always assumed gave onto a garden gave onto emptiness" (66). What Harry learned in *Rabbit, Run,* Janice learns in *Rabbit Redux:* taking off spreads the affliction. In view of these conditions, I am less sanguine than critics like David L. Vanderwerken about the durability of the hope indicated by Harry's "one small step" for unification (Vanderwerken 77).

23. The last lines of the novel—"He. She. Sleeps. O.K.?"—plays off the cadence of the closing of *Rabbit, Run* (as will the third and fourth entries in the novel sequence), and Robert Detweiler interprets them as "a resolution of quietness and equanimity" (134). I am much more guarded about accepting Rabbit's "return to health," an optimism that seems to me to deny the full measure of the image clusters that precede those lines. I would suggest that we not pass too quickly over the novel's concluding question mark—a hook Updike does not, after all, let his protagonist off.

24. From the moment Harry accepts his black coworker's invitation and enters the androgynous lair of the blues bar, he is troubled by the sexual component of his interest, especially in Skeeter, whose "liquidity" proves an oddly tantalizing alternative to the dry salvages of Jill and Peggy (250–51, 283). Skeeter recognizes and exploits this confusion, "feminizing" Harry to assert his privileges in his house—a method most horrifyingly conducted when Skeeter compels Harry to witness his sexual power over the drug-dependent girl.

25. An ironic gloss on this metaphor is provided by the local police chief, who disgustedly comments on Jill's death, which he lays at the door of her rich, negligent parents: "All our bad checks are being cashed" (348).

26. A telling contrast to this interpretation of the stars can be found in Updike's "Made in Heaven," whose protagonist finds them to be a welcoming congregation, an index of belief, and cosmic evidence of his own importance: "How little, little to the point of nothingness, he was beneath those stars! . . . And yet it was he who was witnessing the stars; they knew nothing of themselves, so in this dimension he was greater than they. As far as he could reason, religion begins with this strangeness, this standstill; faith tips the balance in favor of the pinpoint" (195). It is a faith he keeps until the conclusion of the story, when his dying wife, whose own faith he imagined to be "like water sealed into an underground cistern, unchangingly pure" (196), reveals to him that she has *not* been a believer for many years.

27. As it happens, Jill finds all this false, gaudy bliss marvelous: "Isn't it beautiful, all goldy and plasticky with that purple fire inside?" (139). The thinness of her diction bears out the shallowness of her appreciation, as well as adding to our understanding that Jill will prove no ideal reprieve for Harry from his tribulations.

28. Jill echoes Harry when she describes people to Nelson as motes in God's eye, as mirrors tilted the wrong way so that He cannot see Himself in them; meanwhile, our egos blind us to God's presence. It is ironic, of course, that Jill discusses our ruinous self-involvement while playing Monopoly, and that when she looks up from her disquisition her face looks blank as a mirror (159–60).

29. "Whatever else God may be, He shouldn't be pat" (*Roger's Version* 24). Anybody's *real* God "will *not* be deduced, will *not* be made subject to statistics and bits of old bone and glimmers of light in some telescope!" rages Roger Lambert, defending God against the arrogant violations of Dale Kohler, a student who proposes to expose God to view on his computer (*Roger's Version* 88). For a thorough and convincing summary of the influences of Barth and Kierkegaard on Updike, see Hunt (13–48), in which the theological underpinning of Updike's art of "open dialectic" is revealed.

30. Not only the memento mori of wrinkles around Peggy's eyes but the eyes themselves disturb Rabbit. The reference to her one good eye recalls Polyphemus, making the drifting Rabbit an Odysseus intent on escaping her clutches—her exasperating, ironic constancy. Less polished than the professional call girl Mim, she is just as primed for illicit behavior.

31. In place of that magic touch, Updike offers Rabbit the Magic Fingers of the motel bed to help keep the romance going.

32. Janice leads them to a Greek restaurant, where they "accidentally" encounter Charlie Stavros and where she recruits Nelson in the disparagement of "gooey" Chinese food (36)—significantly, a source of warm, lyrical pleasures for Harry in *Rabbit, Run*. Now the introduction of a new exotic cuisine confuses and depresses him. (It also bears mention that Jill finds all but the simplest nourishment repellent, having opted for other appetites.)

33. Factors contributing to Janice "redux" are Stavros's sleeping with Mim and her having to see him through a seizure that convinces her that their affair could kill him. So

despite his differences from Harry in terms of politics, personality, and sexual responsiveness, Stavros proves to be another man whose heart is on the verge of giving out.

34. Updike's initial vision of a pastoral sequel to *Rabbit Redux,* something on the order of *Rural Rabbit* (interview with Sragow 62–63) has plainly come down to this monetary translation of Wordsworth's field of golden daffodils. Elsewhere in the novel, Harry and Janice arouse one another sexually by talking about their new house and the appreciation of their investments (354–57). Instead of listening in on whispers of love, we eavesdrop on bank statements.

35. Not even wealth is spared the effects of decay. Weighted down by silver dollars, Rabbit "feels as if the sidewalk now is a downslanted plane, the whole year dropping away under him, loss after loss. His silver is scattered, tinsel. His box will break, the janitor will sweep up the coins. It's all dirt anyway" (375).

36. By comparison, the triumph of a long putt made comes complete with a "wooden gobbling sound" at the fall into the hole (60)—a moment of omnipotence, perhaps, but one which resonates with the "sucking down" associated elsewhere in the novel with wives and the bedrock of the dead.

37. On the other hand, Melanie does admire the solid juxtaposition of houses in Brewer—"It's like America used to be"—to which Nelson replies with characteristic Angstrom unease: "I hate it. Everything's so humid and stuffy and, so *closed*" (132).

38. It is suggested that God is entropy, or at least, that He has succumbed to entropy, when Rabbit learns that Peggy Fosnacht has had a mastectomy and shudders to think of the "breast he had sucked" suddenly "Flicked away by God's fingernail with its big moon" (460). Once again, the regenerative symbolism of the moon which America seems to be counting upon is denied.

39. The sentiment is seconded in the story "The Other Side of the Street": "Yes, you grow into the spaces the absent have left you" (145). A parallel point of evidence regarding Janice's growing self-possession in *Rabbit at Rest* will be her admission to herself, substantiating Rabbit's feeling in *Rabbit Is Rich,* that the deaths of her parents have given her sufficient "mental space" to fulfill her managerial talents (*Rabbit at Rest* 312).

40. Not even a vacation trip, a departure to the Poconos designed to verify and reward the Angstroms's financial insulation, escapes the numbing indignities of the wasteland and death's indiscriminate dominion: "[T]hey would enter upon a few stilted hours on the alien beach whose dry sand burned the feet and scratched in the crotch and whose wet ribs where the sea had receded had a deadly bottomless smell, a smell of vast death" (136).

41. As did Jill in *Rabbit Redux,* the sight of the girl stimulates protective and sexual inclinations in Rabbit; as with Jill, albeit less spectacularly, Rabbit fails in an ultimate sense to fulfill consequent responsibilities based on either design.

42. "There is along the way an open space, once a meadow, now spiked with cedars and tassle-headed weeds, where swallows dip and careen, snapping up insects revived in the evening damp." Between images of attrition and sustained effort, Rabbit imitates the mitigated resolve of these birds. "Like these swallows Rabbit, the blue and gold of his new shoes flickering, skims above the earth, above the dead" (141).

43. Thelma Harrison, who has won Rabbit in the Caribbean swapping episode, confesses that part of her long-standing desire for him has had to do with "the way you

never sit down anywhere without making sure there's a way out" (418). But his having anal sex with her is described as a capitulation to the void—not a refuge reached but a raw finitude, an immolating dark.

44. Running again, Rabbit suddenly stops: "His momentum is such that the world for a second or two streams on, seeming to fling all its trees and housetops outward against star-spangled space" (232). Dizzying, how space absorbs and proclaims a patriotic American imperative! Or have we cast our plenty into the void?

45. Judy's survival notwithstanding, numerous references to drowning in *Rabbit at Rest* show water to be Rabbit's nightmare element (54). Shells, seafood, and his own chest X-rays confront Rabbit with a cold, nebulous depth—death's circumambience (106, 113, 230). If we have seen Eliot's Prufrock in several of Rabbit's meditations in these novels, here is the drowned Phlebas the Phoenician from *The Waste Land,* who "passed the stages of his age and youth" as "A current under sea / Picked his bones in whispers" (lines 315–17).

46. Still, even a solid Republican like Harry Angstrom realizes that what rises in Reagan is mostly gas—dreamy anesthesia (62).

47. When Rabbit tells Thelma that he does not believe in God, she quickly shifts into sexual nostalgia: "Before you go, let me see him at least" marks an immediate redirection of Thelma's impulses from God to her lover's genitals (206).

48. Richard Maple is seized by a similar feeling in "Grandparenting": "huddled up, like a homunculous frigidly burning at the far end of God's indifferently held telescope" (314).

49. Strangely, this rueful train of thought almost immediately precedes, even seems to precipitate, a "piece of paradise blundered upon": the sexual episode with Pru.

50. The following comments by reviewer Garry Wills are representative of the opposition: "By succumbing to his own stylistic solipsism, Updike ends up exemplifying what is wrong. Description makes up for analysis; detail for design; inclusiveness for rigor; and mere length for moral heft or grip. . . . The endless verbal cleverness of Updike can run unimpeded by the weights of moral insight or of judgment" (14).

CONCLUSION

1. "Sound is audible metaphor, which does as form what imagery (always in danger of becoming too predictable) must try for as content" (Jonathan Bishop 24).

2. I have also employed this delightful and, in my experience, continually apt quotation, taken from Thoreau's 1848 address to the Harvard graduation class, to introduce *Designs of Darkness in Contemporary American Fiction* (Philadelphia: University of Pennsylvania Press, 1990).

3. More recently, Sontag has offered this gloss, which hews to similar criteria: "I believe in right action. But, as a writer, it's far more complicated. Literature is not about doing the right thing—though it is about expressiveness (language) at a noble level and wisdom (inclusiveness, empathy, truthfulness, moral seriousness)" ("Singleness" 172).

4. Elsewhere and often in his introduction to *The Western Canon* ("An Elegy for the Canon"), Bloom redirects our predilection for making it "useful": "Reading deeply in the Canon will not make one a better or a worse person, a more useful or more harm-

ful citizen. The mind's dialogue with itself is not primarily a social reality. All that the Western Canon can bring one is the proper use of one's own solitude" (30).

The study of literature, however it is conducted, will not "save any individual, any more than it will improve any society. Shakespeare will not make us better, and he will not make us worse, but he may teach us how to overhear ourselves when we talk to ourselves" (31).

The Western Canon, despite the limitless idealism of "those who would open it up, exists precisely in order to impose limits, to set a standard of measurement that is anything but political or moral" (35).

5. I borrow this phrase from Mark Edmundson, who uses it to describe a moralizing brand of criticism identified with Matthew Arnold and T. S. Eliot, and which he opposes with critics descended from Montaigne and Emerson, who "aren't primarily interested in being anyone's source of secure authority" (68), and with whose assumptions, obviously, the fictions covered in this study resonate very nicely.

6. This line comes from Jorie Graham's *Region of Unlikeness* (1991), a collection of poetry whose title not only attests to the difficulty of finding one's way through the confusion of the poet's and history's thickets but also serves as a sobering contrast to, say, Richard Wilbur's suggestion of the inevitability of *likeness* in "Praise in Summer," the poem from which I have taken the title of this book.

Works Cited

Acker, Kathy. "A Conversation with Kathy Acker." With Ellen G. Friedman. *Review of Contemporary Fiction* 9.3 (1989): 12–22.

———. *Don Quixote*. New York: Grove, 1986.

———. *Empire of the Senseless*. New York: Grove, 1988.

———. *Great Expectations*. New York: Grove, 1982.

———. "An Interview with Kathy Acker." By Larry McCaffery. *Mississippi Review* 20.1–2 (1991): 83–97.

———. "Kathy Acker: An Interview." By Paul Perilli. *Poets & Writers* 21.2 (March/April 1993): 28–33.

———. "Kathy Acker: From Mascot to Doyenne of the Avant-Garde." Interview with Judy Stone. *Publishers Weekly* (11 December 1995): 53–54.

———. "Kathy Acker: Where Does She Get Off?" Interview with R. U. Sirius. *io* 2 (1994): 18–23.

———. "The Language of the Body." *CTHEORY* (1992): Internet. 21 February 1996.

———. *Literal Madness: Kathy Goes to Haiti; My Death My Life by Pier Paolo Pasolini; Florida*. New York: Grove, 1988.

———. "Models of Our Present." *Artforum* (February 1984): 62–65.

Ackerman, Diane. "A. R. Ammons Amid the Fungi." In *Jaguar of Sweet Laughter: New and Selected Poems*, 171–72. New York: Random, 1991.

———. "Diffraction." In *Jaguar of Sweet Laughter: New and Selected Poems*, 111–12. New York: Random, 1991.

———. "Halley's Comet." In *Jaguar of Sweet Laughter: New and Selected Poems*, 12–14. New York: Random, 1991.

———. *Jaguar of Sweet Laughter: New and Selected Poems*. New York: Random, 1991.

Albee, Edward. *The Zoo Story. Modern and Contemporary Drama*. Ed. Miriam Gilbert, Carl H. Klaus, and Bradford S. Field Jr., 490–99. New York: St. Martin's, 1994.

Alter, Robert. "The Leveling Wind." Review of *The Tunnel*. *The New Republic* (27 March 1995): 29–32.

Ammons, A. R. *Collected Poems, 1951–1971*. New York: Norton, 1972.

———. "Corson's Inlet." In *Collected Poems, 1951–1971*, 147–51. New York: Norton, 1972.

———. "Poetics." In *Collected Poems, 1951–1971*, 199. New York: Norton, 1972.

———. "The Unifying Principle." In *Collected Poems, 1951–1971*, 287. New York: Norton, 1972.

Auster, Paul. *City of Glass*. New York: Viking Penguin, 1985.

———. "Disappearances." In *Ground Work: Selected Poems and Essays, 1970–1979*, 61–68. London: Faber & Faber, 1990.

———. "Fore-shadows." In *Ground Work: Selected Poems and Essays, 1970–1979*, 40. London: Faber & Faber, 1990.

———. *Ground Work: Selected Poems and Essays, 1970–1979*. London: Faber & Faber, 1990.

———. "Incendiary." In *Ground Work: Selected Poems and Essays, 1970–1979*, 49. London: Faber & Faber, 1990.

———. "An Interview with Paul Auster." By Larry McCaffery and Sinda Gregory. *Contemporary Literature* 33.1 (1992): 1–23.

———. *The Invention of Solitude*. New York: Viking Penguin, 1988.

———. *Leviathan*. New York: Viking, 1992.

———. *The Locked Room*. New York: Viking Penguin, 1986.

———. *The Music of Chance*. New York: Viking, 1990.

———. "Unearth." In *Ground Work: Selected Poems and Essays, 1970–1979*, 7–28. London: Faber & Faber, 1990.

———. "White Spaces." In *Ground Work: Selected Poems and Essays, 1970–1979*, 81–88. London: Faber & Faber, 1990.

Bailey, Peter J. *Reading Stanley Elkin*. Urbana: University of Illinois Press, 1985.

Bair, Deidre. *Samuel Beckett: A Biography*. New York and London: Harcourt Brace Jovanovich, 1978.

Baker, Nicholson. *U and I: A True Story*. New York: Random, 1991.

Barth, John. "The Literature of Exhaustion." In *The Friday Book: Essays and Other Nonfiction*, 62–76. New York: G. P. Putnam's Sons, 1984.

———. "Lost in the Funhouse." In *Lost in the Funhouse: Fiction for Print, Tape, Live Voice*, 69–94. New York: Doubleday/Bantam, 1969.

Baudrillard, Jean. "The Ecstasy of Communication." Trans. John Johnston. In *The Anti-Aesthetic: Essays on Postmodern Culture*, ed. Hal Foster, 126–34. Port Townsend, Wash.: Bay Press, 1983.

Bawer, Bruce. "Don DeLillo's America." *New Criterion* 3 (April 1985): 34–42.

Bellow, Saul. *Herzog*. New York: Viking, 1964.

Birkerts, Sven. "Second Thoughts." *Review of Contemporary Fiction* 16 (1): 7–12.

Bishop, Elizabeth. *The Complete Poems 1927–1979*. New York: Farrar, Straus and Giroux / Noonday, 1980.

———. "The Fish." In *The Complete Poems 1927–1979*, 42–44. New York: Farrar, Straus and Giroux / Noonday, 1980.

———. "Sandpiper." In *The Complete Poems 1927–1979*, 131. New York: Farrar, Straus and Giroux / Noonday, 1980.

Bishop, Jonathan. "The Individual Thing." *Renascence* 45 (fall 1992–winter 1993): 17–33.

Black, Max. "More about Metaphor." In *Metaphor and Thought,* ed. Andrew Orotny, 19–43. London and New York: Cambridge University Press, 1979.

Bloom, Harold. *The Western Canon: The Books and the School of the Ages.* New York: Harcourt Brace, 1994.

Boorstein, Daniel J. "Darwinian Expectations." In *Cleopatra's Nose: Essays on the Unexpected,* 125–40. New York: Random, 1994.

Borges, Jorge Luis. "The Analytical Language of John Wilkins." In *Borges, A Reader: A Selection from the Writings of Jorge Luis Borges,* ed. Emir Rodriguez Monegal and Alastair Reid, trans. Ruth L. C. Simms, 141–43 New York: Dutton, 1981.

———. "The Circular Ruins." In *Labyrinths: Selected Stories and Other Writings,* ed. Donald A. Yates and James E. Irby, trans. James E. Irby, 45–50. New York: New Directions, 1964.

———. "Funes, the Memorious." In *Labyrinths: Selected Stories and Other Writings,* ed. Donald A. Yates and James E. Irby, trans. James E. Irby, 59–66. New York: New Directions, 1964.

———. *Labyrinths: Selected Stories and Other Writings.* Ed. Donald A. Yates and James E. Irby. Trans. James E. Irby. New York: New Directions, 1964.

Boruch, Marianne. "On Metaphor." *Ohio Review* 52 (1994): 104–19.

Brennan, Karen. "The Geography of Enunciation: Hysterical Pastiche in Kathy Acker's Fiction." *Boundary 2* 21.2 (1994): 243–68.

Brenner, Gerry. *"Rabbit, Run:* John Updike's Criticism of the 'Return to Nature.'" In *Critical Essays on John Updike,* ed. William R. Macnaughton, 91–104. Boston: G. K. Hall, 1982.

Brown, E. K. *Rhythm in the Novel.* Lincoln: University of Nebraska Press, 1978.

Burhans Jr., Clinton S. "Things Falling Apart: Structure and Theme in *Rabbit, Run.*" In *Critical Essays on John Updike,* ed. William R. Macnaughton, 148–62. Boston: G. K. Hall, 1982.

Burke, Kenneth. "Semantic and Poetic Meaning." In *The Philosophy of Literary Form: Studies in Symbolic Action.* 2d ed. 1–137. Baton Rouge: Louisiana State University Press, 1967.

Burroway, Janet. "Trash Talk." *New Letters* 60.4 (1994): 11–19.

Cable, Lana. *Carnal Rhetoric: Milton's Iconoclasm and the Poetics of Desire.* Durham and London: Duke University Press, 1995.

Canetti, Elias. *Crowds and Power.* Trans. Carol Stewart. New York: Viking, 1963.

Carr, C. "Text and Violence: Kathy Acker Strikes Again." *Voice Literary Supplement* 53 (March 1987): 9–10.

Cary, Joyce. *The Horse's Mouth.* New York: Harper, 1957.

Cixous, Hélène. "The Character of 'Character.'" *New Literary History* 5 (1974): 383–402.

Clayton, Jay. *The Pleasures of Babel: Contemporary American Literature and Theory.* New York: Oxford University Press, 1993.

Colley, Ann C. *The Search for Synthesis in Literature and Art: The Paradox of Space.* Athens: University of Georgia Press, 1990.

Conrad, Joseph. Preface to *The Nigger of the "Narcissus."* Ed. Robert Kimbrough, 145–48. New York: Norton, 1979.

Cooper, Rand Richards. "Rabbit Loses the Race: John Updike's 'Small Answer of a Texture.'" *New Republic* (17 May 1991): 315–21.

Crews, Frederick. "Mr. Updike's Planet." Review of *Roger's Version,* by John Updike. *New York Review of Books* (4 December 1986): 7+.

Cullen, Countee. "Only the Polished Skeleton." In *On These I Stand: An Anthology of the Best Poems of Countee Cullen,* 146. New York and London: Harper & Brothers, 1947.

Dane, Gabrielle. "Hysteria as Feminist Protest." *Women's Studies* 23 (1994): 231–56.

DeBellis, Jack. "The 'Extra Dimension': Character Names in Updike's 'Rabbit' Trilogy." *Names* 36 (1988): 29–42.

DeLillo, Don. *Americana.* Boston: Houghton Mifflin, 1971.

———. "The Art of Fiction CXXXV." Interview with Adam Begley. *Paris Review* 128 (fall 1993): 275–306.

———. *End Zone.* Boston: Houghton Mifflin, 1972.

———. "The Engineer of Moonlight." *Cornell Review* 5 (winter 1979): 21–47.

———. *Great Jones Street.* Boston: Houghton Mifflin, 1973.

———. "An Interview with Don DeLillo." With Tom LeClair. In *Anything Can Happen: Interviews with Contemporary American Novelists,* ed. Tom LeClair and Larry McCaffery, 79–90. Urbana: University of Illinois Press, 1983.

———. "An Interview with Don DeLillo." With Maria Nadotti. Trans. Peggy Boyers. *Salmagundi* 100 (fall 1993): 86–97.

———. *Libra.* New York: Viking, 1988.

———. *Mao II.* New York: Viking, 1991.

———. *The Names.* New York: Knopf, 1982.

———. "'An Outsider in This Society': An Interview with Don DeLillo." With Anthony DeCurtis. In *Introducing Don DeLillo,* ed. Frank Lentricchia, 43–66. Durham and London: Duke University Press, 1991.

———. *Pafko at the Wall.* Harper's (October 1992): 35–70.

———. *Players.* New York: Knopf, 1977.

———. *Ratner's Star.* New York: Knopf, 1976.

———. *Underworld.* New York: Scribner, 1997.

———. *White Noise.* New York: Viking, 1985.

Derrida, Jacques. "White Mythology: Metaphor in the Text of Philosophy." Trans. F. C. T. Moore. *New Literary History* 6.1 (1974): 5–74.

Dickinson, Emily. "There's a Certain Slant of Light." In *The Poems of Emily Dickinson,* ed. Thomas H. Johnson, 1:185. Cambridge: Harvard University Press, 1963.

Dillard, Annie. *Holy the Firm.* New York: Harper & Row, 1977.

———. *Living by Fiction.* New York: Harper & Row, 1982.

Dix, Douglas Shields. "Kathy Acker's *Don Quixote:* Nomad Writing." *Review of Contemporary Fiction* 9.3 (1989): 56–62.

Doctorow, E. L. *The Book of Daniel.* New York: Random, 1971.

Donoghue, Denis. Review of *All the Pretty Horses,* by Cormac McCarthy. *The New York Review of Books* (24 June 1993): 5–6, 8–10.

Doty, Mark. "Difference." In *My Alexandria,* 52–54. Urbana and Chicago: University of Illinois Press, 1993.

Duemer, Joseph. "To Make the Visible World Your Conscience." *New England Review* 14.4 (1992): 268–85.

Dunn, Stephen. *Loves. New and Selected Poems, 1974–1994,* 275–87. New York and London: Norton, 1994.

Edmundson, Mark. "The Human Factor." Review of *The Scandal of Pleasure: Art in an Age of Fundamentalism.* By Wendy Steiner. *Lingua Franca* (January/February 1996): 64–68.

Eliot, T. S. *The Complete Poems and Plays, 1909–1950.* New York: Harcourt, Brace and World, 1962.

———. "The Love Song of J. Alfred Prufrock." In *The Complete Poems and Plays, 1909–1950,* 3–7. New York: Harcourt, Brace and World, 1962.

———. "The Waste Land." In *The Complete Poems and Plays, 1909–1950,* 37–55. New York: Harcourt, Brace and World, 1962.

Elkin, Stanley. *The Franchiser.* Boston: Godine, 1976.

Embler, Weller. *Metaphor and Meaning.* DeLand, Fla.: Everett/Edwards, 1966.

Federman, Raymond. "Imagination as Plagiarism [an unfinished paper]." *New Literary History* 7 (1976): 563–78.

Fleischauer, John F. "John Updike's Prose Style: Definition at the Periphery of Meaning." *Critique* 30.4 (1989): 277–89.

Forché, Carolyn. "The Colonel." In *The Country Between Us,* 16. New York: Harper & Row, 1981.

Freeman, Barbara Claire. *The Feminine Sublime: Gender and Excess in Women's Fiction.* Berkeley: University of California Press, 1995.

Friedman, Ellen G. "'Now Eat Your Mind': An Introduction to the Works of Kathy Acker." *Review of Contemporary Fiction* 9.3 (1989): 37–49.

———. "'Utterly Other Discourse': The Anticanon of Experimental Women Writers from Dorothy Richardson to Christine Brooke-Rose." *Modern Fiction Studies* 34.3 (1988): 353–70.

Friedrich, Hugo. *Montaigne.* Ed. Philippe Desan. Trans. Dawn Eng. Berkeley: University of California Press, 1991.

Frost, Robert. *Complete Poems of Robert Frost.* New York: Holt, Rinehart and Winston, 1958.

———. "Education by Poetry." In *Selected Prose of Robert Frost.* Ed. Hyde Cox and Edward Connery Lathem, 33–46. New York: Holt, Rinehart and Winston, 1966.

———. "For Once, Then, Something." In *Complete Poems of Robert Frost,* 276. New York: Holt, Rinehart and Winston, 1958.

———. "Mending Wall." In *Complete Poems of Robert Frost,* 47–48. New York: Holt, Rinehart and Winston, 1958.

Frow, John. "The Last Things before the Last: Notes on *White Noise.*" In *Introducing Don DeLillo,* ed. Frank Lentricchia, 175–91. Durham and London: Duke University Press, 1991.

Fulton, Alice. "The Fractal Lanes." In *Powers of Congress,* 23. Boston: Godine, 1990.

Gass, William. "The Artist and Society." In *Fiction and the Figures of Life,* 276–88. Boston: Godine, 1971.

———. "Carrots, Noses, Snow, Rose, Roses." In *The World within the Word,* 280–307. New York: Knopf, 1978.

———. "Culture, Self, and Style." In *Habitations of the Word,* 185–205. New York: Simon and Schuster, 1985.

———. "Emerson and the Essay." In *Habitations of the Word,* 9–49. New York: Simon and Schuster, 1985.

———. *Fiction and the Figures of Life.* Boston: Godine, 1971.

———. "Groping for Trouts." In *The World within the Word,* 262–79. New York: Knopf, 1978.

———. *Habitations of the Word.* New York: Simon and Schuster, 1985.

———. "The High Brutality of Good Intentions." In *Fiction and the Figures of Life,* 177–90. Boston: Godine, 1971.

———. "The Imagination of an Insurrection." In *Fiction and the Figures of Life,* 263–67. Boston: Godine, 1971.

———. *In the Heart of the Heart of the Country.* Boston: Godine, 1968.

———. "In Terms of the Toenail: Fiction and the Figures of Life." In *Fiction and the Figures of Life,* 55–76. Boston: Godine, 1971.

———. "An Interview with William Gass." With Regis Durand. *Delta* 8 (May 1979): 7–19.

———. "The Medium of Fiction." In *Fiction and the Figures of Life,* 27–33. Boston: Godine, 1971.

———. "Monumentality/Mentality." *Oppositions* 25 (fall 1982): 126–44.

———. *Omensetter's Luck.* New York: New American Library, 1966.

———. "The Ontology of the Sentence, or How to Make a World of Words." In *The World within the Word,* 308–38. New York: Knopf, 1978.

———. "Philosophy and the Form of Fiction." In *Fiction and the Figures of Life,* 3–26. Boston: Godine, 1971.

———. "Representation and the War for Reality." In *Habitations of the Word,* 73–112. New York: Simon and Schuster, 1985.

———. A Revised and Expanded Preface. *In the Heart of the Heart of the Country,* xiii–xlvi. Boston: Godine, 1981.

———. "The Soul Inside the Sentence." In *Habitations of the Word,* 113–40. New York: Simon and Schuster, 1985.

———. "Tribalism, Identity, and Ideology." *Profession* 94 (1994): 54–56.

———. "Tropes of the Text." In *Habitations of the Word,* 141–59. New York: Simon and Schuster, 1985.

———. *The Tunnel.* New York: Knopf, 1995.

———. *Willie Masters' Lonesome Wife.* TriQuarterly Supplement 2. Evanston, Ill.: Northwestern University Press, 1968.

———. *The World within the Word.* New York: Knopf, 1978.

Gelfant, Blanche H. *Women Writing in America: Voices in Collage.* Hanover, N.H.: University Press of New England, 1984.

Glück, Louise. "Mock Orange." *The First Four Books of Poems: Firstborn, The House on*

Marshland, Descending Figure, The Triumph of Achilles, 155. Hopewell, N.J.: Ecco, 1995.

Goldbarth, Albert. "Donald Duck in Danish." In *Popular Culture,* 3–12. Columbus: Ohio State University Press, 1990.

———. "Some Things." In *Heaven and Earth: A Cosmology,* 104. Athens: University of Georgia Press, 1991.

Graham, Jorie. "Who Watches from the Dark Porch." In *Region of Unlikeness,* 97–108. Hopewell, N.J.: Ecco, 1991.

Greene, Gayle. *Changing the Story: Feminist Fiction and the Tradition.* Bloomington: Indiana University Press, 1991.

Harries, Karsten. "Metaphor and Transcendence." In *On Metaphor,* ed. Sheldon Sacks, 71–88. Chicago and London: University of Chicago Press, 1979.

Hawkes, John. *Virginie: Her Two Lives.* New York: Harper, 1982.

Hawkes, Terence. *Metaphor.* The Critical Idiom No. 25. Ed. John J. Jump. London: Methuen, 1972.

Heaney, Liam F. "The Essence of Language: Metaphorically Speaking." *Contemporary Review* 266.1553 (1995): 313–19.

Heaney, Seamus. "Joy or Night: Last Things in the Poetry of W. B. Yeats and Philip Larkin." In *The Redress of Poetry,* 146–63. New York: Farrar, Straus & Giroux, 1995.

Heffernan, James A. W. "Ekphrasis and Representation." *New Literary History* 22 (1991): 297–316.

Hulley, Kathleen. "Transgressing Genre: Kathy Acker's Intertext." In *Intertextuality and Contemporary American Fiction,* ed. Patrick O'Donnell and Robert Con Davis, 171–90. Baltimore and London: Johns Hopkins University Press, 1989.

Hunt, George W. *John Updike and the Three Great Secret Things: Sex, Religion, and Art.* Grand Rapids, Mich.: Eerdmans, 1980.

Irigaray, Luce. *This Sex Which Is Not One.* Trans. Catherine Porter. With Carolyn Burke. Ithaca, N.Y.: Cornell University Press, 1985.

Jacobs, Naomi. "Kathy Acker and the Plagiarized Self." *Review of Contemporary Fiction* 9.3 (1989): 50–55.

Keesey, Douglas. *Don DeLillo.* Twayne's United States Authors Series 629. New York: Macmillan/Twayne, 1993.

Kinzie, Mary. "The Cure of Poetry." In *The Cure of Poetry in an Age of Prose: Moral Essays on the Poet's Calling,* 271–90. Chicago and London: University of Chicago Press, 1993.

———. "Succeeding Borges, Escaping Kafka: On the Fiction of Steven Millhauser." *Salmagundi* 92 (fall 1991): 115–44.

Klinkowitz, Jerome. *Literary Subversions: New American Fiction and the Practice of Criticism.* Carbondale: Southern Illinois University Press, 1985.

———. *The Self-Apparent Word: Fiction as Language/Language as Fiction.* Carbondale: Southern Illinois University Press, 1984.

Krieger, Murray. *Ekphrasis: The Illusion of the Natural Sign.* Baltimore: Johns Hopkins University Press, 1992.

Kristeva, Julia. *Desire in Language: A Semiotic Approach to Literature and Art.* Ed. Leon

S. Roudiez. Trans. Thomas Gora, Alice Jardine, and Leon S. Roudiez. New York: Columbia University Press, 1980.

————. "The Ethics of Linguistics." In *Desire in Language: A Semiotic Approach to Literature and Art,* ed. Leon S. Roudiez. Trans. Thomas Gora, Alice Jardine, and Leon S. Roudiez, 23–35. New York: Columbia University Press, 1980.

————. "The Novel as Polylogue." In *Desire in Language: A Semiotic Approach to Literature and Art,* ed. Leon S. Roudiez. Trans. Thomas Gora, Alice Jardine, and Leon S. Roudiez, 159–209. New York: Columbia University Press, 1980..

Kuehl, John. *Alternate Worlds: A Study of Postmodern Antirealistic American Fiction.* New York: New York University Press, 1989.

Kuhns, Richard. "Metaphor as Plausible Inference in Poetry and Philosophy." *Philosophy and Literature* 3.2 (1979): 225–38.

Kundera, Milan. *The Book of Laughter and Forgetting.* Trans. Michael Henry Heim. New York: Knopf, 1980.

Lakoff, George, and Mark Turner. *More than Cool Reason: A Field Guide to Poetic Metaphor.* Chicago and London: University of Chicago Press, 1989.

Lane, Anthony. "The Top Ten." *New Yorker* (27 June–4 July 1994): 79+.

Langer, Lawrence L. *Admitting the Holocaust: Collected Essays.* New York: Oxford University Press, 1995.

LeClair, Tom. *In the Loop: Don DeLillo and the Systems Novel.* Urbana: University of Illinois Press, 1988.

Lehman, David. "Three Meditations on Wallace Stevens." In *The Line Forms Here,* 35–52. Ann Arbor: University of Michigan Press, 1992.

Lentricchia, Frank, ed. *Introducing Don DeLillo.* Durham and London: Duke University Press, 1991.

Macnaughton, William R., ed. *Critical Essays on John Updike.* Boston: G. K. Hall, 1982.

Martin, Ronald E. *American Literature and the Destruction of Knowledge.* Durham and London: Duke University Press, 1991.

Massey, Irving. *Find You the Virtue: Ethics, Image, and Desire in Literature.* Fairfax, Va.: George Mason University Press, 1987.

Melville, Herman. *Moby Dick.* Ed. Harrison Hayford and Hershel Parker. New York: Norton, 1967.

Miller, J. Hillis. *Poets of Reality: Six Twentieth-Century Writers.* Cambridge, Mass.: Harvard University Press, 1965.

Millhauser, Steven. "Alice, Falling." In *The Barnum Museum,* 163–81. New York: Penguin/New American Library, 1991.

————. *The Barnum Museum.* New York: Penguin / New American Library, 1991.

————. "The Barnum Museum." In *The Barnum Museum,* 73–91. New York: Penguin/New American Library, 1991.

————. "Behind the Blue Curtain." In *The Barnum Museum,* 61–71. New York: Penguin/New American Library, 1991.

————. *Catalogue of the Exhibition. Salmagundi* 92 (fall 1991): 55–109.

————. "Cathay." In *In the Penny Arcade,* 147–64. New York: Knopf, 1986.

————. "The Dream of the Consortium." *Harper's* (March 1993): 62–70, 72.

————. *Edwin Mullhouse: The Life and Death of an American Writer, 1943–1954,* by *Jeffrey Cartwright.* New York: Knopf, 1972.

————. "The Eighth Voyage of Sinbad." In *Barnum Museum,* 111–40. New York: Penguin/New American Library, 1991.

————. "Eisenheim the Illusionist." In *Barnum Museum,* 215–37. New York: Penguin/New American Library, 1991.

————. "A Game of Clue." In *Barnum Museum,* 9–60. New York: Penguin/New American Library, 1991.

————. *In the Penny Arcade.* New York: Knopf, 1986.

————. "In the Penny Arcade." In *In the Penny Arcade,* 135–45. New York: Knopf, 1986.

————. Interview by Jean W. Ross. *Contemporary Authors,* ed. Hal May, 111:325–27. Detroit: Gale Research, 1984.

————. "The Invention of Robert Herendeen." In *Barnum Museum,* 183–214. New York: Penguin/New American Library, 1991.

————. *Portrait of a Romantic.* New York: Knopf, 1977.

————. "Replicas." *Yale Review* 83.3 (1995): 50–61.

————. "The Sepia Postcard." In *Barnum Museum,* 93–110. New York: Penguin/New American Library, 1991.

Moi, Toril. *Sexual / Textual Politics: Feminist Literary Theory.* New Accents. Gen. ed. Terence Hawkes. London and New York: Methuen, 1985.

Mooney, William. "Those Pearls His Eyes: Paul West's Blind Monologuists and Deaf Auditors." *Review of Contemporary Fiction* 11.1 (1991): 267–79.

Morse, Samuel. "The Motive for Metaphor—Wallace Stevens: His Poetry and His Practice." *Origin* 2 (spring 1952): 3–65.

Nabokov, Vladimir. "Signs and Symbols." In *Writing Fiction: A Guide to Narrative Craft.* 3d ed. Ed. Janet Burroway, 283–87. New York: Harper Collins, 1992.

Nemerov, Howard. *The Collected Poems of Howard Nemerov.* Chicago: University of Chicago Press, 1977.

————. "Holding the Mirror Up to Nature." In *The Collected Poems of Howard Nemerov,* 207. Chicago: University of Chicago Press, 1977.

————. "Inside the Onion." In *Trying Conclusions: New and Selected Poems, 1961–1991,* 117–18. Chicago and London: University of Chicago Press, 1991.

————. "Lion & Honeycomb." In *The Collected Poems of Howard Nemerov,* 277. Chicago: University of Chicago Press, 1977.

————. "Unscientific Postscript." In *The Collected Poems of Howard Nemerov,* 48. Chicago: University of Chicago Press, 1977.

Newman, John Henry. *The Uses of Knowledge: Selections from* The Idea of a University. Ed. Leo L. Ward. New York: Appleton-Century-Crofts, 1948.

O'Connor, Flannery. *Wise Blood.* In *Three by Flannery O'Connor,* 1–120. New York: New American Library, 1962.

Olds, Sharon. "The Swimmer." In *The Father,* 56. New York: Knopf, 1992.

Osborne, John. *Look Back in Anger.* New York: Bantam, 1957.

Ozick, Cynthia. "The Moral Necessity of Metaphor." *Harper's* (May 1986): 62–68.

Percy, Walker. "Metaphor as Mistake." In *The Message in the Bottle: How Queer Man Is, How Queer Language Is, and What One Has to Do with the Other,* 64–82. New York: Farrar, Straus and Giroux, 1975.

Piercy, Marge. "You Ask Why Sometimes I Say Stop." In *Contemporary American Poetry,* ed. A. Poulin Jr. 6th ed. 458–59. Boston: Houghton Mifflin, 1996.

Plath, James, ed. *Conversations with John Updike.* Jackson: University of Mississippi Press, 1994.

Plimpton, George, ed. *The Writer's Chapbook.* New York: Viking, 1989.

Poirier, Richard. *Poetry and Pragmatism.* Cambridge, Mass.: Harvard University Press, 1992.

———. *Robert Frost: The Work of Knowing.* New York: Oxford University Press, 1977. Reprint, Stanford, Calif.: Stanford University Press, 1990.

Powers, Richard. "Bordercrossings: A Conversation in Cyberspace." With N. Katherine Hayles, Jay Labinger, and Richard Powers. Moderated by Janet Stites. *Omni* (November 1993): 38+.

———. *Galatea 2.2.* New York: Farrar Straus Giroux, 1995.

———. *The Gold Bug Variations.* New York: William Morrow, 1991.

———. *Operation Wandering Soul.* New York: William Morrow, 1993.

———. *Prisoner's Dilemma.* New York: Macmillan, 1988.

———. "PW Interviews Richard Powers." By John F. Baker. *Publishers Weekly* (16 August 1991): 37–38.

———. *Three Farmers on Their Way to a Dance.* William Morrow/Harper Collins, 1985.

Pritchett, V. S. Review of *Rabbit Is Rich.* By John Updike. *New Yorker* (9 November 1981): 201–6.

Prunty, Wyatt. *"Fallen from the Symboled World": Precedents for the New Formalism.* New York: Oxford University Press, 1990.

Pynchon, Thomas. *The Crying of Lot 49.* Philadelphia: J. B. Lippincott, 1966.

Redding, Arthur F. "Bruises, Roses: Masochism and the Writing of Kathy Acker." *Contemporary Literature* 35.2 (1994): 281–304.

Rich, Adrienne. "When We Dead Awaken: Writing as Re-Vision." In *On Lies, Secrets, and Silence: Selected Prose 1966–1978,* 33–49. New York: Norton, 1979.

Ricouer, Paul. *The Rule of Metaphor.* Trans. Robert Czerny with Kathleen McLaughlin and John Costello. Toronto: University of Toronto Press, 1975.

Rogers, Pattiann. "Twentieth-Century Cosmology and the Soul's Habitation." In *Writing It Down for James: Writers on Life and Craft,* ed. Kurt Brown, 186–97. Boston: Beacon, 1995.

Rosenfeld, Alvin H. "The Virtuoso and the Gravity of History." *Salmagundi* 55 (winter 1982): 103–9.

Ruskin, John. "Of the Pathetic Fallacy." In *Of Many Things.* 4th ed. Vol. 3, *Modern Painters.* 161–77. London: Allen, 1897–1904.

Salinger, J. D. "Teddy." In *Nine Stories,* 166–98. Boston: Little, Brown / Bantam, 1953.

Schnitzer, Deborah. *The Pictorial in Modernist Fiction.* Ann Arbor, Mich.: UMI Research Press, 1988.

Sciolino, Martina. "Confessions of a Kleptoparasite." *Review of Contemporary Fiction* 9.3 (1989): 63–67.

Sheehan, Donald. "Wallace Stevens' Theory of Metaphor." *Papers on Language and Literature* 2 (1966): 57–66.

Simic, Charles. *Dime-Store Alchemy: The Art of Joseph Cornell*. Hopewell, N.J.: Ecco, 1992.

Singer, Alan. *A Metaphorics of Fiction: Discontinuity and Discourse in the Modern Novel*. Tallahassee: University Presses of Florida, 1983.

Sontag, Susan. "On Style." In *Against Interpretation and Other Essays*, 15–36. New York: Dell, 1966.

———. "Singleness." In *Who's Writing This? Notations on the Authorial I with Self Portraits*, ed. Daniel Halpern, 171–74. Hopewell, N.J.: Ecco, 1995.

Stein, Gertrude. "Pictures." In *Lectures in America*, 59–90. New York: Random, 1962.

Steiner, Wendy. *The Colors of Rhetoric: Problems in the Relation between Modern Literature and Painting*. Chicago: University of Chicago Press, 1982.

Stern, Chaim, ed. *Gates of Prayer: The New Union Prayerbook*. New York: Central Conference of American Rabbis, 1975.

Stevens, Wallace. *Adagia* (1934–40?). In *Opus Posthumous*, ed. Milton J. Bates, 184–202. New York: Knopf, 1989.

———. "About One of Marianne Moore's Poems." In *The Necessary Angel*, 91–103. New York: Knopf, 1951.

———. "Add This to Rhetoric." In *The Collected Poems*, 198–99. New York: Random, 1954.

———. "Bouquet of Roses in Sunlight." In *The Collected Poems*, 430–31. New York: Random, 1954.

———. *The Collected Poems*. New York: Random, 1954.

———. *The Comedian as the Letter C*. In *The Collected Poems*, 27–46. New York: Random, 1954.

———. "Description without Place." In *The Collected Poems*, 339–469. New York: Random, 1954.

———. "Effects of Analogy." In *The Necessary Angel: Essays on Reality and the Imagination*, 105–30. New York: Random, 1951.

———. "A High-Toned Old Christian Woman." In *The Collected Poems*, 59. New York: Random, 1954.

———. "How to Live. What to Do." In *The Collected Poems*, 125–26. New York: Random, 1954.

———. "Man Carrying Thing." In *The Collected Poems*, 350–51. New York: Random, 1954.

———. "The Man with the Blue Guitar." In *The Collected Poems*, 165–84. New York: Random, 1954.

———. "Men Made Out of Words." In *The Collected Poems*, 355–56. New York: Random, 1954.

———. "Metaphor as Degeneration." In *The Collected Poems*, 444–45. New York: Random, 1954.

———. "The Motive for Metaphor." In *The Collected Poems,* 288. New York: Random, 1954.

———. *The Necessary Angel: Essays on Reality and the Imagination.* New York: Random, 1951.

———. "Negation." In *The Collected Poems,* 97–98. New York: Random, 1954.

———. *Notes toward a Supreme Fiction.* In *The Collected Poems,* 380–408. New York: Random, 1954.

———. "Nuances of a Theme by Williams." In *The Collected Poems,* 18. New York: Random, 1954.

———. *Opus Posthumous.* Ed. Milton J. Bates. New York: Knopf, 1989.

———. *An Ordinary Evening in New Haven.* In *The Collected Poems,* 465–89. New York: Random, 1954.

———. "Prelude to Objects." In *The Collected Poems,* 194–95. New York: Random, 1954.

———. "Rubbings of Reality" (1946). In *Opus Posthumous,* ed. Milton J. Bates, 244–45. New York: Knopf, 1989.

———. "Someone Put a Pineapple Together." In *The Necessary Angel: Essays on Reality and the Imagination,* 83–87. New York: Random, 1951.

———. "Study of Two Pears." In *The Collected Poems,* 196–97. New York: Random, 1954.

———. *Sunday Morning.* In *The Collected Poems,* 66–70. New York: Random, 1954.

———. "Three Academic Pieces." In *The Necessary Angel: Essays on Reality and the Imagination,* 69–89. New York: Random, 1951.

———. "Williams" (1934). In *Opus Posthumous,* ed. Milton J. Bates, 213–15. New York: Knopf, 1989.

Sturrock, John. *Paper Tigers: The Ideal Fictions of Jorge Luis Borges.* London: Oxford University Press, 1977.

Sukenick, Ronald. "Thirteen Digressions." In *In Form: Digressions on the Act of Fiction,* 16–33. Carbondale: Southern Illinois University Press, 1985.

Tharpe, Jac. *Walker Percy.* Twayne's United States Authors Series 449. Boston: G. K. Hall, 1983.

Theroux, Alexander. "Theroux Metaphrastes: An Essay on Literature." Published with *Three Wogs,* 3–32. Boston: Godine, 1975.

Thompson, Michael. *Rubbish Theory: The Creation and Destruction of Value.* New York: Oxford University Press, 1979.

Thoreau, Henry David. *Walden.* Ed. J. Lyndon Shanley. Princeton, N.J.: Princeton University Press, 1971.

Trachtenberg, Stanley. Introduction to *New Essays on* Rabbit, Run Ed. Stanley Trachtenberg, 1–29. New York: Cambridge University Press, 1993.

Updike, John. "Accuracy." In *Picked-Up Pieces,* 16–17. New York: Knopf, 1975.

———. *The Afterlife and Other Stories.* New York: Knopf, 1994.

———. "The Angels." In *Collected Poems, 1953–1993,* 58. New York: Knopf, 1995.

———. "The Astronomer." In *Pigeon Feathers and Other Stories,* 179–86. New York: Knopf, 1962.

———. "The Blessed Man of Boston, My Grandmother's Thimble, and Fanning Island." In *Pigeon Feathers and Other Stories*, 227–45. New York: Knopf, 1962.

———. "The Bulgarian Poetess." In *The Music School*, 211–31. New York: Knopf, 1966.

———. *The Centaur*. New York: Knopf, 1963.

———. *Collected Poems, 1953–1993*. New York: Knopf, 1995.

———. "Conjunction." In *The Afterlife and Other Stories*, 46–53. New York: Knopf, 1994.

———. "A Conversation with John Updike." With Charlie Reilly. In *Conversations with John Updike*, ed. James Plath, 124–50. Jackson: University of Mississippi Press, 1994.

———. "Deaths of Distant Friends." In *Trust Me: Short Stories*, 83–89. New York: Knopf, 1987.

———. "Ex-Basketball Player." In *Collected Poems, 1953–1993*, 4–5. New York: Knopf, 1995.

———. "Flight." In *Pigeon Feathers and Other Stories*, 49–73. New York: Knopf, 1962.

———. "Forty Years of Middle America with John Updike." Interview with Melvin Bragg. In *Conversations with John Updike*, ed. James Plath, 221–28. Jackson: University of Mississippi Press, 1994.

———. "Grandparenting." In *The Afterlife and Other Stories*, 298–316. New York: Knopf, 1994.

———. "Harv Is Plowing Now." In *The Music School*, 175–82. New York: Knopf, 1966.

———. *Hugging the Shore: Essays and Criticism*. New York: Random/Vintage, 1983.

———. "The Importance of Fiction." In *Odd Jobs: Essays and Criticism*, 84–87. New York: Knopf, 1991.

———. "Intercession." In *The Same Door*, 142–53. New York: Knopf/Fawcett Crest, 1959.

———. "Is There Life After Golf?" Review of *Golf in the Kingdom*, by Michael Murphy. In *Picked-Up Pieces*, 98–103. New York: Knopf, 1975.

———. "John Updike." Interview with Frank Gado. In *First Person: Conversations on Writers & Writing*, ed. Frank Gado, 80–109. Schenectady, N.Y.: Union College Press, 1973.

———. *Just Looking: Essays on Art*. New York: Knopf, 1989.

———. "Made in Heaven." In *Trust Me: Short Stories*, 190–207. New York: Knopf, 1987.

———. *Midpoint*. In *Collected Poems, 1953–1993*, 64–101. New York: Knopf, 1995.

———. *The Music School*. New York: Knopf, 1966.

———. "Novel Thoughts." Review of four novels (including *Galatea 2.2*). *New Yorker* (21/28 August 1995): 105–6, 108–14.

———. *Odd Jobs: Essays and Criticism*. New York: Knopf, 1991.

———. *Of the Farm*. New York: Knopf, 1965.

———. "The Other Side of the Street." In *The Afterlife and Other Stories*, 136–47. New York: Knopf, 1994.

———. "Packed Dirt, Churchgoing, A Dying Cat, A Traded Car." In *Pigeon Feathers and Other Stories,* 246–79. New York: Knopf, 1962.

———. *Picked-Up Pieces.* New York: Knopf, 1975.

———. *Pigeon Feathers and Other Stories.* New York: Knopf, 1962.

———. "The Pro." In *Museums and Women,* 169–74. New York: Knopf, 1972.

———. *Rabbit at Rest.* New York: Knopf, 1990.

———. *Rabbit Is Rich.* New York: Knopf, 1981.

———. *Rabbit Redux.* New York: Knopf, 1971.

———. *Rabbit, Run.* New York: Knopf, 1960.

———. *Roger's Version.* New York: Knopf, 1986.

———. *The Same Door.* New York: Knopf/Fawcett Crest, 1959.

———. "A Sandstone Farmhouse." In *The Afterlife and Other Stories,* 103–35. New York: Knopf, 1994.

———. "A Sense of Shelter." In *Pigeon Feathers and Other Stories,* 83–101. New York: Knopf, 1962.

———. "Seven Stanzas at Easter." In *Collected Poems, 1953–1993,* 20–21. New York: Knopf, 1995.

———. "Short Easter." In *The Afterlife and Other Stories,* 92–102. New York: Knopf, 1994.

———. "A 'Special Message' for the Franklin Library's First Edition Society Printing of *Rabbit at Rest* (1990)." In *Odd Jobs: Essays and Criticism,* 869–72. New York: Knopf, 1991.

———. "Tips on a Trip." In *Picked-Up Pieces,* 95–98. New York: Knopf, 1975.

———. "Tomorrow and Tomorrow and So Forth." In *The Same Door,* 28–37. New York: Knopf/Fawcett Crest, 1959.

———. *Trust Me: Short Stories.* New York: Knopf, 1987.

———. "Trust Me." In *Trust Me: Short Stories,* 3–12. New York: Knopf, 1987.

———. "Twin Beds in Rome." In *The Music School,* 76–86. New York: Knopf, 1966.

———. "Updike Redux." Interview with Michael Sragow. In *Conversations with John Updike,* ed. James Plath, 59–66. Jackson: University of Mississippi Press, 1994.

———. "Upon the Last Day of His Forty-ninth Year." In *Collected Poems, 1953–1993,* 169. New York: Knopf, 1995.

———. "The Virtues of Playing Cricket on the Village Green." Review of *Collected Essays: Volume 2, The American Novel and Reflections on the European Novel.* By Q. D. Leavis. In *Odd Jobs: Essays and Criticism,* 291–301. New York: Knopf, 1991.

———. "Whitman's Egotheism." In *Hugging the Shore: Essays and Criticism.,* 106–17. New York: Random/Vintage, 1983.

———. "Why Rabbit Had to Go." *New York Times Book Review* (5 August 1990): 1, 24–25.

———. "Wife-Wooing." In *Pigeon Feathers and Other Stories,* 109–15. New York: Knopf, 1962.

Vanderwerken, David L. "Rabbit 'Re-Docks': Updike's Inner Space Odyssey." *College Literature* 2.1 (1975): 73–78.

Wagner, Linda Welshimer. "Metaphor and William Carlos Williams." *University Review* (Kansas City) 31.1 (1964): 43–49.

Walker, Nancy A. *Feminist Alternatives: Irony and Fantasy in the Contemporary Novel by Women.* Jackson and London: University Press of Mississippi, 1990.

Walsh, Richard. *Novel Arguments: Reading Innovative American Fiction.* Cambridge Studies in American Literature and Culture 91. New York: Cambridge University Press, 1995.

West, Paul. "Deep-Sixed into the Atlantic." *Review of Contemporary Fiction* 11.1 (1991): 260–62.

———. *Gala.* New York: Harper, 1976.

———. "In Defense of Purple Prose." In *Sheer Fiction,* 47–55.Kingston, N.Y.: McPherson, 1987.

———. "An Interview with Paul West." With David W. Madden. *Review of Contemporary Fiction* 11.1 (1991): 154–76.

———. *Lord Byron's Doctor.* New York: Doubleday, 1989.

———. "Paul West: An Interview." With Bradford Morrow. *Conjunctions* 12 (autumn 1988): 141–71.

———. *The Place in Flowers Where Pollen Rests.* New York: Doubleday, 1988.

———. *Portable People.* New York: Paris Review, 1990.

———. "Short Life of Esteban Fletcher." In *The Universe, and Other Fictions,* 77–89. Woodstock, N.Y.: Overlook, 1988.

———. *A Stroke of Genius: Illness and Self-Discovery.* New York: Viking, 1995.

———. *The Very Rich Hours of Count von Stauffenberg.* New York: Harper, 1980.

———. *The Women of Whitechapel and Jack the Ripper.* New York: Random, 1991.

Whalley, George. "Metaphor." In *Princeton Encyclopedia of Poetry and Poetics.* Enlarged ed. Ed. Alex Preminger, 490–95. Princeton, N.J.: Princeton University Press, 1974.

Wheelwright, Philip. *Metaphor & Reality.* Bloomington: Indiana University Press, 1962.

Wilbur, Richard. "Attention Makes Infinity." In *New and Collected Poems,* 383. San Diego, Calif.: Harcourt Brace Jovanovich, 1988.

———. "Merlin Enthralled." In *New and Collected Poems,* 245–46. San Diego, Calif.: Harcourt Brace Jovanovich, 1988.

———. *New and Collected Poems.* San Diego, Calif.: Harcourt Brace Jovanovich, 1988.

———. "Objects." In *New and Collected Poems,* 360–61. San Diego, Calif.: Harcourt Brace Jovanovich, 1988.

———. "Praise in Summer." In *New and Collected Poems,* 391. San Diego, Calif.: Harcourt Brace Jovanovich, 1988.

———. "A World Without Objects Is a Sensible Emptiness." In *New and Collected Poems,* 283–84. San Diego, Calif.: Harcourt Brace Jovanovich, 1988.

Williams, Tennessee. *Cat on a Hot Tin Roof.* In *Modern and Contemporary Drama,* ed. Miriam Gilbert, Carl H. Klaus, and Bradford S. Field Jr., 384–421. New York: St. Martin's, 1994.

Williams, William Carlos. *Collected Earlier Poems.* New York: New Directions, 1961.

————. "El Hombre." In *The William Carlos Williams Reader,* ed. M. L. Rosenthal, 6. New York: New Directions, 1966.

————. *Imaginations.* Ed. Webster Schott. New York: New Directions, 1970.

————. Prologue to *Kora in Hell* (1918). In *Imaginations,* ed. Webster Schott, 6–28. New York: New Directions, 1970.

————. "Queen-Ann's-Lace." In *Collected Earlier Poems,* 210. New York: New Directions, 1961.

————. "A Sort of a Song." In *The William Carlos Williams Reader,* ed. M. L. Rosenthal, 46–47. New York: New Directions, 1966.

————. *Spring and All* (1923). In *Imaginations,* ed. Webster Schott, 85–151. New York: New Directions, 1970.

————. "Spring and All." In *The William Carlos Williams Reader,* ed. M. L. Rosenthal, 15–16. New York: New Directions, 1966.

————. *The William Carlos Williams Reader.* Ed. M. L. Rosenthal. New York: New Directions, 1966.

————. "The Young Housewife." In *Collected Earlier Poems,* 136. New York: New Directions, 1961.

Wills, Garry. "Long-Distance Runner." Review of *Rabbit at Rest.* By John Updike. *New York Review of Books* (25 October 1990): 11–14.

Wilson, Matthew. "The Rabbit Tetralogy: From Solitude to Society to Solitude Again." *Modern Fiction Studies* 37.1 (1991): 5–24.

Wimsatt Jr., W. K. "Poetry and Morals." In *The Verbal Icon: Studies in the Meaning of Poetry,* 85–100. London: Methuen, 1954.

Woolf, Virginia. *A Room of One's Own.* New York and Burlingame: Harcourt, Brace & World, 1957.

Wordsworth, William. "A Slumber Did My Spirit Seal" (1799). In *The Norton Anthology of English Literature.* Vol. 2. 4th ed. Ed. M. H. Abrams et al. 177. New York: Norton, 1979.

Yeats, William Butler. "Byzantium." In *The Collected Poems of W. B. Yeats,* 243–44. New York: Macmillan, 1956.

Zinman, Toby Silverman. "Gone Fission: The Holocaustic Wit of Don DeLillo." *Modern Drama* 34.1 (1991): 74–87.

Index

Acker, Kathy, 17, 110–28, 182, 185, 186, 199–201; Blood and Guts in High School, 199n. 1; Don Quixote, 113–14, 117–21, 122, 123–28, 199–200n. 6, 200nn.9– 10; Empire of the Senseless, 119, 199n. 4, 200n. 7; Great Expectations, 112–23, 126, 128, 199n. 3; "The Language of the Body," 115; Literal Madness, 118; "Models of Our Present," 118

Ackerman, Diane: "A. R. Ammons Amid the Fungi," 197n. 1; "Diffraction," 95; "Halley's Comet," 95

Albee, Edward: Zoo Story, 155

Alter, Robert, 81–82

Ammons, A. R., 17; "Corson's Inlet," 15; "Poetics," 195n. 11; "The Unifying Principle," 195n. 11, 195n. 4

Anti-realism. See Realism

Anti-transcendence. See Transcendence

Arbitrariness. See Chance

Arnold, Matthew, 208n. 5

Auster, Paul, 17, 63–73, 182, 185–86, 195; The Art of Hunger, 63–64; City of Glass, 65–66, 69, 73, 195n. 5; Disappearances, 64; "Fore-shadows," 68; Ghosts, 195n.1; "Incendiary," 67;

The Invention of Solitude, 72–73; Leviathan, 64–73; The Locked Room, 67, 68, 73, 195n. 3, 195n. 6; The Music of Chance, 68; The New York Trilogy, 63–64, 68, 73; "Unearth," 68; "White Spaces," 69

Bailey, Peter J., 12

Baker, Nicholson: U and I: A True Story, 66, 191n. 5

Barth, John, 194n. 5, 201n. 1; "The Literature of Exhaustion," 113; "Lost in the Funhouse," 1

Barth, Karl, 154–55, 205n. 29

Barthelme, Donald, 104; "At the End of the Mechanical Age," epigraph

Baudelaire, Charles, 113

Baudrillard, Jean, 42, 119, 192n. 4, 193n. 8

Bawer, Bruce, 45, 193n. 12

Beckett, Samuel, 69; Murphy, 76

Bellow, Saul: Herzog, 177, 202n. 7

Bersani, Leo, 123, 200n. 15

Birkerts, Sven, 200n. 8

Bishop, Elizabeth: "The Fish," 189n. 1

Bishop, Jonathan, 57, 207n. 1

Black, Max, 13, 14, 16, 190n. 9

Bloom, Harold, 184, 185, 207–8n. 4
Boorstein, Daniel J., 100
Borges, Jorge Luis: "The Analytical Language of John Wilkins," 55; "The Circular Ruins," 194n. 3; "Funes the Memorious," 56; "Tlon, Uqbar, Orbis Tertius," 52
Boruch, Marianne, 9
Brennan, Karen, 199n. 1
Brenner, Gerry, 203n. 14
Bronowski, Jacob, 94–95
Brookner, Anita, 181
Brooks, Peter, 200n. 15, 201n. 17
Brown, E. K., 130
Burhans Jr., Clinton S., 201n. 4
Burke, Kenneth, 196n. 6
Burroughs, William, 70
Burroway, Janet, 185

Cable, Lana, 123, 187
Canetti, Elias, 35
Cary, Joyce: The Horse's Mouth, 20, 191n. 9
Cervantes, Miguel de: Don Quixote, 113, 118, 127
Cezanne, Paul, 131
Chance, 2; in Acker, 120–22; in Auster, 66–69, 70–73, 195nn. 4–6; in Gass, 76; in Millhauser, 50, 55–56; in Powers, 97, 99, 104, 106–7; in Updike, 132, 133–34, 177; in West, 30, 192n. 12
Cixous, Hélène, 114, 117, 121–22, 199–200nn. 5–6
Clarke, Arthur C.: 2001, 108
Clayton, Jay, 200n. 15, 201n. 17
Closure: versus open texts/narratives, 4, 5–9, 12–13, 15–17, 182, 185; in Acker, 111–12, 116–19, 123–27, 199–200n. 6, 200n. 9; in Auster, 67–68, 72, 195n. 2l; in DeLillo, 33, 35, 37, 39–40, 46–48, 193n. 10; in Gass, 85–87, 90; in Millhauser, 57, 60; in Powers, 94–95, 98, 100, 102, 106–8, 197n. 2, 198n. 5; in Updike,

132–35, 137, 139–40, 142, 145, 149–51, 154, 156–57, 159, 161–62, 166–67, 175–76, 179, 201n. 3, 201–2n. 5, 204n. 20, 204n. 23, 205n. 29, 206n. 37, 207–8nn.42–43; in West, 24, 31–32
Colette, 112
Colley, Ann, 20, 24
Conrad, Joseph: The Nigger of the "Narcissus," 19
Cornell, Joseph, 55, 194n. 8
Crews, Frederick, 154
Cullen, Countee: "Only the Polished Skeleton," 182

Dane, Gabrielle, 124–25
DeBellis, Jack, 203n. 14
DeLeuze, Gilles: and Felix Guattari, 124
DeLillo, Don, 17, 33–48, 182, 185, 192–93; Americana, 44; End Zone, 35, 44, 45, 46; The Engineer of Moonlight, 193n. 9; Great Jones Street, 34, 45, 192n. 3; Libra, 44, 193n. 13; Mao II, 35, 36, 46, 192n. 6; The Names, 33, 45, 46, 47, 192n. 1, 192–93n. 7; Pafko at the Wall, 36, 46–47, 192n. 4; Players, 42, 45, 193n. 12; Ratner's Star, 36, 44; White Noise, 34–48, 96, 129, 185, 197n. 2
Derrida, Jacques, 17
Detection: in Auster, 63–64, 65–66, 70, 72–73, 185–86; in DeLillo, 38, 41; in Updike, 179–80; in West, 29
Dickens, Charles, 112, 183; Great Expectations, 113
Dickinson, Emily: "Tell all the Truth but tell it slant," 7, 73, 182, 183; "There is no Frigate like a Book," 113; "There's a certain Slant of light," 41
Dillard, Annie: Holy the Firm, 10, 17; Living by Fiction, 72
Dix, Douglas Shields, 117, 200n. 9
Doctorow, E. L.: The Book of Daniel, 39

Donne, John, 55
Doty, Mark: "Difference," 187
Duemer, Joseph, 70
Dunn, Stephen: Loves, 97

Edmundson, Mark, 208n. 5
Ekphrasis, 19, 191n. 2
Eliot, T. S., 208n. 5; "The Hollow Men," 39; "The Love Song of J. Alfred Prufrock," 146, 147, 172, 202n. 7, 207n. 45; "Preludes," 150; The Waste Land, 207n. 45
Elkin, Stanley, 21, 44, 49; The Franchiser, 10–13, 17
Embler, Weller, 12, 190n. 8
Emerson, Ralph Waldo, 8, 141, 171, 208n. 5
Emplotment: in Acker, 116, 123, 201n. 17; in Auster, 63, 67; in DeLillo, 40, 193n. 10; in Gass, 75, 83–84; in Millhauser, 52, 56; in Powers, 94–95, 99–100, 197–98n. 4; in Updike, 130, 132; in West, 25, 29
Enargeia: versus energeia, 19–20, 23, 29–30, 80, 82–83, 123–24, 136, 138, 191n. 7
Ethics, 13, 182–87, 207n. 3, 207–8n. 4, 208n. 5; and Acker, 118, 124–25; and Gass, 78–82, 86–87, 92–93, 196nn. 6–7; and Millhauser, 55; and Updike, 142, 143, 158, 179, 207n. 50; and West, 20, 29–31, 191n. 8

Federman, Raymond, 111
Fitzgerald, F. Scott, 184
Flaubert, Gustave: Madame Bovary, 113
Fleischauer, John F., 132
Forché, Carolyn: "The Colonel," 75
Freeman, Barbara Claire, 127
Freud, Sigmund, 58
Friedman, Ellen G., 114, 118, 199n. 4
Frost, Robert, 8; "Birches," 133; "Education by Poetry," 47, 61, 183; "For Once, Then, Something," 8–9; "Mending Wall," 9

Frow, John, 37, 193n. 11
Fulton, Alice: "The Fractal Lanes," 129

Gass, William, 16, 47–48, 74–93, 112, 130, 185, 186, 195–97; "The Artist and Society," 47–48, 196n. 7; "Carrots, Noses, Snow, Rose, Roses," 196n. 4, 196n. 10; "Culture, Self, and Style," 196n. 9; "Emerson and the Essay," 76, 82, 85; Fiction and the Figures of Life, 196n. 10; "Groping for Trouts," 196n. 9; "The High Brutality of Good Intentions,"196n. 6; "Icicles," 197n. 13; "The Imagination of an Insurrection," 77; "In the Heart of the Heart of the Country," 82–83, 88, 90, 91, 197n. 13; "In Terms of the Toenail: Fiction and the Figures of Life," 85, 87; "The Medium of Fiction," 83, 102; "Monumentality/Mentality," 86; "Mrs. Mean," 197n. 13; Omensetter's Luck, 79, 80, 82–83, 196–97n. 11, 197n.13; "The Ontology of the Sentence, or How to Make a World of Words," 196n. 10; "The Order of Insects," 196–97n. 11, 197n. 14; "The Pedersen Kid," 197n. 13; "Philosophy and the Form of Fiction," 82; Preface to In the Heart of the Heart of the Country, 76–77, 80, 92; "Representation and the War for Reality," 195–96n. 1, 196n. 5, 196n.9, 10; "The Soul Inside the Sentence," 196n. 10; "Tribalism, Identity, and Ideology," 92; "Tropes of the Text," 196n. 10; The Tunnel, 75–93, 185, 186; Willie Masters' Lonesome Wife, 82–83, 112
Gelfant, Blanche H., 199n. 2
Genet, Jean, 110, 199n. 1
Gluck, Louise: "Mock Orange," 114
Godwin, Gail: Odd Woman, 199n. 2
Goldbarth, Albert: "Donald Duck in Danish," 74; "Some Things," 50

Goodman, Nelson, 24
Graham, Jorie: Region of Unlikeness,
    208n. 6; "Who Watches from the
    Dark Porch," 186

Harries, Karsten, 14, 190n. 11
Hawkes, John: Virginie: Her Two Lives,
    191n. 10
Heaney, Seamus, 183, 185
Heffernan, James A. W., 191n. 2
Hemingway, Ernest: A Farewell to Arms,
    196n. 9
History, 208n. 6; in Acker, 111, 113,
    114, 122; in Auster, 67; in DeLillo,
    36, 38, 46, 193n. 13; in Gass,
    75–87, 90, 92, 196nn. 2–3, 196n. 5,
    196–97n. 11; in Millhauser, 56; in
    Powers, 95, 99, 105, 197–98n. 4; in
    Updike, 171–72; in West, 21, 22,
    25–26, 29, 30
Hopkins, Gerard Manley, 104
Hopper, Edward, 181
Hulley, Kathleen, 114, 118–19, 120

Identity, 9–10, 13, 15, 190n. 12; in
    Acker, 111, 114–18, 120–23,
    125–28, 199n. 2, 199n. 5, 200nn.
    13–14; in Auster, 64–65, 67–69,
    71–72; in DeLillo, 33, 35–36,
    38–40, 43, 46; in Gass, 75–78, 80,
    82–85, 87–89, 92–93; in Mill-
    hauser, 53, 57; in Powers, 96–105,
    107–8, 198n. 6; in Updike, 135–36,
    140–41, 161, 168–69, 171–73,
    203n. 14, 205n. 28; in West, 23
Ionesco, Eugene: The Bald Soprano, 101
Irigaray, Luce, 115–16, 117, 121, 199n.
    5, 200nn. 13–14, 200–201n. 16

Jacobs, Naomi, 111, 121
Jakobson, Roman, 198n. 5
James, Henry, 45, 58, 196n. 6
James, William, 8
Joyce, James: A Portrait of the Artist as a
    Young Man, 133; Ulysses, 113

Keats, John, 112, 198n. 8, 199n. 13
Kierkegaard, Soren, 205n. 29
Kinzie, Mary, 9, 194n. 6
Klinkowitz, Jerome, 201n. 1
Krantz, Judith, 181
Krieger, Murray, 19, 20, 191n. 2
Kristeva, Julia, 124, 201n. 18
Kuhns, Richard, 15, 190n. 11
Kundera, Milan: The Book of Laughter
    and Forgetting, 186

Lakoff, George, and Mark Turner, 13
Lane, Anthony, 181
Langer, Lawrence L., 77
Language, 1–18, 181–87, 189nn. 2–4,
    190nn. 6–12, 190–91n. 13, 207n. 3;
    in Acker, 111–12, 115–25, 199n. 4,
    200n. 8, 200n. 13; in Auster, 64–6,
    71, 195n. 1; in DeLillo, 33–34,
    36–38, 41–48, 192–93n. 7, 193nn.
    9–12; in Gass, 74–77, 79–89,
    92–93, 195–96n. 1, 196nn. 5–6,
    196nn. 8–10, 196–97n. 11; in Mill-
    hauser, 49–50, 52–53, 55–62,; in
    Powers, 95–97, 99–102, 104–9,
    197–98n. 4, 198nn. 6–8, 198nn.
    10–11, 199n. 15; in Updike,
    129–34, 136, 139–41, 143, 146–52,
    153, 164–65, 173–74, 177–78,
    179–80, 201nn. 1–4, 202n. 6, 204n.
    23, 205n. 25, 205n. 32, 206n. 38,
    206n. 42, 207n. 50; in West,
    19–25, 29–30, 191nn. 2–5
Leavis, F. R., 199n. 4
LeClair, Tom, 37
Lehman, David, 189n. 3
Levi-Strauss, Claude, 67

Magritte, René, 19, 20
Martin, Ronald E., 194n. 9
Massey, Irving, 20
Melville, Herman: Moby Dick, 50, 66, 72
Miller, J. Hillis, 190n. 10
Millhauser, Steven, 17, 49–62, 182,
    185, 193–95; "Alice, Falling," 53,

54, 58; "The Barnum Museum,"
50–51, 53–57, 59; The Barnum
Museum, 50–62; "Behind the Blue
Curtain," 53, 59, 194n. 2; Catalogue of the Exhibition, 194–95n.
10; "Cathay," 194n. 4; "The Dream
of the Consortium," 50, 51, 53,
194n. 4; Edwin Mullhouse, 59–60;
"The Eighth Voyage of Sinbad,"
51–52, 55, 56–57, 194n. 4, 194n.
6; "Eisenheim the Illusionist," 51,
59; "A Game of Clue," 57–59,
194n. 2; "In the Penny Arcade,"
61; "The Invention of Robert
Herendeen," 62, 194n. 3; Portrait
of a Romantic, 52–53, 194n. 7;
"Replicas," 52; "The Sepia Postcard," 53, 194n. 2
Milton, John: Paradise Lost, 196n. 7
Moi, Toril, 200n. 12
Montaigne, Michel de, 80, 208n. 5
Moore, Marianne, 16, 61
Morality. See Ethics

Nabokov, Vladimir, 195n. 2; "Signs and
Symbols," 2
Nietzsche, Friedrich, 6
Nemerov, Howard: "Holding the Mirror
Up to Nature," 16–17; The Image
and the Law, 190n. 6; "Inside the
Onion," 190n. 6; "Lion & Honey-
comb," 8; "Unscientific Postscript,"
1, 9
Newman, John Henry, 61
Newton, Isaac, 95

O'Connor, Flannery: Wise Blood, 158
Olds, Sharon: "The Swimmer," 39
Osborne, John: Look Back in Anger, 148
Other, the, 2–3, 7, 8–9; in Acker,
113–15, 118–24, 126–27, 199n. 5;
in Auster, 65–68, 195n. 1; in
DeLillo, 35, 43; in Gass, 92–93; in
Millhauser, 194–95nn. 8–10; in
Powers, 99, 102–3; in Updike,

134–35, 147–48, 155, 161, 169–70,
172; in West, 30
Ozick, Cynthia, 92–93

Paley, Grace, 201n. 1
Parody: in Acker, 110–12, 127, 200n. 12,
201n. 18; in Auster, 63; in Mill-
hauser, 56
Percy, Walker, 104–5, 198n. 11
Piercy, Marge: "You Ask me Why Some-
times I Say Stop," 115
Plagiarism. See Parody
Plath, Sylvia: "Daddy," 81
Poirier, Richard, 8, 48
Pound, Ezra, 113
Powers, Richard, 17, 94–109, 182, 185,
197–99; Galatea 2.2, 97–109, 186;
The Gold Bug Variations, 96–97,
98, 100, 198n. 7; Operation Wandering Soul, 97, 197–98n. 4; Prisoner's Dilemma, 197–98n. 4; Three
Farmers on Their Way to a Dance,
97
Pritchett, V. S., 179
Process: versus product, 9, 14–15, 189n.
5, 190n. 6, 186–87; in Acker,
119–24, 126, 200nn. 9–10; in
Auster, 67–68, 70; in DeLillo, 40,
44; in Gass, 76, 77–78, 83–84,
86–87; in Millhauser, 49, 50–51,
56–57, 60–61, 193n. 1, 195n. 11; in
Powers, 100, 102, 104, 198nn. 6–7;
in Updike, 131–32, 138, 144,
149–51, 156–57, 159–60, 163–65,
167–69, 171, 175, 178, 202n. 6,
202n. 8; in West, 23–24, 27–28,
29–32
Proust, Marcel, 98, 112, 179
Prunty, Wyatt, 8–9
Pynchon, Thomas, 46; The Crying of Lot
49, 190–91n. 13

Quest: in Acker, 114, 115–16, 121–23,
125, 127–28; in Auster, 69; in Powers, 94, 100; in Updike, 132

Randomness. See Chance
Rauschenberg, Robert, 113
Realism: in Acker, 111–12, 117–18, 120;
    and antirealism, 7, 9–10, 183, 186,
    207–8n. 4; in Auster, 64, 67–9, 73;
    in DeLillo, 40–41, 42, 45–47; in
    Gass, 78, 83, 89–93, 196n. 5; in
    Millhauser, 49–61, 194nn. 2–8; in
    Powers, 95–97, 102, 104, 107,
    197–98n. 4, 198n. 9; in Updike,
    130–32, 170, 179–80, 201n. 2,
    203n. 11; in West, 19–20, 25,
    29–30, 32, 192n. 12
Redding, Arthur F., 200n. 12, 201n. 18
Reed, Ishmael, 201n. 1
Referentiality. See Language
Representation. See Language
Revelation. See Transcendence
Rich, Adrienne, 111
Ricoeur, Paul, 186
Rodin, Auguste, 22–23
Rosenfeld, Alvin H., 83
Roth, Philip, 192n. 12
Ruskin, John, 19–20, 191n. 1

Salinger, J. D.: "Teddy," 141
Schnitzer, Deborah, 29–30
Sciolino, Martina, 118
Self. See Identity
Shakespeare, William, 95, 108
Shapiro, Karl, 189n. 4
Shelley, Mary: Frankenstein, 108
Shelley, Percy Bysshe, 1; "Ozymandias,"
    183
Simic, Charles, 194n. 8
Singer, Alan, 16, 190n. 12
Snow, C. P., 103, 198n. 10
Sontag, Susan, 184, 185, 207n. 3
Sprat, Thomas, 13
Stein, Gertrude, 8; "Pictures," 20, 21
Stern, Chaim, 78–79
Stevens, Wallace, 2, 4–8, 9, 10, 13–15,
    189n. 3, 189n. 5; "About One of
    Marianne Moore's Poems," 61; Ada-
    gia, 6–7; "Add This to Rhetoric," 6;

"Bouquet of Roses in Sunlight,"
    9–10; The Comedian as the Letter C,
    6, 66; "Description without Place,"
    10; "Effects of Analogy," 13–14; "A
    High-Toned Old Christian
    Woman," 187; "How to Live. What
    to Do," 5; "Man Carrying Thing,"
    61; The Man with the Blue Guitar,
    14; "Men Made Out of Words," 7;
    "Metaphor as Degeneration," 190n.
    9; "The Motive for Metaphor," 15;
    "Negation," 15; Notes Toward a
    Supreme Fiction, 5, 7, 9; "Nuances
    of a Theme by Williams," 4–5, 17;
    An Ordinary Evening in New Haven,
    10, 14, 61, 85, 87; "Prelude to
    Objects," 8; "Rubbings of Reality,"
    5; "Someone Put a Pineapple
    Together," 7; "Study of Two Pears,"
    189n. 2; Sunday Morning, 135, 164;
    "Three Academic Pieces," 7;
    "Williams," 5
Storification. See Emplotment
The Story of O, 114, 120
Sturrock, John, 57
Style, 181–84; in Acker, 110–13,
    116–17, 119–20; in Auster, 68–69;
    in DeLillo, 45–46, 193nn.11–12; in
    Elkin, 12–13, 49; in Gass, 79–81,
    83–84, 93, 195–96n. 1, 196n. 4,
    196n. 6, 196nn. 9–10; in Mill-
    hauser, 49, 55, 57–58; in Powers,
    96–97, 198n. 10; in Updike,
    129–32, 137–38, 179–80, 201nn.
    1–2, 204n. 23, 205n. 32, 207n. 50;
    in West, 20–22, 25, 28
Sukenick, Ronald, 21
Swift, Jonathan: Gulliver's Travels, 54
Symbol. See Language

Technique. See Style
Theroux, Alexander, 191n. 4
Thoreau, Henry David, 182, 207n. 2;
    Walden, 20–21, 68
Trachtenberg, Stanley, 139–40, 202n. 6

Transcendence: or its failure, through
metaphor / words, 1, 5–6, 11,
13–14, 16–18; in Acker, 117–19,
123–24; in Auster, 68–69, 72–73;
in DeLillo, 33–37, 39, 40–43, 47,
192n. 3, 193n. 14; in Gass, 75,
83–85, 88–89; in Millhauser, 53,
61–62; in Powers, 96–97, 100–109,
198n.8, 198n.11; in Updike, 130,
137–43, 145, 147, 151–55, 163–67,
169–79, 202n. 9, 203nn. 11–12,
205nn. 26–29, 206nn. 36–38, 206n.
42, 206–7n. 43, 207nn. 47–49; in
West, 20, 24, 27

Updike, John, 17, 129–80, 182, 185,
186, 191n. 7, 199n. 14, 201–7;
"Accuracy," 131; "The Angels," 139;
"The Astronomer," 176–77; "The
Blessed Man of Boston, My Grand-
mother's Thimble, and Fanning
Island," 138; "The Bulgarian Poet-
ess," 170; The Centaur, 131; "Con-
junction," 176; "Deaths of Distant
Friends," 170; "Ex-Basketball
Player," 203n. 16; "Flight," 201n. 3;
"Grandparenting," 207n. 48; "Harv
Is Plowing Now," 175–76; "The
Importance of Fiction," 201n. 2; "Is
There Life After Golf?," 203n. 11;
Just Looking, 191n. 7; "Made in
Heaven," 205n. 26; Midpoint, 151,
159; Of the Farm, 142; "The Other
Side of the Street," 206n. 39;
"Packed Dirt, Churchgoing, a Dying
Cat, a Traded Car," 179; "The Pro,"
203n.11; Rabbit Redux, 129–30,
143–58, 160, 161, 167, 168,
174–75, 179–80, 202n. 7,
204–6nn.17–34, 206n. 41; Rabbit at
Rest, 129–30, 131, 168–80, 206n.
39, 207nn. 45–47, 207n. 49; Rabbit
Is Rich, 129–30, 157–67, 168, 169,
176, 179–80, 206–7nn.35–44; Rabbit, Run, 129–30, 131, 132–43,

146, 150–52, 153–57, 159, 160,
161–62, 163, 167–70, 175, 179–80,
201–2nn. 3–15, 204nn. 22–23,
205n. 32; Roger's Version, 154–55,
180, 205n. 29; "A Sandstone Farmhouse," 164, 173; "A Sense of Shelter," 135–36; "Seven Stanzas at
Easter," 140; "Short Easter," 154; "A
'Special Message' for the Franklin
Library's First Edition Society Printing of Rabbit at Rest," 132, 167–68;
"Tips on a Trip," 203n. 11; "Tomorrow and Tomorrow and So Forth,"
138–39; "Trust Me," 165; "Twin
Beds in Rome," 168; "Upon the
Last Day of His Forty-ninth Year,"
158; "The Virtues of Playing Cricket
on the Village Green," 179; "Whitman's Egotheism," 130; "Why Rabbit Had to Go," 131;
"Wife-Wooing," 185

Vonnegut Jr., Kurt, 201n. 1

Walker, Nancy A., 111
Walsh, Richard, 118, 119, 126, 127,
200nn. 10–11, 201n. 19
West, Paul, 17, 19–32, 95–96, 120, 130,
182, 191–92; "Deep-Sixed into the
Atlantic," 191n. 8; "In Defense of
Purple Prose," 21, 22, 191n. 4;
Gala, 21; Lord Byron's Doctor, 21;
The Place in Flowers Where Pollen
Rests, 23; Portable People, 22–23;
Sheer Fiction, 21; "Short Life of
Esteban Fletcher," 23; A Stroke of
Genius: Illness and Self-Discovery,
191n. 3; The Universe, and Other
Fictions, 95–96; The Very Rich
Hours of Count von Stauffenberg,
21; The Women of Whitechapel and
Jack the Ripper, 25–32, 120, 185
Whalley, George, 44–45
Whitman, Walt, 49, 130, 194n. 9
Wheelwright, Philip, 14–15, 183, 185

Wilbur, Richard, 191n. 6; "Attention
    Makes Infinity," 49; "Merlin
    Enthralled," 135; "Objects," 193n.
    1; "Praise in Summer," 13, 23–24,
    208n. 6; "A World without Objects
    Is a Sensible Emptiness," 49
Williams, Tennessee: Cat on a Hot Tin
    Roof, 158
Williams, William Carlos, 2–5, 7–8, 10,
    11–12, 17, 189n. 1, 189nn. 4–5; "El
    Hombre," 2–3, 5; Prologue to Kora
    in Hell, 2–3, 24–25; "Queen-Ann's-
    Lace," 189n. 2; "A Sort of a Song,"
    7–8, 190n. 10; "Spring and All," 4;
    Spring and All, 3; "The Young
    Housewife," 3–4

Wills, Gary, 207n. 50
Wilson, Matthew, 171
Wilson, Robley, 201n. 1
Wimsatt Jr., W. K., 183, 185
Woolf, Virginia, 201n. 2; A Room of
    One's Own, 126
Words. See Language
Wordsworth, William, 75, 206n. 34;
    "A Slumber Did My Spirit Seal,"
    178

Yeats, William Butler: "Byzantium," 169

Ziegler, Jack, 182
Zinman, Toby Silverman, 193n. 10